HATRED IN THE HALLWAYS

Violence and Discrimination Against Lesbian, Gay, Bisexual, and Transgender Students in U.S. Schools

Human Rights Watch
New York · Washington · London · Brussels

ISBN: 1-56432-259-9
Library of Congress Catalog Card Number: 2001089868

Cover and internal photographs copyright © Patricia Williams for Human Rights Watch, 2001. Photographs were taken at high schools and at lesbian, gay, bisexual, and transgender youth groups in California.

Cover design by Rafael Jiménez

Addresses for Human Rights Watch
350 Fifth Avenue, 34th Floor, New York, New York 10118-3299
Tel: (212) 290-4700, Fax: (212) 736-1300, E-mail: hrwnyc@hrw.org

1630 Connecticut Avenue, N.W., Suite 500, Washington, D.C. 20009
Tel: (202) 612-4321, Fax: (202) 612-4333, E-mail: hrwdc@hrw.org

33 Islington High Street, N1 9LH London, UK
Tel: (171) 713-1995, Fax: (171) 713-1800, E-mail: hrwatchuk@gn.apc.org

15 Rue Van Campenhout, 1000 Brussels, Belgium
Tel: (2) 732-2009, Fax: (2) 732-0471, E-mail:hrwatcheu@skynet.be

Web Site Address: http://www.hrw.org

Listserv address: To subscribe to the list, send an e-mail message to majordomo@igc.apc.org with "subscribe hrw-news" in the body of the message (leave the subject line blank).

Human Rights Watch is dedicated to
protecting the human rights of people around the world.

We stand with victims and activists to prevent
discrimination, to uphold political freedom, to protect people from inhumane
conduct in wartime, and to bring offenders to justice.

We investigate and expose
human rights violations and hold abusers accountable.

We challenge governments and those who hold power to end abusive practices
and respect international human rights law.

We enlist the public and the international
community to support the cause of human rights for all.

HUMAN RIGHTS WATCH

Human Rights Watch conducts regular, systematic investigations of human rights abuses in some seventy countries around the world. Our reputation for timely, reliable disclosures has made us an essential source of information for those concerned with human rights. We address the human rights practices of governments of all political stripes, of all geopolitical alignments, and of all ethnic and religious persuasions. Human Rights Watch defends freedom of thought and expression, due process and equal protection of the law, and a vigorous civil society; we document and denounce murders, disappearances, torture, arbitrary imprisonment, discrimination, and other abuses of internationally recognized human rights. Our goal is to hold governments accountable if they transgress the rights of their people.

Human Rights Watch began in 1978 with the founding of its Europe and Central Asia division (then known as Helsinki Watch). Today, it also includes divisions covering Africa, the Americas, Asia, and the Middle East. In addition, it includes three thematic divisions on arms, children's rights, and women's rights. It maintains offices in New York, Washington, Los Angeles, London, Brussels, Moscow, Dushanbe, and Bangkok. Human Rights Watch is an independent, nongovernmental organization, supported by contributions from private individuals and foundations worldwide. It accepts no government funds, directly or indirectly.

The staff includes Kenneth Roth, executive director; Michele Alexander, development director; Reed Brody, advocacy director; Carroll Bogert, communications director; Barbara Guglielmo, finance director; Jeri Laber, special advisor; Lotte Leicht, Brussels office director; Michael McClintock, deputy program director; Patrick Minges, publications director; Maria Pignataro Nielsen, human resources director; Jemera Rone, counsel; Dinah PoKempner, general counsel; Malcolm Smart, program director; Wilder Tayler, legal and policy director; and Joanna Weschler, United Nations representative. Jonathan Fanton is the chair of the board. Robert L. Bernstein is the founding chair.

The regional directors of Human Rights Watch are Peter Takirambudde, Africa; José Miguel Vivanco, Americas; Sidney Jones, Asia; Holly Cartner, Europe and Central Asia; and Hanny Megally, Middle East and North Africa. The thematic division directors are Joost R. Hiltermann, arms; Lois Whitman, children's rights; and Regan Ralph, women's rights.

The members of the board of directors are Jonathan Fanton, chair; Lisa Anderson, Robert L. Bernstein, David M. Brown, William Carmichael, Dorothy Cullman, Gina Despres, Irene Diamond, Adrian W. DeWind, Fiona Druckenmiller, Edith Everett, Michael E. Gellert, Vartan Gregorian, Alice H. Henkin, James F. Hoge, Stephen L. Kass, Marina Pinto Kaufman, Bruce Klatsky, Joanne Leedom-Ackerman, Josh Mailman, Yolanda T. Moses, Samuel K. Murumba, Andrew Nathan, Jane Olson, Peter Osnos, Kathleen Peratis, Bruce Rabb, Sigrid Rausing, Orville Schell, Sid Sheinberg, Gary G. Sick, Malcolm Smith, Domna Stanton, John J. Studzinski, and Maya Wiley. Robert L. Bernstein is the founding chair of Human Rights Watch.

ACKNOWLEDGMENTS

This report was written by Michael Bochenek, counsel to the Children's Rights Division of Human Rights Watch, and A. Widney Brown, advocacy director of the Women's Rights Division, based on information the authors gathered during visits to California, Georgia, Kansas, Massachusetts, New York, Texas, and Utah between October 1999 and October 2000. Melanie Breen, Rook Campbell, Sam David, Derek R. Henkle, Tejal Jesrani, Rachel Lanzerotti, Kerry McArthur, Shalu Rozario, and Sadie Zea Ishee provided additional research assistance.

Lois Whitman, executive director of the Children's Rights Division; Regan Ralph, executive director of the Women's Rights Division; Michael McClintock, deputy program director of Human Rights Watch; and Wilder Tayler, legal and policy director, edited the report. Pamela Bruns, California director for Human Rights Watch; David Buckel, senior staff attorney, Lambda Legal Defense and Education Fund; Allyson Collins, Human Rights Watch senior researcher; Joanne Csete, Children's Rights Division researcher; M.K. Cullen, director of advocacy, Gay, Lesbian, and Straight Education Network (GLSEN); Kate Frankfurt, a consultant and former advocacy director for GLSEN; John Green, Human Rights Watch director of operations; John F. Sherwood, Jr., teacher, Waverly Middle School, Lansing, Michigan; and Saman Zia-Zarifi, Human Rights Watch academic freedom director, also reviewed and commented on the manuscript. Pamela Bruns, Adam Greenfield, Rona Peligal, and Robert Peterson helped secure development support for this research. Sobeira Genao, Fitzroy Hepkins, Veronica Matushaj, and Patrick Minges provided production assistance.

We wish to express our deep appreciation, above all, to the many courageous and resilient youth who spoke with us, particularly the members of our youth advisory committee. This report would not have been possible without their willingness to share their experiences with us. The names of all of the youth we interviewed have been changed to protect their privacy.

David Buckel; Kate Frankfurt; Shannon Minter, staff attorney, National Center for Lesbian Rights (NCLR), San Francisco; and Gretchen Noll, National Network for Youth, Washington, D.C., were instrumental in helping us formulate the scope of this research project. We also received early advice and input from Cynthia Brown, former program director of Human Rights Watch; Rea Carey; Melisa Casumbal, National Youth Advocacy Coalition, Washington, D.C.; Arthur Coleman, Esq.; M.K. Cullen; Michael Kaplan, National Youth Advocacy Coalition, Washington, D.C.; Gara LaMarche, Open Society Institute, New York; Jennifer Middleton, staff attorney, American Civil Liberties Union (ACLU), New York; John Spear, director of field services, GLSEN, New York; and Hector Vargas and Blake Cornish, National Gay and Lesbian Task Force, Washington D.C.

Susan Fineran, assistant professor, Boston University School of Social Work; Ramona Faith Oswald, assistant professor of family studies, Department of Human and Community Development, University of Illinois at Urbana-Champagne; Virginia J. Mahan, doctoral candidate, Texas Tech University; Caitlin Ryan, director of policy studies, Research Institute on Sexuality, Social Inequality and Health, San Francisco State University; and Stephen T. Russell, assistant cooperative extension specialist, University of California, Davis, shared their unpublished research with us.

In addition, we are grateful to the members of the advisory committees for the Children's Rights and Women's Rights Divisions, the Human Rights Watch California Committee (South), and the Human Rights Watch Young Advocates for their input on this project.

In the course of our field research, we were assisted by the following individuals and organizations: Katrina Avila, director, Boston Alliance of Gay, Lesbian, Bisexual, and Transgendered Youth, Boston; Jerry Battey, Eagles Academy, Los Angeles; Brenda Barron, assistant field director for southern organizing, GLSEN, Atlanta; Kirk Bell, assistant field director for western organizing, GLSEN, San Francisco; Dr. Roberta Benjamin, Los Angeles Unified School District (LAUSD); Steve Bewsey, director of homeless and housing services, Lifeworks, Austin, Texas; Brent Boultinghouse, Project 10, Los Angeles; David Bowden; Ralph T. Bowden, Jr., Esq.; Julie Browne, crisis line coordinator, Community United Against Violence (CUAV), San Francisco; Conni Champagne, Speakers Bureau coordinator, CUAV, San Francisco; Chattahoochee Valley Parents, Families and Friends of Lesbians and Gays (PFLAG), Columbus, Georgia; Emma Cherniavsky, associate California director, Human Rights Watch, Los Angeles; Adam Christian, Human Rights Watch, Los Angeles; Brian Chue, executive director, Lavender Youth Recreation and Information Center (LYRIC), San Francisco; Stephen Clark, legal director, ACLU of Utah, Salt Lake City; Chris Coggins, Macon Pride, Macon, Georgia; Judy Colbs, PFLAG, Atlanta; Larry Crane, development director, Youth First Texas, Dallas; Heather G. Daims, principal, Fairfax High School, LAUSD; Betty Dotts, PFLAG, Lubbock, Texas; Emma Dumont, Human Rights Watch, Los Angeles; Linda Ellis, executive director, Youth Pride, Atlanta; Bill Farrick, North Shore Alliance of Gay/Lesbian Youth, Beverly, Massachusetts; Fenway Community Health Center, Boston; Tina Fernandez, program director, Orange County Human Relations, Santa Ana, California; Michael Ferrera, clinical director of group homes, Gay and Lesbian Adolescent Social Services (GLASS), Los Angeles; Scott Fitzmaurice, Cape and Islands Gay and Straight Youth Alliance, Hyannis, Massachusetts; J. Robert Force, Esq., Human Rights Watch Young Advocates, Los Angeles; Jill Francis, Cathedral of Hope MCC, Dallas; GLSEN, Kansas City; GLSEN Utah, Salt Lake City; Wes Giles, Gay and Lesbian Community Center, San Antonio, Texas; Carol Gnade, executive director, ACLU of Utah, Salt Lake City; Kevin Gogin, director, Support Services for Sexual Minority Youth, San Francisco Unified School District; Michelle Golden, Boston Gay and Lesbian Adolescent Social Services, Boston;

Gail Goodman, executive director, Out Youth, Austin, Texas; Janet Glass; Anna Gregory, board member, Dimensions, San Francisco; Louis Harvey III, Anti-Violence Project, L.A. Gay and Lesbian Center, Los Angeles; Richard Haynes, executive director, New York City Gay and Lesbian Anti-Violence Project; Steven Hicks, co-chair, GLSEN, Los Angeles; Elle Hills, Macon Pride, Macon, Georgia; Matt Humphrey, Athens GLBT Youth Support Group, Athens, Georgia; Christine Hwang, staff attorney, NCLR, San Francisco; Robert M. Ivancic, executive director, Youth First Texas, Dallas; Cristal Jang, Support Services for Gay and Lesbian Youth, San Francisco Unified School District; Pamela K. Johnson, executive director, Men of Color Against Aids, Roxbury, Massachusetts; Jaron Kanegson, TransYouth, Berkeley, California; Mike Kennedy, Larkin Street Youth Center, San Francisco; Joseph Kosciw, research program manager, GLSEN, New York; Caroline Laub, director, Bay Area Gay-Straight Alliance Network, San Francisco; Camille Lee, teacher, Salt Lake City School District; Carol Lee, volunteer coordinator, L.A. Gay and Lesbian Center, Los Angeles; Julie Leinert, Catholic Charities of the East Bay, Oakland, California; Asha Leong, program manager, Youth Pride, Atlanta; Robin Levi, advocacy director, Women's Institute for Leadership Development in Human Rights, San Francisco; Vern Lewis, Georgia Equality Project, Atlanta; Anne Lundbom, youth services coordinator, CUAV, San Francisco; Gerald P. Mallon, Green Chimneys Children's Services, New York; Dion Manley, FTM International, San Francisco; Terry Maroney, staff attorney, Urban Justice Center, New York; Ronnie Mendoza, Lifeworks, Austin, Texas; Sandy Miller, Out Adolescents Staying in Schools (OASIS), Long Beach, California; Carla P. Moniz, youth coordinator/outreach worker, Boston Gay and Lesbian Adolescent Social Services, Boston; Alex Night, Lambda GLBT Community Services, El Paso, Texas; Seana O'Farrell, member services coordinator, Bay Positives, San Francisco; Nancy Otto, ACLU of Northern California, San Francisco; Felicia Park-Rogers, director, Children of Lesbians and Gays Everywhere, San Francisco; Julie Parker, Human Rights Watch Young Advocates, Los Angeles; Robert Peterson, Human Rights Watch, Los Angeles; Carol Petrucci, Houston Area Teenage Coalition of Homosexuals (HATCH), Houston; Merle Price, LAUSD; Eric A. Pliner, Learning Support Services, Massachusetts Department of Education, Malden, Massachusetts; Jennifer Rakowski, CUAV, San Francisco; Patrick Rauber, Eagles Academy, Los Angeles; Andrea Reece, youth counselor, Franklin Community Action Corporation Youth Programs, Greenfield, Massachusetts; Eli Reyna, community building program coordinator, Orange County Human Relations, Santa Ana, California; Diane Ritchie, Esq; Gail R. Rolf, coordinator, Project 10, Los Angeles; Joe Salvemini, OASIS, Los Angeles; Victor Sanchez, Bienestar, Los Angeles; Christine Sartiaguda, GLASS, Los Angeles; Steve Scarborough, staff attorney, Southern Regional Office, Lambda Legal Defense and Education Fund, Atlanta; Jack Siebert, GLSEN, San Francisco; Zak Sinclair, youth leadership coordinator,

LYRIC, San Francisco; Sierra Spingarn, Queer Youth Leadership Project at LYRIC, San Francisco; Anne Stanton, executive director, Larkin Street Youth Center, San Francisco; Erik R. Stegman, GLSEN, Whittier, California; Kate Stern, coordinator for the Safe Schools Initiative for GLBT students, Boston Public Schools; Becky Thompson, director, The Walt Whitman Community School, Dallas; Erik Travis, GLSEN, Los Angeles; Luis Torres, co-chair, GLSEN Orange County; Clayton Vetter, Planned Parenthood Association of Utah; Shawna Virago, domestic violence client advocate and hate violence victim advocate, CUAV, San Francisco; Ofelia Virtucio, Aqua, San Francisco; Vitaly, staff attorney, Legal Services for Children, San Francisco; John Volpe, director, Green Chimneys Children's Services Gramercy Residence, New York; Wendy Weaver, teacher, Nebo School District, Utah; Shannan Wilber, staff attorney, Youth Law Center, San Francisco; Paula Wolfe, Gay and Lesbian Center, Salt Lake City; Rob Woronoff, director of LGBT services, Home for Little Wanderers, Boston; Doug Wortham, GLSEN Utah, Salt Lake City; Manson Yew, Human Rights Watch Young Advocates, Los Angeles; and Caprice Young, LAUSD Board of Education.

In addition, we thank those who asked not to be named.

Grants and other support from the Susan A. and Donald P. Babson Fund, the Paul and Edith Babson Fund, the David Bohnett Foundation, the Evelyn and Walter Haas, Jr., Fund, the Liberty Hill Foundation, the Leo Model Foundation, The New York Community Trust—The Paul Rapoport Fund, the Snowdon Foundation, and An Uncommon Legacy Foundation and Barbara Dobkin made this investigation possible.

TABLE OF CONTENTS

GLOSSARY

Bisexual	Attracted to persons of both sexes.
Butch	A common term used to describe both males and females who act and dress in stereotypically masculine ways. This term has traditionally been used as a pejorative term to refer to lesbians who do not conform to traditional notions of femaleness.
Closeted	The experience of living without disclosing one's sexual orientation or gender identity (also referred to as being "in the closet").
Coming Out	Becoming aware of one's sexual orientation or gender identity and beginning to disclose it to others. A person may be selectively "out" in some situations or to certain people without generally disclosing his or her sexual orientation or gender identity. "Coming out" is a process that takes place over time, in some cases over many years.
Femme	A common term used to describe both males and females who act and dress in stereotypically feminine ways. This term has traditionally been used as a pejorative term to refer to gay men who do not conform to traditional notions of maleness.
Gay	Attracted to a person of the same sex. This term is sometimes used to refer only to males who are attracted to other males, but it may also be used as a synonym for the more clinical term *homosexual.*
Gay-Straight Alliance (GSA)	A student club for lesbian, gay, bisexual, transgender, and straight (heterosexual) youth.

Gender expression	All of the external characteristics and behaviors that are socially defined as masculine or feminine, including dress, mannerisms, speech patterns, and social interactions.
Gender identity	A person's internal, deeply felt sense of being male or female (or something other than or in between male and female).
Heterosexual	Attracted exclusively to the opposite sex (also referred to as being "straight").
Homosexual	Attracted to a person of the same sex. Most lesbian, gay, bisexual, and transgender persons in the United States prefer the more contemporary terms *lesbian* and *gay.*
In the closet	The experience of living without disclosing one's sexual orientation or gender identity.
Intersex	The term used for the approximately one in two thousand people who are born with sexual anatomy that mixes male and female characteristics or is otherwise atypical.
Lesbian	A female who is attracted to other females.
LGBT	A common abbreviation for "lesbian, gay, bisexual, and transgender." The abbreviation may include a *Q,* for "questioning," or occasionally two *Q*s, for "queer and questioning."
Out	The experience of living openly as lesbian, gay, bisexual, or transgender individual. There are many degrees of being "out"; for example, one may tell one's friends, family, coworkers, neighbors, or the public.

Queer	Often used as a slur to refer to lesbian, gay, bisexual, and transgender persons, the term *queer* has been reclaimed by many lesbian, gay, bisexual, and transgender individuals in the United States—particularly by youth—as an expression of pride in one's sexual orientation and gender identity.
Questioning	Uncertain of one's sexual orientation or gender identity.
Sexual Orientation	One's attraction to the same sex, the opposite sex, or both sexes.
Straight	Attracted exclusively to the opposite sex (also termed "heterosexual").
Transgender	One whose identity or behavior falls outside of stereotypical gender norms. This term is often shortened to "trans."
Transitioning	In the process of bringing one's appearances and body into alignment with one's gender identity through dress, hormone therapy, and sex reassignment surgery.
Transsexual	One who has undergone sex reassignment surgery so that one's physical sex corresponds to one's gender identity. Female-to-male transsexual (FTM) people were born with female bodies but have a predominantly male gender identity; male-to-female transsexual (MTF) people were born with male bodies but have a predominantly female gender identity.

U.S. School Grades

Elementary school is composed of grades one through six with students of ages five through twelve. Middle school is composed of eighth and ninth grades with students aged twelve through fourteen. High school is composed of freshman, sophomore, junior and senior years with students aged fourteen through eighteen.

Dylan N., Nevada

Dylan N. told his family that he was gay when he was twelve, but that fact came as no surprise to them. "From a young age, I was set aside as different," he explained when we interviewed him in December 1999 in Atlanta, Georgia.

During the first semester of his sophomore year, Dylan appeared on a local public access television program as a participant in a discussion about the experiences of lesbian, gay, bisexual, and transgender students at high school. When word spread among his classmates that he was gay, they subjected him to constant harassment because of his sexual orientation. Some of his peers began to taunt him routinely by calling him a "fag," "butt pirate," "fairy," "homo," "queer," "sissy," "ass licker," "AIDS whore," and other derogatory terms. "It was all part of the normal daily routine," said Dylan.

The verbal harassment escalated almost immediately into physical violence. Other students began spitting on him and throwing food at him.

One day in the parking lot outside his school, six students surrounded him and threw a lasso around his neck, saying, "Let's tie the faggot to the back of the truck."

He escaped from his tormentors and ran inside the school. Finding one of the vice-principals, he tried to tell her what had just happened to him. "I was still hysterical," he said. "I was trying to explain, but I was stumbling over my words. She laughed."

The school took no action to discipline Dylan's harassers. Instead, school officials told him not to discuss his sexual orientation with other students.

"Looking back on it, I was *so* out," he said. "I tried to start GSAs [gay-straight alliances]. Like, I tried to do so much."

After the lasso incident, the harassment and violence intensified. "I was living in the disciplinary office because other harassment was going on. Everyone knew," he said. "It gave permission for a whole new level of physical stuff to occur."

To escape the relentless harassment, Dylan asked for a transfer to another school in the district. When the semester ended, the district placed him in an alternative school for students with poor academic records or behavioral problems.

"The principal [at the alternative school] had a real issue with me," Dylan said. "The principal told me he wouldn't have me acting like a faggot at school. After a semester there, I realized that it was not a place where I could get an education."

Dylan was successful in securing a transfer to a traditional school the following year, when he was fifteen, but school officials again directed him not to discuss his sexual orientation with other students.

The gag rule imposed on him by the school did not protect him from his peers, who learned that he was gay from his former classmates at his first school. "It was the same thing all over again," he said. "They'd push me up against the lockers and call me a fag. They'd chase me around campus in their cars, screaming and yelling 'fag' out the windows." Once, he told us, a teacher walked out of the room while some of his classmates were throwing things at him.

On another occasion, a group of students surrounded him outside the school, punching him, shouting that he was a "bitch," and jeering while security officers stood nearby. When the fight ended, he related, "I was completely bloody. I was bleeding from both lips, my nose, behind my ear."

Dylan tried to return to his second school, the alternative school, but school officials turned down his request to be placed there again. "What they did was they put me in the adult education program. Their justification was, I would be around people who were much more accepting. What they didn't tell me was I would have no chance of getting a high school diploma," he said.

I. INTRODUCTION

To the more than two million lesbian, gay, bisexual, and transgender youth of school age living in the United States and to those who are questioning their sexual orientation or gender identity, Dylan N.'s story is all too familiar. It is a story of harassment, abuse, and violence; a story of deliberate indifference by school officials who disclaim any responsibility for protecting Dylan or ensuring his right to an education; a story of escalating violence; a story of the failure of legal protection; and finally, a story of a young man denied an education because of his sexual orientation. In this report, Human Rights Watch documents attacks on the human rights of lesbian, gay, bisexual, and transgender youth who are subjected to abuse on a daily basis by their peers and in some cases by teachers and school administrators. These violations are compounded by the failure of federal, state, and local governments to enact laws providing students with express protection from discrimination and violence based on their sexual orientation and gender identity, effectively allowing school officials to ignore violations of these students' rights. Gay youth spend an inordinate amount of energy plotting how to get safely to and from school, how to avoid the hallways when other students are present so they can avoid slurs and shoves, how to cut gym class to escape being beaten up—in short, how to become invisible so they will not be verbally and physically attacked. Too often, students have little energy left to learn. In interviews, lesbian, gay, bisexual, and transgender youth explained how teachers and administrators turned their backs, refusing to take reports of harassment, refusing to condemn the harassment, and failing to hold accountable students who harass and abuse. Some school officials blame the students being abused of provoking the attacks because they "flaunt" their identity. Other school officials justify their inaction by arguing that students who "insist" on being gay must "get used to it." And finally, some school officials encourage or participate in the abuse by publicly taunting or condemning the students for not being "normal." For gay youth who survive by carefully concealing their sexual orientation or gender identity, they learn that they will be protected only if they deny who they are—a message that too often leads to self-hatred and a fractured sense of identity.

In violation of its obligations under international law to provide protection from discrimination, the federal government has failed to enact measures that would explicitly provide protection from violence and discrimination based on sexual orientation and gender identity. Only four states have enacted laws that explicitly prohibit harassment of gay and lesbians students. As a result, the vast majority of lesbian, gay, bisexual, and transgender youth are not only left unprotected by school policies but are treated as if they are the problem when they report harassment and violence to school officials. This denial by school officials

3

that they have any responsibility or duty to protect lesbian, gay, bisexual, and transgender students from harassment and violence stands in sharp contrast to their response to other forms of discrimination. For example, virtually every public school in the United States has a policy prohibiting race-based discrimination. Every student, teacher, and administrator we interviewed was clear that as a matter of school policy and usually of practice, race-based attacks on students will be condemned and punished.

In contrast, the vast majority of lesbian, gay, bisexual, and transgender youth trying to escape the hostile hallways of their schools confront school officials who refuse to recognize the serious harm inflicted by the attacks and to provide redress for them. In fact, there is not even a token consensus among public school officials that gay youth deserve to be treated with dignity and respect.

The systematic failure of the public school system in the United States to protect these students means that they are left to choose between struggling in isolation to survive the harassment as they seek an education or escaping the hostile climate by dropping out of school. The burden these students bear is exacerbated in many cases by the rejection of their families, condemnation within their communities, being demonized by individual teachers and administrators, and rejection by members of the adult lesbian, gay, bisexual, and transgender communities who are too scared of being identified themselves to offer support to gay youth.

But societal discomfort with the existence of gay youth in no way excuses the failure of the state to protect these students from discrimination, harassment, and violence in public schools. Society's deeply held prejudices against marginalized groups can never justify violations of the principle of nondiscrimination.

In this report, we document the devastating impact of pervasive animus towards lesbian, gay, bisexual, and transgender youth. The problem is not that these youth are lesbian, gay, bisexual, or transgender. The problem is impunity for school officials who, through acts of commission and omission, violate these students' right to be free from persecution and discrimination.

Furthermore, at the local, state, and federal level, the government has failed to address these deep-seated prejudices against lesbian, gay, bisexual, and transgender people. Few jurisdictions have enacted laws prohibiting discrimination on the basis of sexual orientation or gender identity. In fact, government at all levels has repeatedly bowed to pressure from society to allow explicit discrimination against gay people.

This report contains stories of pain and rejection, resilience and defiance, courage and grace. A common thread running through virtually all these stories is isolation and the almost total failure of the public school system to take seriously the human rights of these students. Each day, most gay youth walk into their schools wondering what they will have to face—taunts, food thrown in the face, lewd mockery in the locker room, being slammed "accidentally" against lockers during the change in classes—all in front of teachers who hear and see no evil. For some, the burden of coping each day with the endless harassment is too much. They drop out of school. Some commit suicide. Others just barely survive as they navigate the open hostility of peers and the deliberate indifference of school officials. They try to do well academically, but much of their energy is focused on surviving another day. A few fight back, demanding that the school administration take the harassment seriously, that recognition of gays and lesbians be integrated into the curriculum, that they be allowed to organize gay-straight alliances, and that they be encouraged to celebrate their identities.

This report is about the failure of the government, specifically public school officials, teachers, and administrators, to fulfill their obligation to ensure that all youth enjoy their right to education in an environment where they are protected from discrimination, harassment, and violence. No child should have to go to school in survival mode. No school district should heave a sigh of relief when yet another gay student has dropped out, allowing the district to claim that "there are no homosexuals here."

Despite what some adults may want to believe, lesbian, gay, bisexual, and transgender youth are everywhere—growing up in rural communities, in small towns, in suburbs, in immigrant communities, in communities of color, in inner cities, in religious communities, and on the streets. Their sexual orientation and gender expression are two pieces of the mosaic of their identity. Every youth deserves to be treated with respect and to be protected from violations of their human rights, including to be free from discrimination, harassment, and violence and to be encouraged to learn and to grow intellectually and emotionally without being asked to deny an essential component of his or her identity.

Methods

Human Rights Watch conducted research for this study from October 1999 to October 2000 during visits to California, Georgia, Kansas, Massachusetts, New York, Texas, and Utah. Two researchers from two divisions of Human Rights Watch interviewed 140 youth between the ages of twelve and twenty-one for this report. We also interviewed 130 adults, including youth service providers, teachers, administrators, counselors, and parents.

We developed a list of questions on key topics for these interviews in consultation with a youth advisory group and based on discussions with attorneys, researchers, and advocates and a review of news accounts, academic research, and legal cases. Guided by our checklist, we asked open-ended questions, with the exception of a few queries for demographic information such as age, school grade, and self-identified sexual orientation and gender identity. While we did not adhere formulaically to our questionnaire in every interview, we did ask each person about every one of the subjects addressed in this report. Most of our individual interviews with youth lasted between forty minutes and one hour.

We attempted to interview youth of diverse ethnic and racial, socioeconomic, and geographic backgrounds, including youth who lived in rural areas as well as in urban and suburban locations. We identified youth through local service providers, attorneys, and local chapters of the Gay, Lesbian, Straight Education Network (GLSEN) and Parents and Friends of Lesbians and Gays (PFLAG). We chose this approach because we wanted to be able to refer youth to appropriate resources if we found that they were in immediate need of support, and we wanted to ensure that we interviewed a large number of youth in each of the states we visited.

We arranged interviews through youth groups and other support groups in two ways. Some groups permitted us to make presentations at their regular meetings after discussing our project and the purpose of our visit at prior meetings. In those cases, we introduced ourselves, described the work of Human Rights Watch, outlined the scope of our research, and invited those who were interested to speak with us individually after the presentation and a general question-and-answer session. Other groups identifed youth who were willing to speak with us and arranged individual appointments for us.

In our discussions with group coordinators and in our introductory presentations, we attempted to ensure that youth understood that they were free not to participate, that they could end the interview at any time, that we would publish a report based on our interviews, and that we would not publish their names or other identifying information . We also repeated these statements at the beginning of each interview before asking youth whether they were willing to talk with us. We did not keep track of the number of youth who declined to be interviewed, but we observed at many group meetings that between one quarter and one half of those who heard our introductory presentations chose not to speak with us individually.

We recognize that youth who are likely to participate in the groups we met with are not representative of the population of lesbian, gay, bisexual, and transgender youth as a whole. Our reliance on youth and other support groups meant that we conducted most of our interviews in urban areas, although we discovered that youth who are able to do so often travel great distances to attend these meetings—from other neighborhoods or remote counties, across state lines, and sometimes from hundreds of miles away. Our focus on such groups also meant that we did not interview youth who had not disclosed their sexual orientation or gender identity to others. In addition, the youth we saw had access to support from peers and adults that youth in more isolated areas generally lacked.

We occasionally interviewed youth in pairs at their request. In a few cases, time constraints or the policies of a particular group did not permit us to interview youth individually. Wherever quotations or other information cited in this report came from joint interviews or group discussions, we note that fact.

The names of all youth have been changed to protect their privacy. In addition, we did not name teachers and administrators when they requested confidentiality.

International Standards

We assess the treatment of youth according to international law, as set forth in the International Covenant on Civil and Political Rights (ICCPR); the International Covenant on Economic, Social, and Cultural Rights; the Convention on the Rights of the Child; the Convention on the Elimination of All Forms of Discrimination against Women; and other international human rights instruments. These instruments establish that students have the right to protection from mental or physical harm, the right to freedom from discrimination based on their sexual orientation or gender identity, the right to an education, and the rights to freedom of expression, association, and peaceful assembly. Chapter XI discusses the scope of these rights and the protection they are accorded under U.S. law.

In this report, the word "child" refers to anyone under the age of eighteen. Article 1 of the Convention on the Rights of the Child defines as a child "every human being under the age of eighteen years unless, under the law applicable to the child, majority is attained earlier."

II. RECOMMENDATIONS

This report contains evidence of the substantial failure of the government at the local, state, and federal level to protect lesbian, gay, bisexual, and transgender students from human rights violations, including harassment, violence, and deprivation of the right to education. Human Rights Watch calls for immediate actions by the state to end these abuses.

Key Recommendations
- All school districts should review their nondiscrimination policies for inclusion of protection based on sexual orientation and gender identity. If such protections are missing, they should immediately amend the policy to include explicit language prohibiting discrimination based on sexual orientation and gender identity.
- All school districts should immediately evaluate the effectiveness of the implementation of their nondiscrimination policies and, where there exists a gap between policy and practice, take immediate measures to close the gap by training all school staff and students.
- State legislatures should enact legislation to protect students from harassment and discrimination on the basis of sexual orientation and gender identity.
- The United States Department of Education should monitor school districts for compliance with the principle of nondiscrimination, intervene where the policies are failing, and include sexual orientation and gender identity in any data collection tools measuring discrimination in education.
- State governments should ensure that all university programs for the education of state-certified teachers include mandatory training on working with diverse students, including those who are lesbian, gay, bisexual, and transgender and those who are questioning their sexual orientation or gender identity.
- Federal and state governments should enact legislation to protect administrators, teachers, counselors, other school staff, and all other employees from discrimination in employment on the basis of sexual orientation or gender identity.

Additional Recommendations
To Local School Boards and Individual Schools
Policies Against Harassment and Violence
Schools should review and, where necessary, develop and implement written policies that prohibit discrimination, harassment, and abuse of students based on

their actual or perceived sexual orientation or gender identity. At a minimum, these policies should:

- Explicitly prohibit discrimination and harassment on the basis of sexual orientation and gender identity.
- Define harassment based on sexual orientation and gender identity to include unwelcome verbal, written, or physical conduct, such as negative name calling or imitating mannerisms, directed at a person because of his or her actual or perceived sexual orientation or gender identity.
- Prohibit such harassment by all employees and students, providing graduated consequences, proportionate to the seriousness of the harassment, for violations of this policy.
- Ensure that policies cover harassment by persons who are not employees or students when they are engaged in school-sponsored activities.
- Establish procedures for addressing complaints.
- Identify a school official or officials who will be responsible for handling complaints.
- Ensure that all students have a meaningful opportunity to report instances of harassment.
- Require staff to report harassment when they become aware of it.
- Prevent retaliation against those who report harassment or who take part in disciplinary proceedings (for example, as witnesses). Schools should advise students of the steps to take to report further harassment, and school officials should follow up with students to see if they have suffered additional harassment or retaliation.
- Require a response to all reported incidents of harassment, including those in which a student does not file a written complaint.
- Require schools to document all incidents of harassment and record the ways in which the harassment was addressed. Documentation should include physical evidence of the harassment, if any. For example, school officials should photocopy threatening or discriminatory letters or notes and should photograph graffiti. When harassment results in physical injuries to the student, the school should arrange for the student to receive medical attention. School officials should note the physical injuries and the need for medical attention in the incident report. If the student consents, school officials should include the medical report and photographs of the injuries among the documentation of the incident.
- Require referral to law enforcement officials when a reported incident of harassment appears to be a crime.

Other Steps to Provide Protection from Harassment and Violence
- Provide introductory and ongoing training to all staff—teachers, administrators, support staff, cafeteria personnel, and maintenance workers—on addressing the needs of lesbian, gay, bisexual, and transgender youth.
- Provide training to all staff on how to intervene to stop harassment that occurs in their presence. Other students may take the failure of staff to respond immediately to harassment as an indication that the staff member approves of the harassment or that the student deserves to be harassed.
- Ensure that all staff are trained on antidiscrimination laws and policies.
- Provide appropriate training for noninstructional staff. For example, bus drivers should receive training on addressing harassment that occurs in transit to and from school or other locations. School security officers should receive training that includes information on the settings in which harassment is most likely to occur.
- Establish and enforce a policy that administrators, teachers, counselors, and other school staff should never disclose information concerning a student's sexual orientation or gender identity to other students, his or her parents or guardians, or the local community.
- Evaluate existing policies and practices to ensure that the burden of ending harassment is not placed on the student who has been subjected to harassment. For example, schools should not move a harassed student to another class or school unless the student specifically requests such action, and then only after exploring other options to end the harassment.
- Introduce students to the principles of respect and tolerance at an early age, starting with elementary school. General programs on tolerance and respect should integrate the idea of tolerance and respect for lesbian, gay, bisexual, and transgender persons in an age-appropriate manner.

Protection from Discrimination in Employment
- In states that have not acted to protect teachers, administrators, and other employees from discrimination in employment on the basis of sexual orientation and gender identity, school districts should provide such protection in written policies and in employee contracts.

Teachers, Administrators, and Other Staff
- Provide training for faculty and staff on lesbian, gay, bisexual, and transgender issues. Because many schools rely on volunteers to assist in the

classroom and with other school activities, they should be included in training sessions on these issues.

- Provide lesbian, gay, bisexual, and transgender staff who wish to be open about their sexual orientation or gender identity with the institutional support to make them feel safe to do so.

Counseling

- Provide specialized training for school counselors on lesbian, gay, bisexual, and transgender issues.
- Establish and implement policies providing confidentiality in discussions between counselors and students. School counselors should advise students of the existence and limits, if any, on counselor-student confidentiality. Policies should include a prohibition on disclosing information concerning students' sexual orientation or gender identity to their classmates, parents or guardians, or local communities. School counselors should be guided by the ethical standards of the American School Counselor Association, the American Counseling Association, the National Board for Certified Counselors, and the National Association of Social Workers.

Access to Information

- Ensure that guidance counselors, school nurses, school social workers, and school psychologists receive special training on providing support and information for gay, lesbian, bisexual, and transgender youth and their families.
- Make information about gay, lesbian, bisexual, and transgender issues available in school libraries. This information should include videos, pamphlets, and books, including those written by youth, for the use of students, teachers, and parents.
- Develop reading lists of books on gay issues, periodically displaying these materials in a visible way.
- Ensure that library holdings are up to date and present accurate information about lesbian, gay, bisexual, and transgender issues.
- Ensure that library holdings are catalogued and shelved so that students can access the materials easily. For example, cataloguing systems should use contemporary subject headings such as "lesbian" and "gay" rather than outdated and potentially derogatory terminology such as "homosexual" or "homophile." Books on lesbian, gay, bisexual, and transgender issues should be kept in the same manner as other holdings, preferably on open shelves,

rather than being kept in the librarian's office and made available only on request.

- Ensure that students are able to borrow materials on issues related to sexual orientation and gender identity in a confidential manner. In some schools, for example, students are able to borrow books on these and other adolescent development issues from their counselors rather than checking them out from the school library.
- Develop local guides to organizations for lesbian, gay, bisexual, and transgender youth, those who are questioning their sexual orientation or gender identity, and their family members.
- Invite local speakers' bureaus or university groups to make presentations or conduct workshops on lesbian, gay, bisexual, and transgender issues.

Gay-Straight Alliances and Other School-Based Support Groups
- Develop gay-straight alliances or other in-school support groups for gay, lesbian, bisexual, transgender, heterosexual, and questioning students who want to talk to each other about issues related to sexual orientation and gender identity.
- Facilitate the formation and operation of these groups on equal terms with other student groups. For instance, schools should appoint faculty advisors, compensating them on an equal basis with other faculty advisors; permit groups to meet on school grounds; allow groups to bring in outside speakers if they wish; and allow groups to participate in schoolwide activities. Schools should accord gay-straight alliances the same privileges that are routinely granted to other student groups.
- Publicize the existence of these groups on equal terms with other student groups. For example, schools should permit gay-straight alliances to have the use of school bulletin boards and access to the public address system if other groups are permitted such use or access.

Transgender Youth
- Ensure that all existing and model complaint mechanisms at the school district and individual school level include provisions for complaints by transgender youth.
- Allow all transgender and questioning youth the means to define themselves in the manner most appropriate for them. This includes allowing them to choose appropriate names and gender classifications.
- Where schools have dress codes, apply those codes in a gender-neutral manner.

Curriculum

- Integrate age-appropriate discussion about gay issues into relevant core subject areas, such as literature, history, and current affairs.
- Include information that is specific to the needs of lesbian, gay, bisexual, and transgender youth in health education on sexuality and sexually transmitted diseases. Such information should not be presented with the implicit message that being gay, lesbian, bisexual, or transgender is itself a health problem.
- Evaluate materials currently in use to ensure that they do not present outdated information or stereotypical messages.

Recommendations to State Governments

To State Legislatures

- Enact legislation to protect students from harassment and discrimination on the basis of sexual orientation and gender identity.
- Enact legislation to protect teachers, counselors, administrators, and other employees from discrimination in employment on the basis of sexual orientation and gender identity.
- Include sexual orientation and gender identity in hate crimes legislation.
- In all legislation relating to diversity issues, include lesbian, gay, bisexual, transgender, and questioning youth.
- Repeal laws and regulations that prevent teachers and service providers from including information relevant to lesbian, gay, bisexual, transgender, and questioning youth in health education on sexuality and sexually transmitted diseases.
- Repeal legislation that criminalizes consensual sexual relations between consenting adults of the same gender. These laws violate the right to privacy and may be used to justify dismissing teachers, administrators, and staff who provide information or support to lesbian, gay, bisexual, transgender, or questioning youth or disclose their own sexual orientation or gender identity.
- Provide funding and additional support for lesbian, gay, bisexual, and transgender community groups that serve youth.

To State Governors

- Until state legislatures have taken the steps outlined above, state governors should issue executive orders to provide such protections.

To State Departments of Education

- Notify school districts of state and local laws prohibiting discrimination based on sexual orientation, reminding districts that sexual orientation discrimination is prohibited under federal law when it constitutes sexual harassment.

- Analyze existing legislation, regulations, and policies relating to diversity issues and nondiscrimination on the basis of sex or gender for effectiveness in protecting transgender youth from discrimination based on gender identity.
- Include in its regular accreditation process a review of each school district's policies and practices to protect students and staff from discrimination, harassment, and violence, including on the basis of sexual orientation and gender identity.
- Ensure that all existing and model complaint mechanisms include provisions for complaints by lesbian, gay, bisexual, transgender, and questioning youth.
- Monitor and enforce compliance with state and federal laws that protect students from discrimination, harassment, and violence, including on the basis of sexual orientation and gender identity.
- Ensure that all university programs for the education of state-certified teachers include mandatory training on working with diverse students, including lesbian, gay, bisexual, transgender, and questioning students
- If states have continuing education requirements for state-certified teachers, require that some of the continuing education credits address issues related to working with diverse students, including lesbian, gay, bisexual, transgender and questioning students.

Recommendations to the Federal Government
To the Executive Branch
- Submit the International Covenant on Economic, Social and Cultural Rights, the Convention on the Rights of the Child, and the Convention on the Elimination of All Forms of Discrimination against Women to the United States Senate for ratification.

To the United States Congress
- Enact federal legislation to protect administrators, teachers, counselors, other school staff, and all other employees from discrimination in employment on the basis of sexual orientation or gender identity.
- Enact implementing legislation for all human rights treaties ratified by the United States such that persons in the United States could legally enforce the protections of these treaties in U.S. courts.
- Enact federal nondiscrimination legislation that explicitly prohibits discrimination on the basis of sexual orientation and gender identity.

To the United States Senate

- Ratify and implement the International Covenant on Economic, Social and Cultural Rights, the Convention on the Rights of the Child, and the Convention on the Elimination of All Forms of Discrimination against Women.
- Review and withdraw the restrictive reservations, declarations, and understanding that it has attached to the International Covenant on Civil and Political Rights and the Convention against Torture and other Cruel, Inhuman and Degrading Treatment or Punishment.

To the United States Department of Education

- Explicitly notify school districts that Title IX of the Education Amendments of 1972 and some state and local laws prohibit discrimination based on sexual orientation when the discrimination constitutes sexual harassment. The department can direct school districts to *Protecting Students from Harassment and Hate Crime,* the 1999 guide developed by the department's Office for Civil Rights and the Bias Crimes Task Force of the National Association of Attorneys General, which provides step-by-step guidance, sample school policies and checklists, and reference materials that can assist school districts in protecting students from discrimination based on sexual orientation.
- The Office for Civil Rights should increase its monitoring of school districts, vigorously enforcing Title IX and other applicable federal laws against school districts that fail to protect students and employees from discrimination on the basis of sexual orientation that constitutes sexual harassment. When federal legislation is enacted to provide explicit protection from discrimination based on sexual orientation and gender identity, the Office for Civil Rights should monitor compliance and enforce this legislation.
- Include lesbian, gay, bisexual, transgender, and questioning youth in all regulations and policies related to diversity issues.
- Analyze all regulations and policies addressing nondiscrimination on the basis of sex or gender for effectiveness in recognizing lesbian, gay, bisexual, transgender, and questioning youth.
- Ensure that all existing and model complaint mechanisms include provisions for complaints by lesbian, gay, bisexual, transgender and questioning youth.

III. YOUNG AND QUEER IN AMERICA

Estimates of the number of lesbian, gay, and bisexual youth in the United States vary, but most researchers believe that between 5 and 6 percent of youth fit into one of these categories. Based on the 1990 census, there are more than 45 million school-age children in the United States.[1] This means that as many as two million school age children in the United States are dealing with issues related to their sexual orientation. No definitive data on the prevalence of people who identify as transgender exist.[2] However, regardless of the number of school age youth who identify as transgender or are perceived to be transgender, there is no dispute that these students are particularly vulnerable to being attacked both by their peers and by adults. Furthermore, as youth explore their sexual orientation and gender identity at younger and younger ages, school officials can no longer plausibly claim that this is not an issue for the students in their schools. Nor can school officials continue to ignore the pervasiveness of the harassment and the constant hostility that lesbian, gay, bisexual, transgender, and questioning youth face.

"They're here. They're queer. They're thirteen," a recent issue of *Nerve* magazine announced.[3] Recent studies confirm that youth are "coming out"—identifying themselves as gay, lesbian, bisexual, or transgender—at younger ages. "The world, schools, and businesses will have to adapt," said Leslie H., a sixteen-year-old student in Dallas. "They can't keep things the way they were and expect us to conform."[4]

A 1996 study of youth found that, on average, girls are aware of an attraction to other girls at age ten and have their first same-sex experience at age fifteen. Boys now have their first awareness of same-sex attraction at age nine and their

---

[1]The Census Bureau reports that in 1990 the population of children between the ages of five and seventeen was 45,249,989. *See* U.S. Census Bureau, "General Population and Housing Characteristics: 1990," factfinder.census.gov/servlet/BasicFactsServlet (accessed on March 28, 2001).

[2]However, the DSM-IV suggests that 1 per 30,000 adult males is male-to-female transsexual and 1 per 100,000 adult females is female-to-male transsexual. *See* American Psychiatric Association, *Diagnostic and Statistical Manual of Mental Disorders: DSM-IV,* 4th ed. (Washington, D.C.: American Psychiatric Association, 1994).

[3]*See* Stacey D'Erasmo, "Getting Out Early: They're Here. They're Queer. They're Thirteen," *Nerve,* August/September 2000, p. 100.

[4]Human Rights Watch interview, Dallas, Texas, March 27, 2000.

first same-sex experience at age thirteen. Both girls and boys begin to identify themselves as lesbian or gay at age sixteen.[5]

The youth we interviewed fit the trend. Many said they realized that they were lesbian, gay, bisexual, or transgender in elementary school or middle school. "I knew when I was thirteen," Casey G. told us.[6] "I knew when I was eight," Jerome B. said.[7] "I realized in first grade," said Payton R., a Los Angeles County high school student.[8] These findings mean that children are beginning to be aware of their sexual orientation by the third or fourth grade.

Lesbian, gay, bisexual, and transgender youth are often disclosing their sexual orientation or gender identity to their peers, teachers, and families in middle school or early high school. When she was twelve, Gina T. told her classmates that she was a lesbian.[9] Jobey L., a twelve-year-old in Texas, described one of his seventh-grade classmates as "really, really gay—completely out."[10] Erin B., an eighth grade student in DeKalb County, Georgia, started to tell her friends that she was a lesbian when she was in the sixth grade.[11]

In some cases, youth accept their lesbian, gay, bisexual, and transgender peers more readily than the adults in their schools and communities. Discussing the decision she made at the end of her sophomore year to be open about her sexual orientation, Andy J., a seventeen-year-old lesbian, told us, "I think the teachers care

---

[5]See G. Herdt and A. Boxer, *Children of Horizons*, 2d ed. (Boston: Beacon Press, 1996). In contrast, adults surveyed for a 1988 study reported an average age of thirteen for men and between fourteen and sixteen for women for their first awareness of an attraction to a person of the same sex. The average age for the first same-sex experience was fifteen for men and twenty for women. The adults who participated in the study identified themselves as gay or lesbian, on average, when they were between nineteen and twenty-one, for men, and between twenty-one and twenty-three, for women. *See* R.R. Troiden, "Homosexual Identity Development," *Journal of Adolescent Health,* vol. 9 (1988), p. 105. Troiden's study is based on retrospective assessments—that is, on adults' recollections of these developmental milestones—while Herdt and Boxer surveyed youth who were reporting on relatively recent events in their lives.

[6]Human Rights Watch interview, Los Angeles, California, January 20, 2000.

[7]Human Rights Watch interview, Los Angeles, California, January 20, 2000.

[8]Human Rights Watch interview, Long Beach, California, October 21, 1999.

[9]Human Rights Watch interview, Houston, Texas, March 17, 2000.

[10]Human Rights Watch interview, Austin, Texas, March 15, 2000.

[11]Human Rights Watch interview, Atlanta, Georgia, March 2, 2000.

about it more than the students."[12] Steve Bewsey, who works with homeless and runaway youth in Texas, agreed: "The crap comes from the staff."[13]

Some students are able to find acceptance within their school districts after initial challenges of being identified. "The kids are really open," Eric C. said of the last San Francisco school he attended. "All of the gay students there were really open with themselves, and there were a lot of gay kids there. The straight kids don't see the gay kids as a problem. Like, in my leadership class I talked about some problems I was having with my boyfriend. The other kids just acted like it was completely normal."[14]

Although some lesbian, gay, bisexual, and transgender students in the United States experience a positive, welcoming environment at school, the vast majority are not so fortunate. Lesbian, gay, and bisexual youth are nearly three times as likely as their heterosexual peers to have been assaulted or involved in at least one physical fight in school, three times as likely to have been threatened or injured with a weapon at school, and nearly four times as likely to skip school because they felt unsafe, according to the 1999 Massachusetts Youth Risk Behavior Survey.[15] As Human Rights Watch documents in this report, many are targeted for harassment and violence from their peers because of their sexual orientation or gender identity.

In many instances, teachers, administrators, and other staff fail to protect youth from harassment. "The teachers didn't care," Danny W. stated, an assessment we heard frequently from the youth and adults we interviewed.[16] "My kids complain a lot about the teachers turning a blind eye. They'll hear things like 'faggot' and 'suck my dick' in the classroom, and the teacher won't address it," says Michael Ferrera, clinical director of group homes at Gay and Lesbian Adolescent Social Services (GLASS) in Los Angeles.

"The kids will say that if the comments were racial, the teachers would stop them. Because the comments are about sexuality, they don't," Ferrera continued.[17]

---

[12]Human Rights Watch interview, Austin, Texas, March 15, 2000.

[13]Human Rights Watch interview with Steve Bewsey, director of housing and homeless services, Lifeworks, Austin, Texas, March 23, 2000.

[14]Human Rights Watch interview, San Francisco, California, January 27, 2000.

[15]*See* Massachusetts Department of Education, *1999 Massachusetts Youth Risk Behavior Survey* (Boston: Massachusetts Department of Education, 2000), www.doe.mass.edu/lss/yrbs99/ (accessed on April 3, 2001).

[16]Human Rights Watch interview, Dallas, Texas, March 27, 2000.

[17]Human Rights Watch interview with Michael Ferrera, clinical director of group homes, Gay and Lesbian Adolescent Social Services, Los Angeles, California, October 22, 1999.

Of course, the mere existence of school policies to address racial discrimination does not mean that implementation is automatic; in fact, a March 2001 report of the California Attorney General's Civil Rights Commission on Hate Crimes relates numerous accounts of racial or ethnic bias that went unaddressed by school officials.[18] But because such policies exist, and are backed up by state and federal law, teachers and administrators are accountable for their failure to respond to incidents of racial and ethnic discrimination. There is no such accountability in most states if school officials fail to protect students from harassment based on their actual or perceived sexual orientation or gender identity.

Some school districts recognize the importance of addressing all forms of verbal harassment, including harassment directed at students or teachers because of their actual or perceived sexual orientation or gender identity. In Denver, for example, a May 1998 memo on the district's antiharassment policy asked the district's high school principals to "ensure that students are informed that intolerance against others, including gay and lesbian students, will not be tolerated. . . . Remind staff members that they should not ignore inappropriate remarks or slurs, for in doing so, they endorse them."[19] And when teachers and administrators fail to respond to verbal harassment, it can often escalate into physical abuse.

This failure on the part of many adults means that youth are forced to advocate for their safety and well-being and educate their peers and their teachers at the same time that they are developing their identity. "It forces us to take on the role of adults," observed Dylan N., nineteen.[20] "I learned about the cruel politics of high school bureaucracy," Gabriel D., sixteen, told us. He summarized the lessons he learned: "You need to put constant pressure on them. Don't yell, don't be angry, don't be emotional, but be persistent. . . . Document everything: the incidents of harassment, who was there, who was a witness."[21]

Some school officials expect lesbian, gay, bisexual, and transgender youth to take the lead in providing information to their peers about sexual orientation or gender identity issues. After Anika P. was identified as transgender by her peers, school officials asked her to give a talk to her classmates about her gender identity. Anika felt that the school officials neither recognized how vulnerable speaking

---

[18]*See* California Attorney General's Civil Rights Commission on Human Rights, *Reporting Hate Crimes: Final Report* (Sacramento, California: Attorney General's Civil Rights Commission on Hate Crimes, 2001), p. 16.

[19]Brian Weber, "Students Start Club for Gays at East High," *Rocky Mountain News,* September 30, 1998, p. 5A.

[20]Human Rights Watch interview, Atlanta, Georgia, December 15, 1999.

[21]Human Rights Watch interview, San Francisco, California, January 28, 2000.

before the hostile students would feel to her nor were they willing to lay the groundwork to make it safe for her to be open about her identity. "They wanted me to go in front of all the kids," she told us. "They told me, 'We have a few gay students who are also willing to go talk to them.' But I just chose not to tell my personal business." When she refused to take the lead in educating her peers, she felt that the school administration wanted her to leave, so she dropped out of school.[22]

Youth have been a driving force behind many of the positive changes in recent years. Beginning in 1996, youth activists in California have held Queer Youth Lobby Day; in 1999, youth played a critical role in securing the enactment of the state's Student Safety and Violence Prevention Act of 2000 after the measure was initially defeated by one vote.[23] In May 2000, students in Naperville, Illinois, called on their district's school board to include protection against discrimination on the basis of sexual orientation in its policies.[24] And in September 2000, students prevailed over hostile schoolboards in California and Utah that had sought to deny them the right to form clubs known as gay-straight alliances, in violation of the federal Equal Access Act. California's Orange Unified School District settled a lawsuit with El Modena High School students, permitting their group to meet on school grounds and use the school's public address system to announce club meetings. The same month, Utah's Salt Lake City School Board voted to permit student noncurricular groups to meet on school grounds, reversing a 1995 decision that had abolished all noncurricular clubs in an effort to prevent students from forming a gay-straight alliance at East High School.[25]

In fact, most of the youth we interviewed for this report were involved in school gay-straight alliances, student clubs that provide peer support for lesbian, gay, bisexual, transgender, and questioning youth. Many had started their school's gay-straight alliance, often in the face of opposition from school administrators, the local school board, and the community.

Every state we visited had groups for lesbian, gay, bisexual, and transgender youth. Youth with computer access can find a community on the world wide web

---

[22]Human Rights Watch interview, Austin, Texas, March 23, 2000.

[23]See "The Story Behind the Student Safety and Violence Prevention Act of 2000," in *Make It Real: A Student Organizing Manual for Implementing California's New School Nondiscrimination Law (AB 537)* (Los Angeles: Bay Area Gay-Straight Alliance Network/Tides Center and L.A. Gay and Lesbian Center, 2000), p. 11.

[24]See Tracy Dell'Angela, "Students Push for Policy Against Homophobia," *Chicago Tribune,* May 24, 2000.

[25]See Chapter IX, "Efforts to Suppress Gay-Straight Alliances" section.

through gay youth oriented web sites.[26] By talking with their peers on the web, gay youth can escape the isolation many report feeling at school, and they can talk with other gay youth on the web without being publicly identified. And about fifteen cities around the country hold proms for lesbian, gay, bisexual, and transgender youth—not only Boston, Los Angeles, New York, and San Francisco, but also places such as Hartford, Connecticut, and Lincoln, Nebraska.

"I look around at kids today and I feel really envious," a twenty-four-year-old college activist commented to us. "I mean, when I came out in high school there was *nothing.* "[27]

Legal Developments

The increasing awareness of lesbian, gay, bisexual, and transgender issues has fostered a public debate that is playing out in courtrooms and statehouses around the country. A small but increasing number of states have made it unlawful to discriminate on the basis of sexual orientation in the workplace. California, Connecticut, Massachusetts, Vermont, and Wisconsin explicitly prohibit harassment and discrimination in public schools based on sexual orientation.

Several states have programs in place to address harassment and violence against lesbian, gay, bisexual, and transgender youth. Massachusetts and Vermont, the only states that include questions relating to students' sexual orientation on state youth risk behavior surveys, have state programs that provide support to lesbian, gay, and bisexual youth.[28] (Neither program explicitly includes transgender youth.)

In the absence of explicit legal protection from discrimination against lesbian, gay, bisexual, and transgender students, some school districts attempt to protect students from antigay harassment through their policies and codes of conduct. In February 2001, however, a federal court of appeals found that a Pennsylvania school's policy impermissibly restricted students' freedom of speech, basing its holding in part on the fact that the policy "prohibits harassment based on personal characteristics that are not protected under federal law."[29] Although the court recognized that school regulations may offer students greater protection than that

---

[26]*See* Jennifer Egan, "<lonely gay teen seeking same>," *New York Times Magazine,* December 10, 2000, p. 110.

[27]Human Rights Watch interview, Chicago, Illinois, October 6, 2000.

[28]In addition, Oregon and Wisconsin include a question asking students if they have been harassed in the previous thirty days because they were *perceived* to be lesbian, gay, or bisexual.

[29]*Saxe v. State College Area School District,* 240 F.3d 200, 210 (3d Cir. 2001).

in existing federal and state law, its decision raises the prospect of similar constitutional challenges to school policies in other districts. These difficulties underscore the need for federal protection from discrimination based on sexual orientation and gender identity.

Moreover, antigay sentiment flourishes in much of the country. Efforts to provide a safe, supportive environment for lesbian, gay, bisexual, and transgender students are hampered by discriminatory legislation in some states—sometimes referred to as "no promo homo" laws—that restrict student access to information relating to sexual orientation or gender identity. These laws prohibit school officials and teachers from acknowledging that homosexuality exists or saying anything which could be perceived as either neutral or positive about homosexuality.[30]

The Boy Scouts of America, traditionally viewed as an organization open to all boys, secured approval from the U.S. Supreme Court to discriminate against lesbian, gay, bisexual, and transgender youth if it wishes to do so.[31]

In Vermont, a campaign against civil unions legislation began to target a youth group for lesbian, gay, bisexual, and transgender teens. Referring to materials that provide information on avoiding sexually transmitted diseases, the campaign charged that Outright Vermont "could expose our children to the gay sex life" by telling youth "exactly how to perform gay sex acts." Outright director Keith Elston notes that the group does not distribute the materials in schools and does not do safer sex work in schools; instead, it makes brochures—approved by the Centers for Disease Control and Prevention—available to youth who come to the group's drop-in center and request information on safer sex practices.[32]

Lesbian, gay, bisexual, and transgender youth are aware of—and will soon confront, if they haven't already—other legal barriers to equality. These barriers include state prohibitions on same-sex marriage and on adoption by same-sex couples and the military's ban on lesbian, gay, and bisexual individuals serving openly.

The Lesbian, Gay, and Bisexual Youth Population

Estimates of the number of gay, lesbian, and bisexual youth in the United States range from just over 1 percent to just under 9 percent, with the best estimates at 5 to 6 percent of the total population. These figures depend in part on whether

---

[30]See Chapter X, "Health Education" section.
[31]See Boy Scouts of America v. Dale, 530 U.S. 640 (2000).
[32]See Kai Wright, "Youth Group Under Attack in Vermont," New York Blade News, October 27, 2000, p. 8.

the studies measure same-sex attraction, same-sex behavior, or both, whether they ask youth if they are unsure of or questioning their sexual orientation, and whether they ask youth to label themselves as gay, lesbian, or bisexual.

The nature of adolescence complicates any attempt to assess the sexual orientation of youth. Adolescence is a time of exploration and experimentation, a period in which youth begin to develop a sexual identity. As Ritch Savin-Williams has noted, many gay, lesbian, bisexual, and transgender youth are not sexually experienced. Many have heterosexual experiences, and heterosexual youth may have same-sex experiences. Some youth identify as lesbian, gay, or bisexual without having had any same-sex sexual experiences nor, for that matter, any heterosexual experiences.[33]

Asking about same-sex attraction is a way of measuring the incidence of sexual orientation in a group that includes individuals who are not sexually active. The National Longitudinal Study of Adolescent Health, perhaps the most comprehensive of the studies that include questions about same-sex attraction, includes over 12,000 youth in grades seven through twelve drawn from high schools and middle schools across the United States. Six percent of participants between the ages of thirteen and eighteen reported same-sex romantic attraction, with 1 percent identifying same-sex attraction only and 5 percent reporting attraction to both sexes.[34]

Studies that ask youth how they identify themselves yield lower figures, a result that is consistent with research finding that youth are generally reluctant to label themselves as lesbian or gay.[35] Of those who completed the 1995 Massachusetts Youth Risk Behavior Survey, 2.5 percent identified themselves as gay, lesbian, or bisexual; when those who described themselves as unsure of their

[33]*See* Ritch C. Savin-Williams, "Gay and Lesbian Adolescents," in F.W. Bozett and M.B. Sussman, eds., *Homosexuality and Family Relations* (Binghamton, N.Y.: Harrington Park Press, 1990).

[34]Of the remaining youth, 82.6 percent reported opposite-sex attractions only and 11.4 percent reported attractions to neither sex. *See* Stephen T. Russell and Brian D. Franz, "Violence in the Lives of Sexual Minority Youth: Understanding Victimization and Violence Perpetration" (paper presented at the annual meeting of the American Sociological Association, Chicago, Illinois, August 1999), p. 6.

[35]*See, for example,* R.C. Savin-Williams and R.E. Lenhart, "AIDS Prevention Among Lesbian and Gay Youth: Psychosocial Stress and Health Care Intervention Guidelines," in David G. Ostrow, ed., *Behavioral Aspects of AIDS* (New York: Plenum Publishing, 1990).

sexual orientation were included, the figure was 3.8 percent.[36] A 1992 study of junior and senior high school students in Minnesota yielded an even lower incidence of sexual minorities, with 1.1 percent describing themselves as bisexual or predominantly homosexual, 10.7 percent as "unsure" of their sexual orientation, and 88.2 percent as predominantly heterosexual.[37] As might be expected, younger youth are more likely to be unsure of their sexual orientation. The 1992 Minnesota study found, for example, that one in four twelve-year-olds was unsure of his or her sexual orientation, while only one in twenty was questioning his or her sexual orientation at age eighteen.[38]

As a percentage of all youth surveyed, the figures for those that have engaged in same-sex behavior does not differ markedly from measures of same-sex attraction. In Vermont, for example, the 1999 Youth Risk Behavior Survey found that about 3 percent of youth had engaged in same-sex behavior.[39]

A different picture emerges if one examines only those youth who are sexually active. The majority of youth surveyed in Vermont's 1999 Youth Risk Behavior Survey—64 percent of girls and 59 percent of boys—had never had sex. Of those who were sexually active, an analysis of Vermont's 1995 Youth Risk

---

[36]The 1995 Massachusetts Youth Risk Behavior Survey also asked youth if they had ever had same-sex sexual experiences. See Robert Garofolo et al., "The Association Between Health Risk Behaviors and Sexual Orientation Among a School-Based Sample of Adolescents," *Pediatrics,* vol. 101 (1998), p. 895; Robert Garofalo et al., "Sexual Orientation and Risk of Suicide Attempts Among a Representative Sample of Youth," *Archives of Pediatrics and Adolescent Medicine,* vol. 153 (1999), p. 487.

Similarly, in a New Zealand study, 2.8 percent of those questioned at age twenty-one either identified themselves as gay, lesbian, or bisexual or reported relationships with same-sex partners between the ages of sixteen and the time of the survey. See David M. Fergusson, L. John Horwood, and Annette L. Beautrais, "Is Sexual Orientation Related to Mental Health Problems and Suicidality in Young People?," *Archives of General Psychiatry,* vol. 56 (1999), p. 876. These data were gathered as part of the Christchurch Health and Development Study, a twenty-one-year longitudinal study of 1,265 children born in Christchurch, New Zealand.

[37]G. Remafedi et al., "Demography of Sexual Orientation in Adolescents," *Pediatrics,* vol. 89 (1992), p. 714. The sample was representative of youth in Minnesota, consisting of 34,706 students in grades seven through twelve of diverse ethnic, geographic, and socioeconomic backgrounds.

[38]Ibid. See also Gary Hollander, "Questioning Youths: Challenges to Working with Youths Forming Identity," *School Psychology Review,* vol. 29 (2000), p. 173.

[39]Vermont Department of Health, Office of Alcohol and Drug Abuse Programs, *1999 Vermont Youth Risk Behavior Survey* (Montpelier, Vermont: 2000), p. 62, www.state.vt.us/adap/1999YRBS/YRBSST991.htm (accessed on April 3, 2001).

Behavior Survey found that 8.7 percent of boys in the eighth through twelfth grades reported that they had had one or more male sexual partners.[40]

The 1999 Massachusetts Youth Risk Behavior Survey asked students if they had had any same-sex sexual contact and if they identified themselves as gay, lesbian, or bisexual, finding that 5.5 percent of students participating in the survey fit one or both of those categories.

Transgender Youth

We interviewed eight youth who identified themselves as transgender, the umbrella term used to describe the identities and experiences of people whose gender identity in some ways does not conform to society's stereotypical concepts of "maleness" or "femaleness."[41] It includes transsexuals who may or may not have had or plan to have sex reassignment surgery, male and female cross-dressers, and intersex persons.[42]   Both self-identified transgender people and people perceived to be transgender are subject to discrimination and persecution. Gender identity is separate from sexual orientation, though many people who are wrongly perceived to be transgender are gay or lesbian. Human Rights Watch uses the term *transgender* in this report to refer to any youth we interviewed who were questioning their gender identity, challenging gender norms, intersex, or transsexual.

Children of Lesbian, Gay, Bisexual, and Transgender Parents

An estimated two million to eight million parents in the United States are lesbian or gay.[43] Their children are no more likely than any other youth to be

---

[40]*See also* Robert H. DuRant, Daniel P. Krowchuk, and Sara H. Sinal, "Victimization, Use of Violence, and Drug Use at School Among Male Adolescents Who Engage in Same-Sex Sexual Behavior," *Journal of Pediatrics,* vol. 132 (1998), p. 13.

[41]*See* Jamison Green, "Introduction to Transgender Issues," introduction to Paisley Currah and Shannon Minter, *Trangender Equality, A Handbook for Activist and Policymakers* (San Francisco and New York: National Center for Lesbian Rights and National Gay and Lesbian Task Force Policy Institute, 2000), pp. 1-6.

[42]Intersex individuals are people born with "ambiguous" genitalia and who, under existing though controversial medical practices, are often "assigned" a gender by their doctor.

[43]*See* C.J. Patterson, "Lesbian Mothers, Gay Fathers, and Their Children," in A.R. D'Augelli and C.J. Patterson, eds., *Lesbian, Gay and Bisexual Identities over the Lifespan* (New York: Oxford University Press, 1995), p. 262. *See also* Virginia Casper and Steven B. Schultz, *Gay Parents/Straight Schools: Building Communication and Trust* (New York: Teachers College Press, 1999), p. 4.

lesbian, gay, bisexual, or transgender, but they are often targeted for harassment and violence because of their parents' sexual orientation or because their peers believe that they share their parents' sexual orientation. "My mom's a lesbian. I used to get a lot of crap for it," said Leslie H., sixteen. "They'd say, 'Yeah, the lesbian's daughter. Does it run in the family?'"[44]

Children of lesbian, gay, bisexual and transgender parents are enrolled in school districts throughout the United States, not only in urban areas. In primarily rural central Illinois, for example, a February 2001 study of lesbian, gay, bisexual, and transgender persons found that 22 percent of those who responded were parents.[45] "This group of kids is suffering many of the same repercussions that LGBT kids do, and in much higher numbers," says Felicia Park-Rogers, director of Children of Lesbians and Gays Everywhere.[46]

---

[44]Human Rights Watch interview, Dallas, Texas, March 27, 2000.

[45]*See* Ramona Faith Oswald, Eileen Gebbie, and Linda Sue Culton, *Report to the Community: Rainbow Illinois: A Survey of Gay, Lesbian, Bisexual, and Transgender People in Central Illinois* (Urbana, Illinois: Department of Human and Community Development, University of Illinois, 2001), p. 11.

[46]Human Rights Watch interview with Felicia Park-Rogers, director, Children of Lesbians and Gays Everywhere, San Francisco, California, October 26, 1999.

Gabriel D., California

Gabriel D., a sixteen-year-old in the San Francisco area, reported that he had been consistently harassed since his last year in elementary school. "I wasn't labeled until early middle school.

"After that, I've always been harassed," he told us. "I was a little femme kid. It happened when I walked around, whatever I did. It started in junior high, in sixth grade.

"It would happen when I walked down the hall. People would yell or comment 'faggot'-type things.

"I decided this kind of treatment wasn't right. I started looking for some way to deal with it. I decided to complain, based on the comments and the fact that they were repeatedly harassing me. I made complaints about two people. At the time I didn't have an understanding about how the process works.

"They decided to give the kids a little talking to. They weren't walking the halls with me; they couldn't understand what was going on. I was really frustrated.

"It led to the kids increasing the harassment, I realized. The same comments, but it became more and more people. It was always, like, ten people or, like, thirteen very fervent, active harassers. It climaxed two weeks after the end of the first quarter this year. It went from whispers into these comments down the hall, gestures, things that were demeaning to me.

"I try to be fair about things. I tried to talk to one individual. I told him, 'You can apologize.' The next day he threatened to beat me up at the bus.

"I continued to make complaints. Then they started strategically sending different people to harass me. Different people would whistle at me in the hall. In gym, three people yelled across the gym. So when I went to the principal, he said—he said there was no evidence.

"There was one suspension, one day, of a person I didn't really know was involved, but I took that. It was hard to get anything more because they paired off so it was a different person each time.

"These people were in my classrooms. Like, one time, a few of them were on the other team in gym. They would smack the ball really hard toward me, but they had terrible accuracy.

"They take on a stereotypical gay male role. It's extremely sexual a lot of the time, things I don't feel comfortable saying. And hand motions, speaking in an accent.

"Hitting on you, that's a big thing.

"They mimic homoerotic acts. They'll mimic anal sex, mimic oral sex.

"It started at school, but it's even worse off campus. One time, these people sped up in a car and flipped my mom and I off," an obscene hand gesture. "That offends me more, because I was with my parents. I got threatening phone calls too, and one obscene phone call. My sister answered the phone, and they described this explicit sexual act.

"There's nobody out at school. Nobody else is openly gay. There's one vaguely lesbian teacher. It wouldn't make a difference to me if we had an out teacher. Maybe before, yes, but not now."

IV. HATRED IN THE HALLWAYS

I don't feel like adolescents should have to go to school in survival
mode.

—Leon C., Long Beach, California, October 21, 1999

Verbal harassment of lesbian, gay, bisexual, and transgender students is a
serious problem in U.S. high schools and middle schools. One-third of eleventh-
grade students who responded to a 1999 CBS poll said that they knew of incidents
of harassment of gay or lesbian students. Twenty-eight percent admitted to making
antigay remarks themselves.[47] The average high school student in the Des Moines,
Iowa, public schools hears an antigay comment every seven minutes, according to
data gathered by students in a year-long study; teachers intervened only 3 percent
of the time.[48]

Damaging in itself, verbal harassment that goes unchecked may quickly
escalate into physical violence, including sexual assaults. And when teachers and
administrators fail to act to prevent harassment and violence, they send a message
that it is permissible for students to engage in harassment, and they allow the
formation of a climate in which students may feel entitled to escalate their
harassment of gay youth to acts of physical and sexual violence.

Lesbian, gay, bisexual, and transgender youth are not the only victims of
harassment and violence. Because those who commit such acts do so based on
their perception of sexual orientation and gender identity, "straight students are
targets of homophobic harassment," notes Rea Carey, former executive director of
the Washington, D.C.-based National Youth Advocacy Coalition. "A lot of times
it's not until that fact is pointed out to them do school administrators perk up their
ears."[49] Unfortunately, when school officials respond only after a straight student
is "mistakenly" targeted, they reinforce the notion that lesbian, gay, bisexual and
transgender students are not worthy of protection.

When teachers and administrators fail to protect students from peer
harassment and violence, the state violates its obligation under international law to

---

[47]"Out But Not Down," *Anchorage Daily News*, June 24, 1999.

[48]*See* Kelley Carter, "Gay Slurs Abound," *Des Moines Register*, March 7, 1997, p. 1.

[49]Human Rights Watch interview with Rea Carey, then executive director of the
National Youth Advocacy Coalition, New York, New York, March 4, 1999.

31

provide youth with the "measures of protection" they are due as children.[50] In addition, if teachers and administrators extend lesbian, gay, bisexual, or transgender students less protection that they would to heterosexual students in similar circumstances—if, for example, they routinely investigate complaints of sexual harassment by straight girls but brush off such complaints when made by gay boys—the state runs afoul of its duty to respect and ensure the right of youth "without any discrimination to the equal protection of the law."[51]

Unsurprisingly, those who endure such abuse on a daily basis report that it affects their school performance and general well-being. "It was interfering with my education and other students' education. It was interfering with teaching. It was not a good learning environment," said Dempsey H., a sophomore in East Texas.[52]

The failure to address antigay harassment and violence affects the education of all students, not only those who are harassed. Emphasizing "the importance of education to our democratic society," the U.S. Supreme Court has observed that it is "perhaps the most important function of state and local governments," "the very foundation of good citizenship," and "a principal instrument in awakening the child to cultural values."[53] Ultimately, the failure to respond to harassment and violence subverts these principles by sending all students a message that it is permissible to hate.

Verbal and Other Nonphysical Harassment

If the experiences of the youth interviewed by Human Rights Watch are any measure, verbal harassment is very common in U.S. middle schools and high

---

[50]International Covenant on Civil and Political Rights (ICCPR), art. 24(1). Human Rights Watch views the obligation to protect youth from violence as one aspect of the "measures of protection . . . required by [one's] status as a minor." *See* Chapter XI, "Right to Protection from Physical and Mental Violence" section.

[51]ICCPR, art. 26.

[52]Human Rights Watch interview, Lubbock, Texas, March 21, 2000.

[53]*Brown v. Board of Education,* 347 U.S. 483, 493 (1954). Article 29(2) of the Convention on the Rights of the Child notes that one of the purposes of education is "the development of respect for human rights and fundamental freedoms." Ratified by every country in the world with the exception of Somalia and the United States, the convention reflects international consensus on children's human rights. Because the United States has signed but not ratified the convention, it is not generally bound by the convention's terms; as a signatory, however, it has the obligation to refrain from actions that would defeat the convention's object and purpose. *See* Chapter XI, "Right to Protection from Physical and Mental Violence" section.

schools. Nearly every one of the 140 youth we interviewed described incidents of verbal or other nonphysical harassment in school because of their own or other students' perceived sexual orientation. For many lesbian, gay, bisexual, and transgender youth, relentless verbal abuse and other forms of harassment are "all part of the normal daily routine," as Dylan N. notes.[54]

"They used to call me all kinds of names—faggot and stuff like that," said Jesús M., a bisexual seventeen-year-old, in a comment typical of those we heard. "The worst thing about my first school was that they were screaming things to me in the hallways. Sometimes they would say these names in class."[55] "People called everyone 'faggot,'" said Chance M., an eighteen-year-old senior in Massachusetts. "That's like the word of the century. It turned into a routine."[56] "That's how you pick on someone, straight or gay. You call them a fag," said James L., a sophomore in the Los Angeles area. "I hear it a lot of times during the course of the day, a lot, at the very least ten to twenty times a day."[57] "These guys, they'll stand in front of the lockers. They'll be, like, 'Look at that faggot.' You hear it every day," Tommy L. told us.[58]

Most of the other students we spoke with had similar experiences. Aaron G., a twenty-year-old college sophomore, told Human Rights Watch, "I got a lot of harassment in high school. 'Fucking fag,' stuff like that."[59] "I had people harass me for liking girls," recounted Kimberly G., a nineteen-year-old who graduated from a Texas high school in 1999. "I got a lot of that during my senior year. . . . It got to the point with me during the last three months before graduation, it probably happened every day."[60] When Casey G.'s classmates at his North Carolina school discovered that he was gay, they harassed him daily. "They'd come up to me and say, 'I'll pray for you tonight.' Or just call me 'faggot,'" he told us.[61] The same thing happened to Dalia P. when her classmates learned she was a lesbian during her sophomore year; "people would be yelling 'dyke' down the hall," she said.[62] And Erin B., an eighth grader in Georgia, told us about the

---

[54]Human Rights Watch interview, Atlanta, Georgia, December 15, 1999.

[55]Human Rights Watch interview, Long Beach, California, January 19, 2000.

[56]Human Rights Watch interview, Barnstable County, Massachusetts, May 10, 2000.

[57]Human Rights Watch interview, Los Angeles, California, January 19, 2000.

[58]Human Rights Watch telephone interview, March 24, 2000.

[59]Human Rights Watch interview, Barnstable County, Massachusetts, May 10, 2000.

[60]Human Rights Watch interview, Austin, Texas, March 15, 2000 (we interviewed Kimberly G. and Shelby L. together at their request).

[61]Human Rights Watch interview, Los Angeles, California, January 20, 2000.

[62]Human Rights Watch interview, Austin, Texas, March 15, 2000.

verbal abuse one of her classmates receives. "Taylor is the only openly gay male student at school," she said. "He gets teased so badly every five seconds."[63]

Whisper campaigns are a related method of harassment. "People will start rumors about me because I'm the only gay person who's out in the whole school," said Miguel S., a New Jersey high school student. "The worst was when people were saying that I had AIDS."[64] Lavonn R. told us, "Sometimes there didn't need to be much said at all. It could be looks, whispering, horrible rumors. In junior high, the rumors can start in sixth grade and haunt you through the rest of junior high."[65]

Drew L. reported that he received obscene telephone calls.[66] Gina T. also told us that she received threatening calls at home, making her "hate every minute of school."[67]

Harassment can also come in the form of written notes, obscene or suggestive cartoons, graffiti scrawled on walls or lockers, or pornography. "Someone wrote 'FAG' on my locker," Chance M. told us.[68] Lavonn R. reported that his classmates "would always be sticking things in my locker."[69]

On another occasion in the school library, Chance told us, "Someone put a book on how to cope with homosexuality into my bookbag. The alarm went off [when he left the library], and the librarian pulled it out of my bag. It was very embarrassing."[70] Dahlia P. had a similar experience.[71]

Beth G. came to school one day to see "large red letters across the wall saying, 'Beth's dead.'"[72] One of Ron T.'s classmates vandalized the school theater, scrawling messages such as "[Ron] is a faggot" and "all gays must die"; to his school's credit, Ron reports that "that was taken care of quickly."[73]

Dylan N. reported that his classmates passed fake love letters to other boys with his name signed at the bottom.[74] Mimicking behaviors are another common

---

[63]Human Rights Watch interview, Atlanta, Georgia, March 2, 2000.

[64]Human Rights Watch interview, Bergen County, New Jersey, October 31, 1999 (group discussion).

[65]Human Rights Watch interview, Austin, Texas, March 23, 2000.

[66]Human Rights Watch interview, Dallas, Texas, March 27, 2000.

[67]Human Rights Watch interview, Houston, Texas, March 17, 2000.

[68]Human Rights Watch interview, Barnstable County, Massachusetts, May 10, 2000.

[69]Human Rights Watch interview, Austin, Texas, March 23, 2000.

[70]Human Rights Watch interview, Barnstable County, Massachusetts, May 10, 2000.

[71]Human Rights Watch interview, Austin, Texas, March 15, 2000.

[72]Human Rights Watch interview, Boston, Massachusetts, May 8, 2000.

[73]Human Rights Watch interview, Lubbock, Texas, March 21, 2000.

[74]Human Rights Watch interview, Atlanta, Georgia, December 15, 1999.

method of harassment. "Lots of straight guys play as if they were gay," Drew L. said.[75]

The Effect of a Hostile Climate

The unrelenting verbal attacks on lesbian, gay, bisexual, and transgender students creates a hostile climate that can be unbearable for them. It can undermine students' ability to focus at school as well as their well-being. When school officials routinely ignore the pervasive verbal harassment or dismiss its seriousness, they create an atmosphere that the gay students are powerless to change and from which they can only escape by dropping out of school. Although the youth we interviewed frequently focused on fear of physical and sexual violence, many noted that the experience of being called "faggot," "queer," "dyke" and other slurs on a daily basis was devastating. One young gay youth who had dropped out of an honors program angrily protested, "Just because I am gay doesn't mean I am stupid," as he told of hearing "that's so gay" meaning "that's so stupid," not just from other students but from teachers in his school.[76]

Many youth we interviewed emphasized that verbal harassment was not harmless behavior. "It's not just name calling," stressed Gabriel D. "I don't know how schools can isolate it like that. When are they going to see it as a problem? When we're bloody on the ground in front of them? In front of the media? It would be a lot more proactive to educate people to stop it now. . . . Otherwise, when is it going to stop?"[77]

Asked if he thought students who used terms like "fag" were just playing around, Chance M. responded, "A few times, I'm sure that's true. But a lot of times it's pure hate . . . . By ninth grade, they're old enough to know that words hurt. They can stop; it's not that hard."[78]

"People do use the term 'gay' as an adjective to describe anybody stupid or crazy or not cool. It's degrading the whole term and what it represents," Melanie S. told us. "Words hurt," she added. "A gay kid could be on the brink, ready to give up, and hears that word all the time. I can be in a conversation down the hall, and I can hear it. It grabs me. You can't avoid it. People should understand not to do that."[79]

---

[75]Human Rights Watch interviews, Dallas, Texas, March 27, 2000.

[76]Human Rights Watch interview, Long Beach, California, October 21, 1999.

[77]Human Rights Watch interview, San Francisco, California, January 28, 2000 (we interviewed Gabriel D. and Jack S. together at their request).

[78]Human Rights Watch interview, Barnstable County, Massachusetts, May 10, 2000.

[79]Human Rights Watch interview, Salem, Massachusetts, May 23, 2000.

"It hurts because it feels like harassment," commented Danny W., a seventeen-year-old in Dallas.[80] "I know that when people do that I get affected," Drew L., fifteen, said of hearing the word "faggot." "It's kind of like if I heard black people called names, I would get offended. It's a word that I've never been taught as meaning something friendly. It's not a gesture that I take lightly."[81]

"It's so persistent," Michelle Golden, of Gay and Lesbian Adolescent Social Services (GLASS), told Human Rights Watch. "People will say, 'It's just a comment,' but it really creates a climate."[82] Every time a slur is ignored by school officials, the students who are targets of those slurs are reminded that neither their teachers nor the school administrators are willing to defend them or to make the school a safe place for them. At the same time that students who are the targets of the harassment get the message that they are not worthy of protection, the students engaging in acts of harassment get the message that they can get away with harassing their gay peers. It is precisely this impunity that those who harass rely on when they escalate their attacks against lesbian, gay, bisexual, and transgender students.

"There's an emotional consequence to name calling," said Jack S., an eighteen-year-old senior. "When is it equal for all?" asked Gabriel. "It's not like someone calling someone else an idiot. Not everyone gets called a faggot."

"It's only for people who are different," said Jack.[83]

Verbal harassment in itself has serious consequences for school performance and general well-being. When Dr. Gerald P. Mallon interviewed fifty-four gay and lesbian youth in the child welfare system, he found that "[f]or many, verbal harassment causes as much hurt as physical violence because it profoundly damages self-esteem."[84]

Many youth find it particularly damaging to be harassed because of their actual or perceived sexual orientation. A 1993 survey by the American Association of University Women Education Foundation found that 86 percent of students—87 percent of girls and 85 percent of boys—stated that they would be very upset if

---

[80]Human Rights Watch interview, Dallas, Texas, March 27, 2000.

[81]Human Rights Watch interview, Dallas, Texas, March 27, 2000.

[82]Human Rights Watch interview with Michelle Golden, Gay and Lesbian Adolescent Social Services, Boston, Massachusetts, May 8, 2000.

[83]Human Rights Watch interviews, San Francisco, January 28, 2000 (we interviewed Gabriel D. and Jack S. together at their request).

[84]Gerald P. Mallon, *We Don't Exactly Get the Welcome Wagon: The Experiences of Gay and Lesbian Adolescents in Child Welfare Systems* (New York: Columbia University Press, 1998), p. 85.

they were identified by their peers as gay or lesbian. "No other type of harassment—including actual physical abuse—provoked a reaction this strong among boys," the study noted.[85]

An atmosphere of discrimination, harassment, and violence is not conducive to learning. "I was conscious of the fact that I was not getting an education," Dylan N. told us.[86] Many of the youth we interviewed told us that they had skipped school because of persistent harassment or threats of violence.

Some youth switch schools to escape harassment and violence. Eric C., for example, was able to graduate after he transferred to a school with a reputation for acceptance of lesbian, gay, bisexual, and transgender youth, but he had to commute across town after his transfer.[87]

Others, such as Alex M. and Anika P., miss a semester or more of classes until they find a school that they can attend without fearing violence or experiencing persistent harassment. When we interviewed Tanika R., a thirteen-year-old in Los Angeles, she had not attended classes for nearly four months.[88]

A few simply drop out of school altogether. Some are able to receive a General Educational Development diploma (GED, often referred to as a graduate equivalency degree), as Dylan N., Kylie T., and Dalhia P. did. But these youth are the exceptional few who are able to manage an independent study schedule while coping with the long-term effects of harassment and violence and, frequently, beginning to adjust to life on their own. Many more youth, such as Lavonn R., never complete their GEDs after dropping out of school.[89]

Human Rights Watch found that some of the students try to match the attitude of the teachers and administrators who ignore the harassment. Faced with school officials who downplay the verbal harassment or who tell the gay youth they must "get used to it," some students internalize the message they are just going to have to learn to live with harassment. "I got 'fag,' 'homo,' all those derogatory terms for people. But I've never been harassed," said Chauncey T., a seventeen-year-old

---

[85]*Hostile Hallways: The AAUW Survey on Sexual Harassment in America's Schools* (Washington, D.C.: The American Association of University Women Educational Foundation, 1993), p. 20.

[86]Human Rights Watch interview, Atlanta, Georgia, December 15, 1999.

[87]Human Rights Watch interview, San Francisco, California, January 27, 2000.

[88]Human Rights Watch interviews, Atlanta, Georgia, December 15, 1999; Austin, Texas, March 23, 2000; Los Angeles, California, January 20, 2000.

[89]Human Rights Watch interviews, Atlanta, Georgia, December 15, 1999; Greenfield, Massachusetts, May 31, 2000; Austin, Texas, March 15, 2000; Austin, Texas, March 23, 2000.

in Georgia. Asked to explain how he defined harassment, he replied, "Well, no one's ever wanted to fight me." Later in our conversation, he returned to the topic of verbal harassment, saying, "I've gotten verbal abuse . . . not once, not twice, but incessantly."[90]

"They don't see it as harassment," says Carol Petrucci of the Houston Area Teenage Coalition of Homosexuals (HATCH). "They see it as what it's like to be a kid—this is what you have to take."[91] They get this message from their teachers. Jesús M. told us that when he was harassed by his classmates, "Nothing happened. The teachers didn't hear or would ignore them."[92] In fact, some of the youth seemed to think it was their fault that they found the hostile climate unbearable. Alex M., a sophomore in Georgia, told us that he missed fifty-six days of school the previous semester. "I'm not proud of that. I know I should've done better. I just couldn't deal with it anymore," he said.[93]

Whether the message is explicit or implied, lesbian, gay, bisexual, and transgender students are being taught that verbal harassment is an inevitable consequence of being gay and that they have no right to expect adults to confront their harassers or condemn the harassment.

---

[90]Human Rights Watch interview, Atlanta, Georgia, March 3, 2000.

[91]Human Rights Watch interview with Carol Petrucci, director, Houston Area Teenage Coalition of Homosexuals (HATCH), Houston, Texas, March 17, 2000. HATCH runs a drop-in center and provides support for lesbian, gay, bisexual, and transgender youth.

[92]Human Rights Watch interview, Long Beach, California, January 19, 2000.

[93]Human Rights Watch interview, Atlanta, Georgia, March 1, 2000.

Matt P., New Hampshire

"I switched to the public school in tenth grade. That was in '95. Most of my friends were there, and it was okay for the first couple of months.

"I broke up with my girlfriend. I met a guy; he was from a rival town. It was cool because we could keep it secret. I told four people. One of the girls wanted to go out with me, so she put it out on the school e-mail system that day.

"From then on it was a nightmare. There were 4,500 people in my town, and one identifiably gay male in town besides me.

"I was harassed every day. They'd say, 'faggot,' 'queer,' stuff like that.

"My place was in the art room. For my next class after art, I had to go up to the third floor to English, past the landing where the rednecks hung out. They tripped me. I never did anything to them. It was always, 'faggot,' 'queer.' I got pushed down the flight of stairs.

"It got so I didn't go to the locker room or the bathroom. I stopped using my locker. My lock started disappearing and reappearing on other people's lockers.

"It wasn't just at school. My father was harassed. People would recognize his car. On the day of his wedding, we were walking back and these people drove by and yelled "faggot" at me. That was the first time that my extended family had heard of it.

"Another time, I kissed my boyfriend in the car at the light, and some people got out of their car and screamed at us. They went driving after us, tailgating us and yelling and screaming.

"It wasn't all bad. A lot of people were very friendly. But the people that weren't were really loud. There are always people with different viewpoints, but these people were obnoxious.

"Nothing was done by the administration. A guy screamed 'queer' down the hall in front of the principal's office, but nothing happened to him. The teachers—yeah, the teachers could have seen what was going on. Nothing happened."

Escalation

When harassment goes unchecked it may escalate into more serious behavior. "It was horrible," said Dexter P., a nineteen-year-old high school senior, who reported that other students started harassing him in the first grade. "At first they made fun of me because I was 'different.' Then it was because I was gay. They'd call me things like 'fag' and 'cocksucker.' It went on through middle school and got really bad in high school."

He publicly identified as gay during the middle of his sophomore year. "After I came out, it was like I had a death wish or something. I was pushed around, thrown into lockers. I can see it all in my head. It was just constant. Everybody was always harassing me."[94]

Not every student reported suffering harassment as early as the first grade, but many agreed that verbal abuse starts by middle school. "Yeah, it started in fourth or fifth grade," said Chance M., an eighteen-year-old senior. "It started between fourth and fifth grade and didn't stop until the second semester of my senior year," when he enrolled in college classes.[95]

Similarly, harassment began in middle school for Kimberly G., a 1999 graduate. "It's weird because I was not out at all then." She described having other students calling her a lesbian after they saw her holding hands with her best friend. "Dyke, lesbian, nasty comments like that. They just screamed stuff down the hall. Basically rumors spread really fast."[96]

Lavonn R., a nineteen-year-old who had quit school three years before, recalled, "Ever since I was in junior high, I was totally just picked on and harassed."[97] "It was the sixth grade when he was most targeted," Tod R.'s mother said of her eleven-year-old son.[98] "I'd been pegged in middle school," said Anisse B., a 1998 high school graduate.[99]

Drew L., fifteen, told us that many of his classmates at his Louisiana middle school harassed him. "A lot of them said I was gay because I didn't play football, no sports," he told us. "You just kind of dealt with it. . . . They'd be like, 'Are you a faggot?'"[100]

---

[94]Human Rights Watch interview, Salem, Massachusetts, May 24, 2000.

[95]Human Rights Watch interview, Barnstable County, Massachusetts, May 10, 2000.

[96]Human Rights Watch interview, Austin, Texas, March 15, 2000 (we interviewed Kimberly G. and Shelby L. together at their request).

[97]Human Rights Watch interview, Austin, Texas, March 23, 2000.

[98]Human Rights Watch telephone interview, February 8, 2000.

[99]Human Rights Watch interview, Houston, Texas, March 17, 2000.

[100]Human Rights Watch interview, Dallas, Texas, March 27, 2000.

Students told us that harassment intensified when they entered high school. "In middle school, it's little remarks: 'fag,' 'you're gay,' stuff like that, nothing violent that I witnessed," said Ashley G., a seventeen-year-old in Massachusetts.[101] "It was a lot more easier to deal with in junior high than in high school," Lavonn R. commented. "As I got older in high school, people tended to get a lot meaner. I'd be walking through the halls, people would say things, they'd laugh. Anyone who was my friend would get accosted and hassled. People would make them feel they shouldn't be seen around me."[102]

Sexual Harassment

Peer harassment and violence against lesbian, gay, bisexual, and transgender youth is often sexualized. Sometimes this takes the form of unwelcome physical contact with sexual overtones. "People would grab my breast area," Leslie H. said.[103] "They'd come up and grab my waist, put their arm around me," Kimberly G. recounted.[104] "They'll flash you, try to chase you down. That's what's going to happen," said Dempsey H.[105]

Sexual harassment may also consist of sexually suggestive remarks or gestures. "Guys will grab themselves, or they'll make kissing noises," said Andre T.[106] "They mimic homoerotic acts. They'll mimic anal sex, mimic oral sex," Gabriel D. told us.[107]

Young lesbians and bisexual girls are more likely than other youth to experience sexual harassment, according to a recent study of peer sexual harassment among high school students. The study found that young lesbians and bisexual girls are more likely than heterosexual girls to be called sexually offensive names, have rumors told about them, be called "gay" or "lesbian" in a derogatory way, receive sexually offensive photographs or messages, and be touched or grabbed in a sexual way.[108]

It goes almost without saying that experiencing sexual harassment has mental health consequences for youth. Many students who are subjected to sexual

---

[101]Human Rights Watch interview, Salem, Massachusetts. May 23, 2000.
[102]Human Rights Watch interview, Austin, Texas, March 23. 2000.
[103]Human Rights Watch interview, Dallas, Texas. March 27. 2000.
[104]Human Rights Watch interview, Austin, Texas, March 15. 2000.
[105]Human Rights Watch interview, Lubbock, Texas, March 21. 2000.
[106]Human Rights Watch interview, Dallas, Texas. March 27. 2000.
[107]Human Rights Watch interview, San Francisco, California. January 28, 2000.
[108]See Susan Fineran, "Sexual Minority Students and Peer Sexual Harassment in High School," *Journal of School Social Work*, vol. 11 (2001).

harassment report symptoms of depression that may include loss of appetite, loss of interest in their usual activities, nightmares or disturbed sleep, feelings of isolation from friends and family, and feelings of sadness or anger. They may also have difficulties at school, such as missing school days, not performing as well in school, skipping or dropping classes, or being late to class.[109]

Physical Abuse

Ultimately, persistent and unchecked harassment may lead to physical abuse. A number of the youth we interviewed reported just one or two attacks. Although limited in number, these assaults had considerable psychological impact, especially because they often came after persistent verbal and other nonphysical harassment that had gone unchallenged by school officials.

For example, Beth G. reported that several months of verbal threats and other harassment culminated in physical violence. "I got hit in the back of the head with an ice scraper," she told us. By that point, she said, she was so used to being harassed that "I didn't even turn around to see who it was."[110]

Chance M. told us, "Somebody threw a beer bottle at me during tenth grade and hit me in the neck. I had to crawl over to a friend's house for help. I don't think it was by accident. And in seventh grade I did get held down while someone punched me."[111]

In other cases, the physical abuse was severe and frequent. "It was small pranks at first, like thumbtacks on my chair. Or people would steal my equipment," explained Zach C., who was put into a drafting class composed mostly of seniors when he was in his freshman year. "Then things elevated. I'd hear 'faggot' and people would throw things at me. They'd yell at me a lot. One time when the teacher was out of the room, they got in a group and started strangling me with a drafting line. That's about the same consistency as a fishing line. It was so bad that I started to get blood red around my neck, and it cut me." Later in the school year, his classmates also cut him with knives. On another occasion, he reports, "I was dragged down a flight of stairs by my feet."[112]

---

[109]See, for example, S. Fineran and L. Bennett, "Gender and Power Issues of Peer Sexual Harassment Among Teenagers," *Journal of Interpersonal Violence*, vol. 14 (1999), p. 6; M. Trigg and K. Wittenstrom, "That's the Way the World Goes: Sexual Harassment and New Jersey Teenagers," *Initiatives*, vol. 57 (1996), p. 55.

[110]Human Rights Watch interview, Boston, Massachusetts, May 8, 2000.

[111]Human Rights Watch interview, Barnstable County, Massachusetts, May 10, 2000.

[112]Human Rights Watch interview, Houston, Texas, March 17, 2000 (group discussion).

In Dylan N.'s case, verbal harassment escalated almost immediately into physical violence. Other students began spitting on him and throwing food at him. One day in the parking lot outside his school, six students surrounded him and threw a lasso around his neck, saying, "Let's tie the faggot to the back of the truck." After that incident, the harassment and violence intensified. "I was living in the disciplinary office because other harassment was going on. Everyone knew," he said. "It gave permission for a whole new level of physical stuff to occur." He was pushed up against lockers by students who shouted "fag" and "bitch" at him. On one occasion, a group of students surrounded him outside the school, punching him and jeering while security officers stood nearby. When the assault ended, he had a split lip and a broken nose and was bleeding profusely from his ear.[113]

A 1996 Wisconsin lawsuit starkly illustrates the escalation from verbal taunts to horrific violence. The suit was brought by a gay student who was repeatedly attacked throughout his middle school and high school years. After he told his seventh grade classmates that he was gay, they referred to him routinely as "faggot" and began to hit him and spit on him. He was subjected to a mock rape in a science lab by two of his classmates, who told him that he should enjoy it; twenty other classmates looked on and laughed. He attempted suicide at the end of his eighth grade year.

In high school, the abuse worsened. He was attacked several times in the school bathroom and urinated on during at least one of the attacks. When he took the bus to and from school, other students regularly called him "fag" and "queer" and often threw objects such as steel nuts and bolts at him. In the ninth grade, he again attempted suicide.

The next year, he arrived at school early one day and was surrounded by eight boys, one of whom kicked him in the stomach for five to ten minutes while the others looked on and laughed. Several weeks later, he collapsed from internal bleeding caused by the attack. He left school in the eleventh grade.[114]

The student testified that he asked the principal to intervene to stop the harassment and explained in detail both the attacks and the antigay bias motivating the attacks. Despite the principal's promises to intervene, she took no action. In its

---

[113]Human Rights Watch interview, Atlanta, Georgia, December 15, 1999.

[114]*See Nabozny v. Podlesny*, 92 F.3d 446, 450-52 (7th Cir. 1996). Complaints filed in other cases around the country show a similar pattern of escalation from verbal harassment to physical violence. *See, for example, Flores v. Morgan Hill Unified School District*, Case No. C-98 20358 JW (N.D. Cal. filed June 4, 1998); *Iversen v. Kent School District*, No. C97-1194 (W.D. Wash. filed July 23, 1997); *McDonald v. Jefferson Township Board of Education*, No. 97-5233 (WGB) (D.N.J. filed October 23, 1997).

decision, the court noted that "after the mock rape, [the student] escaped and fled to [the principal's] office. [Her] alleged response is somewhat astonishing; she said that 'boys will be boys' and told [him] that if he was 'going to be so openly gay,' he should 'expect' such behavior from his fellow students."[115] In November 1996, a federal jury found school officials liable for not protecting the student. The district agreed to pay the student over $900,000 in a settlement reached after the verdict.[116]

Students suggested that most incidents of physical violence are not reported. "I think they're unreported to a great extent," said Renata B., a Georgia senior. "I've had friends harassed and physically hurt. Few of them ever report anything."[117] Many students who have been blamed by school officials for "provoking" verbal harassment believe that if they report physical violence they will just be blamed again. "The principal thought I was a hard ass and to blame for everything that happened before I was hit by a brick—why would he change his mind now?" asked Nikki L., a fourteen-year-old lesbian.[118]

"It's very embarrassing for boys especially. I think the harassment and violence is really underreported," says HATCH director Carol Petrucci. "When a boy is beaten up or threatened because of his sexual orientation, if he's not out, it's going to be very difficult for him to tell anybody about it. If he is out, some are going to be thinking, 'Maybe I deserved it.'"[119]

But the limited data that are available suggest that it is common for lesbian, gay, bisexual, and transgender youth to suffer physical assaults because of their sexual orientation or gender identity. Youth who report same-sex or both-sex romantic attraction are more likely to have been in a fight that resulted in the need for medical treatment, according to a 1999 study that reviewed national data.[120] An analysis of the 1995 Vermont Youth Risk Behavior Survey reached similar conclusions. Not only were boys who have same-sex partners more likely than their heterosexual peers to be involved in fights that required them to get medical

---

[115]*Nabozny,* 92 F.3d at 451.

[116]*See* Patricia M. Logue, "Near $1 Million Settlement Raises Standard for Protection of Gay Youth," January 1, 1997, www.lambdalegal.org/cgi-bin/pages/documents/record?record=56 (accessed on April 10, 2001).

[117]Human Rights Watch interview, Atlanta, Georgia, December 15, 1999.

[118]Human Rights Watch interview, San Francisco, California, November 18, 1999.

[119]Human Rights Watch interview with Carol Petrucci, March 17, 2000.

[120]*See* Stephen T. Russell and Brian Franz, "Violence in the Lives of Sexual Minority Youth: Understanding Victimization and Violence Perpetration" (paper presented at the annual meeting of the American Sociological Association, Chicago, Illinois, August 1999), p. 7.

treatment, they are also more likely to have been threatened or injured with a weapon at school, more likely not to attend school because they felt unsafe, and more likely to carry a weapon themselves.[121]

Where the Harassment Occurs

Harassment and acts of violence occur most frequently out of the direct view of teachers and administrators. As a result, students frequently told us that they tried to spend as little time as possible in the hallways, on the stairs, or in any other "teacher-free" zone. In addition, youth spoke of the risks they faced on their way to and from school; in some cases, their harassers vandalized their homes or targeted their families with obscene telephone calls. But we also heard numerous reports of harassment and physical abuse taking place in the classroom, in front of teachers.

"Most things happen in the hallways," said Andre T., a Dallas sophomore.[122] Sam P., a twenty-year-old Austin, Texas, graduate, made the same observation, telling us, "The name calling happens in the hallways."[123] "In the hallways, it's severe," said Greg Z., a senior in Georgia, speaking of harassment from classmates. "Lots of jocks, they pick on certain people. This one guy, they messed up his locker, they pushed him up against his locker" because they believed he was gay. "A lot of times it's things like yelling 'faggots.' Sometimes they just trip you walking down the hallways. Or they slam you into the locker and shout and keep on walking."[124] Erin B., an eighth grader in Georgia, explained, "In my school, there's nothing the teachers can do in the halls because there's no one monitoring. One time I was shoved in front of a locker because a boy thought I was a boy who was trying to hit on him. I said, 'I'm a girl and definitely not trying to hit on you.'"[125]

As a result, many students treat the hallways as enemy territory. "In the halls, I go from one class to another without wasting time," Chauncey T. says.[126]

Locker rooms, frequently unmonitored, are another part of schools where harassment can be particularly severe. Erin told us of the steps she took in her

---

[121]*See* R.H. DuRant, D.P. Krowchuk, and S.H. Sinal, "Victimization, Use of Violence, and Drug Use at School Among Male Adolescents Who Engage in Same-Sex Sexual Behavior," *Journal of Pediatrics,* vol. 133 (1998), p. 113.

[122]Human Rights Watch interview, Dallas, Texas, March 27, 2000.

[123]Human Rights Watch interview, Austin, Texas, March 15, 2000.

[124]Human Rights Watch interview, Atlanta, Georgia, December 18, 1999.

[125]Human Rights Watch interview, Atlanta, Georgia, March 2, 2000.

[126]Human Rights Watch interview, Atlanta, Georgia, March 3, 2000.

seventh grade gym class to minimize harassment. "It was really, really horrible there. . . . In gym, especially—horrible. I wasn't out, but everyone assumed. They wouldn't say anything to my face. I would change in the bathroom stall because I didn't want to be accused of looking at anyone. I was tardy to class all the time because of how long it took me to get changed."[127]

Youth also repeatedly told us that they avoid other areas where students are likely to congregate in large numbers. "I don't go to lunch because of problems with some kids," Chauncey T. says. But trying to avoid problems with other students has led to run-ins with the school administration. "I used to sit outside the sixth period classroom," he explains, "but they gave me detention."[128]

"I don't like going to school before school starts because I don't want to have to deal with anything someone might say before the teachers get there," Erin B. explained.[129]

Many youth feel most vulnerable outside the school setting. "It's mostly outside school that you end up feeling scared. There's nothing you can do at all," Chance M. said.[130] For instance, many students are harassed on their way to and from school. "You'll have people throwing things at you on the bus," said Ethan J., sixteen.[131] We heard similar accounts from students who rely on public transit to get to and from school.[132] The same was true of those who walked to and from school. Dahlia P. told us, "I was walking home from school one day, and this guy pulled up and flipped me off and said, 'Die, you lesbian.' I cried the whole day."[133]

---

[127]Human Rights Watch interview, Atlanta, Georgia, March 2, 2000.

[128]Human Rights Watch interview, Atlanta, Georgia, March 3, 2000. Detention is a mild form of punishment, requiring students to stay after the school days ends and study or do chores.

[129]Human Rights Watch interview, Atlanta, Georgia, March 2, 2000.

[130]Human Rights Watch interview, Barnstable County, Massachusetts, May 10, 2000.

[131]Human Rights Watch interview, Greenfield, Massachusetts, May 31, 2000.

[132]In Boston, three high school students reportedly attacked one of their classmates on a train ride home from school because they thought she was a lesbian. After the three saw the girl holding hands with another girl, they groped her, ripped her clothes, and pointed at their genitals while shouting, "Do you like this? Do you like this? Is this what you like?," according to the Associated Press. The three were charged with indecent assault and battery and civil rights violations. Boston school officials also began disciplinary proceedings, noting that "the ride home is considered part of the school day." *See* "Teens Arrested for Allegedly Sexually Assaulting Classmate on Train," Associated Press, January 29, 2000.

[133]Human Rights Watch interview, Austin, Texas, March 15, 2000.

Others, such as Matt P., talked of being harassed at local shopping malls or while driving or walking around town.[134]

Finally, some youth find themselves targeted in their own homes. Harassment at home may take the form of obscene telephone calls, as in the cases of Drew L., Gina T., and Gabriel D., described above.[135] It may also consist of vandalism. Dempsey H. recounted, "One day we came home, and the house was wrapped," meaning that it was covered with toilet paper and other trash. "I went to school, and I told them, 'I'm sure you have an idea of who's doing this.' They told me to file a police report. I talked to the cops, and they said there was no evidence." After he returned home that evening, his brother stepped outside and saw that Dempsey's car had been vandalized. "My car had shaving cream, shoe polish, all kinds of crap all over it," said Dempsey. On another occasion, he told us, his phone line was cut.[136] Lavonn R.'s house was also targeted. "There was toilet paper in the trees, all over the yard," he said.[137]

Harassment outside the school, particularly that which takes place at students' homes, poses a challenge for school administrators. In many school districts, however, the commute to and from school is considered part of the school day; school disciplinary policies often cover actions by students that take place outside the school, an extension of the disciplinary process that is particularly appropriate if the acts arise out of harassment that begins at school. In some cases, however, harassment outside the school should be addressed in coordination with or even exclusively by local law enforcement officials.

But our findings reveal that a surprising amount of harassment occurs in public areas such as hallways, classrooms, lunchrooms, athletic fields, and school buses.[138] Accordingly, schools should begin to address harassment and violence by ensuring that these public spaces are safe for all students.

---

[134]Human Rights Watch interview, Salem, Massachusetts, May 24, 2000.

[135]Human Rights Watch interviews, Dallas, Texas, March 27, 2000; Houston, Texas, March 17, 2000; San Francisco, California, January 28, 2000.

[136]Human Rights Watch interview, Lubbock, Texas, March 21, 2000.

[137]Human Rights Watch interview, Austin, Texas, March 23, 2000.

[138]These findings are consistent with studies of sexual harassment. For example, a 1995 Connecticut study reported that sexual harassment occurred most frequently in public and that often teachers or other adults were present but did not intervene to stop the harassment. Permanent Commission on the Status of Women, *In Our Own Backyard: Sexual Harassment in Connecticut's Public High Schools* (Hartford, Connecticut: Permanent Commission on the Status of Women, 1995).

Erin B., Georgia

"There's one boy at my school who is open, out of the closet. He gets it horrible. . . . He gets it bad. He's really feminine.

"If a gay man is butch, they don't mess with him as much. If he's feminine, he gets pushed around. For girls, if you're butch, they say, 'Dyke, you want to be a man.'

"[Taylor,] that boy in school, is out to selected people. It's all about knowing who you can surround yourself with. I came out to him first. I told him about YouthPride. [At first] he told me everyone assumes he's gay, but he's not. Two days later he came out to me.

"He's taunted and teased in gym because he doesn't play football, he hangs out with the girls instead. The girls are even worse to him because it's like they feel he wants to be a girl. Everybody gives him hell because he's feminine. He's a really sweet guy but no one cares about that. They just care about the fact that he's gay.

"My ex-girlfriend has it a lot easier. She's part of the 'in' crowd; she's a cheerleader. . . . She doesn't get it nearly as bad as Taylor and I. She plays female roles, she's not butch, doesn't have weird hair. She doesn't get people confused about whether she's a girl or a guy.

"Her friend, my ex-girlfriend's friend, doesn't get it at all. She's going out with a guy now, but at the beginning of the school year she was dating a girl. . . . She's a sweet person. They see that and don't judge. . . . She's explained bisexuality to people, and they listened to her. But if I did that nobody would listen."

V. GENDER AND HOMOPHOBIA

Human Rights Watch examined the treatment of female students both by peers and administrators, how lesbians may have experienced harassment differently than gay students, and how students who are or are perceived to be transgender were treated. It quickly became obvious from our research that the abuse of lesbian, gay, bisexual, and transgender youth is predicated on the belief that girls and boys must strictly adhere to rigid rules of conduct, dress, and appearances based on their sex. For boys, that means they must be athletic, strong, sexist, and hide their emotions. For girls, that means they must be attentive to and flirtatious with boys and must accept a subordinate status to boys. Regardless of their sexual orientation or gender identity, youth who violate these rules are punished by their peers and too often by adults.

Boys who reported the most harassment were those who were least stereotypically masculine. Transgender youth are the most vulnerable to both violence by peers and harassment from adults.

Harassment of Young Lesbians and Bisexual Girls

Although both girls and boys are exploring their sexual orientation and gender identity at younger ages than previous generations, girls continue to identify openly as lesbian and disclose their sexual orientation to family and friends at a later age than their male peers. Thus it was more difficult to find young women who identify as lesbian or bisexual to interview. Most youth service organizations working with lesbian, gay, bisexual, and transgender youth consistently report serving more gay male youth than lesbians or transgender youth.

Service providers had different explanations for why gay boys are more likely than young lesbians to be open about their sexual orientation and to use their services. "More boys come out to their parents and need our support than girls. Boys can't have sleepovers or be close in the way that girls can be without causing speculation," explained Sara Marxner of the Lavender Youth Recreation and Information Center in San Francisco. "Also girls do seem to come out later than boys."[139] Other service providers expressed concern that there were fewer young lesbians and transgender youth using their services because service providers had failed to understand their needs or make it safe enough for them to participate.

Some youth service providers tended to downplay harassment of lesbians. Many service providers and youth with whom we spoke offered the opinion that

---

[139]Human Rights Watch interview with Sara Marxner, Lavender Youth Recreation and Information Center, San Francisco, California, November 18, 1999.

boys were more often targeted for harassment than girls. "They're a lot more aggressive toward the guys," Shelby L. told us, speaking of students who harassed those whom they perceived to be gay. "They'd try to beat them up, start fights, knock their stuff around."[140] Vega S., a sixteen-year-old lesbian, told us, "I think guys do have it worse than girls, but girls go through a lot too."[141]

"The girls who can pass have an easier time," said Michael Ferrera, clinical director of group homes for Gay and Lesbian Adolescent Social Services, in Los Angeles. "The lipstick lesbians are objectified, but the butch girls get challenged all the time. The butch lesbians have the hardest time, and the teachers just don't know how to deal with them."[142]

Others however, argued that it is not that simple; that in fact, what girls experience is much more complicated. "There's the perception that young gay men are the ones getting harassed," says Linda Ellis, executive director of Youth Pride, an Atlanta youth group. "But this is a difficult place for young gay women."[143]

"Sometimes you get harassed just because you're a woman, but lesbians get harassed more," Dahlia P. told us. "It's degrading. Not necessarily that they're calling me a lesbian or a dyke—but it's the simple fact that they want to give you hell. It's every day."[144]

In fact, we found that young lesbians and bisexual girls are harassed in ways that may be different from but often no less serious than the abuse faced by gay and bisexual boys. "Gay men get more physical threats; female students are more likely to get sexually harassed and be threatened with sexual violence. We'll hear things like, 'I can make you straight' or 'Why don't you get some of your girlfriends and we can have a party,'" Dahlia P. told us.[145]

Young lesbians do not experience sexism and homophobia as separate events; instead, the two forms of harassment are mutually reinforcing. It is simply impermissible, according to rigid rules of social behavior, for girls to reject boys. It is an unforgivable transgression for girls to "compete" with boys for the attention of other girls. Thus lesbians, and particularly lesbians who identify as or are

---

[140]Human Rights Watch interview, Austin, Texas, March 15, 2000 (we interviewed Shelby L. and Kimberly G. together at their request).

[141]Human Rights Watch interview, Long Beach, California, October 12, 2000.

[142]Human Rights Watch interview with Michael Ferrera, clinical director of group homes, Gay and Lesbian Adolescent Social Services, Los Angeles, California, October 22, 1999.

[143]Human Rights Watch interview, Atlanta, Georgia, December 13, 1999.

[144]Human Rights Watch interview, Austin, Texas, March 15, 2000.

[145]Human Rights Watch interview, Austin, Texas, March 15, 2000.

perceived to be "butch," are punished for violating gender norms and because of their sexual orientation. There is a perception that lesbians who are "femme" are punished less by their peers, largely because the harassment takes the form of boys wanting to "watch" and then "join" the girls. Girls perceive this harassment not only as an invasion of their privacy but also as an implicit threat of sexual violence. When adults downplay or ignore this type of harassment, they are downplaying the harassment as merely an expression of desire rather than a threat of violence.[146]

A 2000 study of students in western Massachusetts by social worker Susan Fineran found that young lesbians and bisexual girls experienced more sexual harassment than heterosexual girls did. For example, 72 percent of lesbian and bisexual girls reported that they were "called sexually offensive names" by their peers, compared with 63 percent of heterosexual girls. Lesbians and bisexual girls were significantly more likely than heterosexual girls to be "touched, brushed up against, or cornered in a sexual way" (63 percent, as compared to 52 percent of heterosexual girls) and to be "grabbed or have their clothing pulled in a sexual way" (50 percent compared to 44 percent). And 23 percent of young lesbians and bisexual girls reported that their peers had "attempted to hurt me in a sexual way (attempted rape or rape)," while 6 percent of the heterosexual girls surveyed had experienced sexual violence of this nature.[147]

This study underscores the point several young women made to Human Rights Watch: That the majority of girls, regardless of their sexual orientation, are sexually harassed by their peers. Thus, some girls who identify as lesbian or bisexual are probably already accustomed to hearing sexually harassing slurs and comments. If school officials fail to protect girls from sexual harassment by boys in school, it follows that young lesbians and bisexual girls will not turn to school

---

[146]As one federal district court has noted, "harassment, like other forms of victimization, is often motivated by issues of power and control on the part of the harasser, issues not related to sexual preference." *Tanner v. Prima Donna Resorts, Inc.,* 919 F. Supp. 351, 355 (D. Nev. 1996). The mistaken view that harassment must be motivated by desire is similar to the now-discredited assumption that rape is primarily an act of sexual gratification. *See, for example,* A. Nicolas Groth, *Men Who Rape: The Psychology of the Offender* (New York: Plenum Press, 1979), pp. 12-13; Human Rights Watch Women's Rights Project, *The Human Rights Watch Global Report on Women's Human Rights* (New York: Human Rights Watch, 1995), pp. 1-7; Karen Crawford and Thomas Hutchins, "Eliminating Immigration Judges' Discretion to Mis-Characterize Rape as an Act of Sexual Purpose or Pleasure in Asylum Proceedings," *Bender's Immigration Bulletin,* vol. 5 (2000), p. 669.

[147]Susan Fineran, "Sexual Minority Students and Peer Sexual Harassment in High School," *Journal of School Social Work,* vol. 11 (2001).

officials for help when they are harassed because of their sexual orientation. Furthermore, both students and service providers consistently noted that the girls who are most targeted for abuse were girls who failed to conform to gender stereotypes. But again, girls may be reluctant to turn to school officials for protection, as adults as well as peers are critical of girls for violating gender norms.

"Girls in my school expect to be harassed," explained Sabrina L.[148] "The boys mess with us all the time—I don't even think most of the time that I get it worse because I am a lesbian. But we know not to say anything—it's like, unless you've been raped the administration doesn't want to know about it. They'll just say you are lying," Halona T. told us. "It would have to be really bad before I would even try to tell anyone."[149]

Another way that sexism seemed to impact young lesbians was their lack of support from their gay peers. Unlike young gay men we interviewed, none of the girls Human Rights Watch talked with reported feeling protected or supported by gay male peers. But several students noted that girls support gay and bisexual boys and sometimes even protect them from abusive peers. In fact, one boy suggested that the best way to survive was to become close friends with the girls dating the jocks because they would not let the jocks harass their friends. But most young lesbians interviewed by Human Rights Watch did not receive support either from other girls or boys. Young lesbians who were perceived to be "butch" or "dykes" not only were more vulnerable to harassment and abuse but also were even rejected in some cases by their lesbian peers, who may see them as straying too far beyond the limits of socially acceptable gender roles. "Lesbian girls, we dress like girls. 'Dyke' is out of here," said Marianne T.[150]

As with gay boys, young lesbians may appear to be successful students who are doing well in school even as they struggle internally with self-hatred, depression, isolation, and thoughts of suicide. Julie W. told us that she sank into depression during her freshman and sophomore years of high school at the same time that she was a straight-A student and a star on the basketball team. Even though disclosing her sexual orientation has meant coping with lots of harassment and threats of violence, she felt that it has been better for her mental health.[151]

Similarly, Kellsie N. told us that she watched her life fall apart as she tried to cope with her own fears and harassment at school. "They started calling me a lesbian in fourth grade," she said. By high school, she reported, "The guys called

---

[148]Human Rights Watch interview, Orange County, California, October 22, 1999.
[149]Human Rights Watch interview, San Francisco, California, November 16, 1999.
[150]Human Rights Watch interview, Long Beach, California, October 13, 2000.
[151]Human Rights Watch interview, Austin, Texas, March 15, 2000.

me 'dyke' all the time and grabbed my butt. The girls just had a whisper campaign." She protected herself by always having a boyfriend. Her test scores showed her to be a gifted and talented student when she entered high school, but when she became pregnant she was tracked into a program for pregnant girls and eventually dropped out. She has her graduate equivalency degree now, but she told Human Rights Watch that she did not feel safe enough in school to learn and succeed.[152]

The Relationship Between Sexism and Homophobia

Sexism and homophobia are related. Several of the male students we interviewed described peer pressure to treat their female counterparts in a demeaning manner, implicitly asserting the view that boys are superior to girls. One of the easiest ways for boys to demean girls was to treat girls as sexual objects. A sixteen-year-old girl who identified as heterosexual but was attending a school for mostly gay youth told us that she left her high school because of the way boys treated her. "They would talk about my breast all the time, sometimes they would grab them. They would say 'put a bag over her head and she'll be fine,' meaning to have sex with."[153]

An integral component of antigay harassment is attacking lesbians for "daring or wanting to be like a man" and gay men for being effeminate. In their crudest forms, these attacks are based on the constructions of sexuality as males literally dominating females. A "butch" lesbian must be put in her place because she is perceived to take on a dominant sexual role and a "femme" gay man must be punished for acting emasculated. It is not surprising then that lesbians are frequently threatened with being raped, an act of violence aimed at achieving literal sexual domination while gay men are attacked and challenged to defend themselves "like a real man."

"As a male, I was expected to be misogynistic, aggressive, competitive, and homophobic," Burke D. told us. "I was expected to drink and smoke. To protect myself from being identified as gay, I was supposed to be sexist. In fact, I concentrated on working hard to get good grades, which was unacceptable to my peers. But as bad as it was for me, I would not have wanted to go through my high school as a woman."[154]

Gay boys who were not "out" to their peers and who participated in team sports reported being constantly subjected to abusive locker room banter that

---

[152]Human Rights Watch interview, Austin, Texas, March 15, 2000.
[153]Human Rights Watch interview, Dallas, Texas, March 27, 2000.
[154]Human Rights Watch interview, Decatur, Georgia, December 15, 1999.

focused on sexually objectifying the girls in the school and trashing as "queer" any student who was different. "I felt suicidal, I tried too hard to be perfect, to participate in sports and to hide. My teammates would always talk about how they could tell if someone was a 'faggot' just from the way they walked. They never suspected me—but I heard it [the slurs] every day," explained Luke G., a high school football player.[155]

Halona T., a young African-American lesbian who attends school in a major metropolitan area, talked about how girls get harassed endlessly by male students. Black girls get harassed for "being good," "acting white," and "being political." The boys feel free to grab the girls as they walk down the halls, but when girls complain to the administration, they are accused of lying. She is open about the fact that she is a lesbian, and she plans to start a gay-straight alliance this year. She worries more about the sexual harassment than the random homophobic comments, although she acknowledged that might change if she became involved with another student.[156] Burke also pointed out that, although most of the lesbians he knew in high school were not out, they could not escape being harassed because they were girls.[157]

Some of the girls we interviewed told us that it is much more difficult to reach out to school officials when they are harassed because of their sexual orientation. "Lots of boys would say 'you're a whore' or 'you've got big boobs,'" said Marie J. "But at least when I was harassed as a girl, I could talk to the support counselor—not the principal, but the counselor. When I was harassed as a lesbian, I couldn't talk to anyone . . . . I just lied, lied about everything."[158]

One counselor we interviewed also expressed concern that girls rarely excelled once they were publicly identified as lesbian. Boys were sometimes able to find a niche for themselves in the drama club, as a band major, or even as the class clown to survive, but girls rarely, if ever, seemed able to find such a niche for themselves.[159] Girls at the counselor's school are put down consciously and unconsciously. The boys believe that girls and women should "keep in their place" and believe that place is definitely subordinate to men. A guidance counselor in Texas also noted the relationship between sexual harassment and gay harassment

[155]Human Rights Watch interview, Austin, Texas, March 15, 2000.
[156]Human Rights Watch interview, San Francisco, California, November 17, 1999.
[157]Human Rights Watch interview, Decatur, Georgia, December 15, 1999.
[158]Human Rights Watch interview, Austin, Texas, March 15, 2000.
[159]Human Rights Watch interview, Lubbock, Texas, March 21, 2000.

in the school. She said that she saw a great deal of disrespect of girls by boys. Although some dismiss it as funny, she says it is very hurtful to the girls.[160]

Some lesbians find protection from this double harassment in athletics. But sports is not always a safe haven for lesbians. In some schools particularly "butchy" girls are forced out of sports to protect the reputation of the program. It depends on the tone set by the coaches.[161]

And it is not just heterosexual boys who act disrespectfully toward young women. Several of the young gay men we interviewed expressed very sexist and sometimes homophobic views of lesbians. One young man thought there was nothing wrong with calling girls "bitches" but thought that calling gay men "faggot" was unacceptable.[162]

Lesbians who can prevail against the sexism and homophobia they face report feeling empowered. Alix M. told us that it took her three years to get the courage to start a small gay-straight alliance in her Kansas City school. Faced with deepening depression and painful feelings of isolation, she turned to the Internet to get information on how to start a gay-straight alliance. Although she got some negative responses, including being yelled at by a teacher about sin, she now feels that she has made the school much safer for gay students who come after her and that she has become a strong individual who has conquered her fears.[163]

Gender-Nonconforming Youth

Although gender identity and sexual orientation are distinct, many youth believed that they were being harassed, threatened, and judged for their failure to dress, speak, and act in ways which conform to stereotypical notions of what is appropriate for young men and women. Thus, regardless of their gender identity, they are being harassed and typically assumed to be gay or lesbian.

"There are the ones that can pass and those that can't," Michael Ferrera notes. "Those that can't are unsafe everywhere. They're always worried about making sure they have someone with them."[164]

"I didn't get called faggot that much because I was playing soccer," Andre T. observed.[165] But a boy who is, in Gabriel D.'s words, "a little femme kid," often

---

[160]Human Rights Watch interview, Lubbock, Texas, March 20, 2000.
[161]Human Rights Watch interview, Dallas, Texas, March 26, 2000.
[162] Human Rights Watch interview, Dallas, Texas, March 27, 2000.
[163]Human Rights Watch telephone interview, March 30, 2000.
[164]Human Rights Watch interview with Michael Ferrera, October 21, 1999.
[165]Human Rights Watch interview, Dallas, Texas, March 27, 2000.

finds himself targeted with unrelenting abuse.[166]   Recognizing this dynamic, Lavonn R. told us, "I tried to act butch, more macho, but I guess I was doing something wrong because it never worked."[167]

He concluded, "If you're a flamboyant person, you're pretty much damned to hell. I can't think of any gay flamboyant person who has his education."[168]

---

[166]Human Rights Watch interview, San Francisco, California, January 28, 2000.
[167]Human Rights Watch interview, Austin, Texas, March 23, 2000.
[168]Human Rights Watch interview, Austin, Texas, March 23, 2000.

Anika P., Texas

Anika P., seventeen, a transgender youth who has lived for the last seven years as a girl, was in the Texas foster care system when we spoke with her in March 2000. She attended a small public school in South Texas through the first three years of high school. While a student, she decided to dress as a girl and use the name she has chosen for herself. She was harassed by her peers and unable to get support because teachers and other school officials neither understood her being transgender nor made any effort to understand. Instead, they tried to keep her from expressing her gender identity at school. "I had to quit [school] because the teachers were, like, 'You can't wear a dress, you can't wear your hair like that,'" she told us.

"I was ten when it started. It freaked them out, I guess. . . When I started dressing as a woman, they didn't know what to do. Then they decided they couldn't have that kind of thing going around.

"They started making up rules, like, you can't dress in a way to interrupt class, so no long hair or makeup. The teachers were rude. I had to use the boys' restroom or the nurse's restroom, but if the nurse wasn't there, then I didn't go at all."

Using the restroom was particularly challenging because the nurse's office was so far away from her classes. "They give you three minutes between classes, so I'd have to race from one side of the building to another. The teachers were like, 'What took you so long?'" Her teachers often disciplined her for being late to class.

She wouldn't go to gym. "I'd skip. I had to use the boys' locker room; I'd have to shower in the boys' shower."

The school put her in a special education class. "They didn't know what to do," she recalled. "They said it was for my own safety."

She was attacked physically once. "I got beat over the head with a bottle in gym," she reports.

Verbal threats were much more common. "Mainly guys would be coming up to me, saying, 'What's your problem?'" she said. They'd be, like, 'What are you going to do, faggot? You still a man? Going to kick your ass.'"

And she was often sexually harassed. Many of the boys who threatened her also came on to her sexually, knowing that their advances were unwelcome. "That was mainly the problem, guys who wanted to hit on me," she told us.

When she entered the foster care system during her junior year, she moved through a number of placements and schools. "They moved me from shelter to shelter. They're like, 'We don't want to confuse the other kids.'" She told us that she was scheduled to move to another placement at the end of the month.

"A lot of them refuse to take transgender youth," she said. "For the past seven years I've been dressing as a woman. But they're like, 'You have to cut your hair, you can't put makeup on.' Sometimes they tell me I can't wear a bra."

"The shelters are separated. They put me in the men's shelter. The other kids say, 'She's supposed to be over with the women.'"

Some of the shelters have their own schools, so she often attended school under the same conditions that she faced at the shelters. "The rules were the same as the shelter. I couldn't talk about my life with the other kids. It was the same rules about dress and everything." At one shelter, she chose not to attend school at all. "I knew the principal wouldn't let me dress the way I dress," she explained.

From September to December 1999, however, she attended a regular public school that was generally respectful of her gender identity and her privacy. "The only people that knew were the principal, the counselor, and the nurse," she explained. "They were good with that part."

She also appreciated the fact that the school put the name she uses on her records and her school identification card. "They put my girl name on my ID. That was cool. They put it as my middle name," with the boy's name she was given at birth abbreviated as a first initial. "They put my girl name on everything—like, '[D. Anika.]' It was a really good school."

The other students accepted her as female until some of her classmates saw an old piece of identification. "They looked through my purse and found a picture of me as a boy," said Anika. Until that time, she said, "I used the female dressing room and everything. It was impossible to find out until they looked through my purse.

"The girls kept my picture, they hid it from me. Guys started coming up to me, they said 'faggot' and stuff."

Anika felt that school officials placed the burden of addressing the harassment on her by asking her to take the lead in educating her peers about gender identity issues. "They wanted me to go in front of all the kids," she recounted. "They told me, 'We have a few gay students who are also willing to go talk to them.'"

School administrators failed to appreciate the pressure she would feel from such a request, she told us. "I just chose not to tell my personal business," she explained.

When she balked at speaking at a school assembly, administrators didn't make an effort to explore other options, she said. "They told me it was a good idea to leave the school. They were like, 'We think that's a good idea.'"

Transgender Youth

I was safe as long as I remained quiet and didn't let anyone know. . . .
It was like walking on eggshells.
                              —Jocelyn F., Atlanta, Georgia, December 18, 2000

Although most of the youth Human Rights Watch interviewed identify as gay, lesbian, bisexual, or queer or state that they are questioning their sexual orientation, some identify as transgender. Transgender is an umbrella term used to describe the identities and experiences of people whose gender identity in some ways does not conform to society's stereotypical concepts of "maleness" or "femaleness."[169] Gender identity is separate from sexual orientation, though many people who are wrongly perceived to be transgender are gay or lesbian. Human Rights Watch uses the term transgender in this report to refer to any youth we interviewed who were questioning their gender identities, challenging gender norms, intersex, or transsexual.

If gay and lesbian people have achieved some modicum of acceptance in the United States over the past several decades, transgender people remain misunderstood at best and vilified at worst. Although transgender people have played a significant role in the modern gay and lesbian rights movement in the United States, they are frequently marginalized and sometimes even attacked within the gay rights movement. Not surprisingly, youth who identify as or are perceived to be transgender face relentless harassment and live with overwhelming isolation.

Because so few adults understand the experiences of transgender people, even the hint that a student may identify as transgender makes most teachers and administrators extremely uncomfortable. "Our society hasn't even begun to deal with transgender issues," says Michael Ferrera, clinical director of group homes for the Los Angeles-based Gay and Lesbian Adolescent Social Services. "They're experiencing things no one has begun to consider."[170]

Thus, when students report peer harassment, the student—not the harassment—is thought to be the problem.

---

[169]See Jamison Green, "Introduction to Transgender Issues," introduction to Paisley Currah and Shannon Minter, *Trangender Equality, A Handbook for Activists and Policymakers* (San Francisco and New York: National Center for Lesbian Rights and National Gay and Lesbian Task Force Policy Institute, 2000), pp. 1-6.

[170]Human Rights Watch interview with Michael Ferrera, October 21, 1999.

A teacher in West Texas described the case of one very young transgender student who wore purple and pink to school. The student had a circle of friends who managed to protect her from her peers, but they could not protect her from the teachers. Upset with her behavior, her teachers began to humiliate and embarrass her, telling her to "quit acting like a girl."[171]

Joe Saldimini, a teacher in the Out Adolescents Staying in Schools (OASIS) program in Los Angeles, gave us a similar account of teachers humiliating a seventh grader who later identified as transgender. "One called her a faggot and told her she wouldn't have any problems if she only acted like a boy. The teacher would embarrass her in front of all the kids and call her a sissy," he reported, adding that at least one other teacher in the student's school was "very helpful."[172]

Such policing of appropriate behavior for girls and boys can start at a very young age. A Head Start teacher we interviewed said that kids as young as four years old are being told that their behavior is wrong. Little boys who play house may be told, "That's for girls."[173]

For young people who actively identify as transgender and begin undergoing sex reassignment surgery in their teens, not only does the school system fail them, but they face significant problems at home as well. As a result, many end up homeless or trying to negotiate the foster care system. Anika P. described being shunted from school to school not because of peer harassment—in fact she was able to pass quite well in school—but because the Texas foster care system was unable to place her in a foster care home or facility. She was rejected by several facilities which are run by religious organizations and allowed to discriminate against transgender youth.[174]

Constant rejection takes a tremendous toll on these students, particularly when they hear such messages from adults. Blossom R. grew up in a small rural town and was perceived by the community to be different from an early age. In the absence of any supportive adults and totally ostracized by peers, school was a nightmare. Blossom simply quit participating:

---

[171]Human Rights Watch interview, Lubbock, Texas, March 20, 2000.

[172]Human Rights Watch interview with Joe Saldimini, teacher, Out Adolescents Staying in Schools (OASIS), Los Angeles, California, October 20, 1999. OASIS is a program of the Los Angeles Unified School District, with two schools that predominantly serve lesbian, gay, bisexual, and transgender youth, one in West Hollywood and the other in Long Beach.

[173]Human Rights Watch interview, Lubbock, Texas, May 21, 2000.

[174]Human Rights Watch interview, Austin, Texas, March 23, 2000.

I stopped talking in fifth grade. Just quit participating. I sat alone at lunch. I had absolutely no friends. My grades were bad and I was told my conduct was unacceptable. I felt completely ostracized. I heard the word "fag" every single day. Kids used it as a weapon, but I didn't care.[175]

Sasha R., a recent high school graduate, recounted how he survived high school by hiding his male identity. Being open about his gender identity was inconceivable to him:

No, I wasn't out in high school. My school was horrible for people even out as queer. I would never have been out. I remember one guy was out as gay, and he always had to walk by the gym with two or three friends.[176]

Chantelle J., fifteen, said, "I've gone to school dressed as a girl since I was thirteen. I would just stay in the bathroom the whole time during lunch." Asked about her experience at school, she replied, "I wasn't able to do any work. I was harassed, a lot. I couldn't concentrate."[177]

During the course of our investigation, we had the opportunity to observe interactions between gay boys and transgender youth. In several cases, the gay boys behaved in ways that appeared to be sexually harassing

Lacking an understanding of transgender issues, many teachers are unintentionally offensive when confronted with transgender youth. "In my social science classes, sometimes topics dealing with sexual orientation or gender identity would pop up, and I'd get put on the spot," said Gerald A. "Another time, we were talking in class about what each of us would do if we had $70,000, and when it came to me the teacher said, 'Oh, I know what you're gonna get.' This was for a final project. Mine was really about the Russian economy, but he assumed I was going to write about getting a sex-change operation."[178]

As a result, a counselor with the Lavender Youth Recreation and Information Center (LYRIC) told Human Rights Watch that it is too difficult for most students to come out as transgender:

---

[175]Human Rights Watch interview, Houston, Texas, March 17, 2000.
[176]Human Rights Watch interview, San Francisco, California, January 27, 2000.
[177]Human Rights Watch interview, Long Beach, California, October 21, 1999.
[178]Human Rights Watch interview, San Francisco, California, October 27, 1999.

I only know of one person who transitioned in school. Most people are too afraid to do so. Even if they're out to their family and close friends, they don't come out. They're just afraid to.

I know of another person, in a much more suburban area, who went through a lot of violence, low self-esteem, harassment coming from other students. That person stopped high school and is getting a GED [a General Educational Development diploma], trying to decide whether to go through college at all.[179]

Even youth service providers often misunderstand the needs of transgender youth. Many fail to create the safe and respectful atmosphere that transgender youth desperately need. This means being open to how each individual identifies, including giving questioning youth the space to explore their gender identity. This means using his or her choice of name and pronouns in conversations. This means respecting his or her privacy. In one discussion, a team of service providers repeatedly referred to a transgender youth as "he/she" and "she, or whatever." "Many adults think that all transgender people are prostitutes; they never imagine that we work and study and have friends and family," explained a transgender social worker.[180] "I don't think we've been serving transgender youth well," Goodman candidly admitted. "Now we know what to do a little better."[181]

---

[179]Human Rights Watch interview with a counselor at the Lavender Youth Recreation and Information Center (LYRIC), San Francisco, California, January 28, 2000. LYRIC is a community center for lesbian, gay, bisexual, and transgender youth.

[180]Human Rights Watch interview, San Francisco, California, November 18, 1999.

[181]Human Rights Watch interview with Gail Goodman, executive director, Out Youth, Austin, Texas, March 14, 2000.

Dahlia P., Texas

"I had problems at first," says Dahlia P. "People would yell 'dyke' down the hallway. Someone slipped a card in my locker that said 'KKK' on it, and on the back it said, 'You dyke bitch, die dyke bitch.' I wouldn't go to school for the whole week, I was so scared. That happened in my tenth grade year, when I was sixteen, the '97-'98 school year.

"Another time I was walking home from school one day, and this guy pulled up. He flipped me off and said, 'Die, you lesbian.' I cried the whole day. That was the last week of my tenth grade year.

"Another time that same year, I lost my backpack during lunch. Somebody stole it. I found it in my algebra teacher's class. All my stuff was gone through. My notebook was ripped up. There was liquid paper on my backpack, in big letters that said 'DYKE.' It was really shocking."

Asked whether she'd experienced any other incidents of harassment because of her sexual orientation, Dahlia hesitated before replying, "I've had other things happen to me, but I don't know for sure if they were because I'm gay. Like in the lunchroom, I've had people squash ketchup all over me."

She described getting into fights frequently during the year. "One girl, she was egging me on, saying, 'If you're such a big bad dyke, why don't you kick my ass?,'" she said of one incident.

Because of these repeated incidents of harassment, she told us that during her tenth grade year, "I really didn't talk to anyone."

When she heard antigay comments at school, "I tried to deny that I was the lesbian. I tried to deny that they were talking to me." she said. "For a long time I wanted to be straight to make everybody happy. I had a boyfriend. Inside I was hurting. I was afraid of being left out, but it just wasn't working. I was in denial totally."

In addition to abuse from her peers, one of her teachers also harassed her verbally, calling her a lesbian and linking her sexual orientation to her performance in class. "He'd say, 'Well, if you weren't a lesbian you might pass this class,' or 'If you'd get your head out from between those girls' thighs, maybe you'd pass.' The message was I would be so much better off if I weren't gay."

Another of her teachers never addressed her by name, although Dahlia was reluctant to assume that the teacher's behavior was motivated by her sexual orientation. "She would point at me and say 'hey, you,' said Dahlia. "If she wanted me to stop doing something, she would tell my friend to tell me to please be quiet. She would just say 'hey' to me."

She was most affected by the verbal harassment she received from the first teacher. "It really discouraged me from going to algebra class," she said. "I didn't go, and I started failing. I really started slipping.

"I started hanging out with friends who were doing drugs, doing all the things you weren't supposed to do," she recounted.

"I skipped school pretty much half the year, during the last half of that year," she told us. "The teacher was always on my case, so I'd skip algebra because of that. . . .

"Mostly it was the fact that I was scared. It wasn't even the verbal abuse. It was the fact that at any time people could walk up to me and knock the crap out of me because I'm gay. I always had to watch my back," said Dahlia, telling us that she quit school halfway through her junior year.

"I stole a truck and went to a different state. I tried to live as somebody who's straight. It wasn't really me. I got tired of pretending, so I moved to Austin[, Texas,] and found my niche."

Dahlia noted wryly that she fit the profile of youth who turn to drugs in an effort to escape their circumstances. "Yeah, that's me," she said. She described her mother as having "problems with drugs," telling us that she used to get angry about her mother's drug use. "Then, my last year in school, I don't know what happened to me. I went into my mom's room, and I rolled up a joint and started smoking weed. Then I started drinking beer most of the week.

"I felt like every time I took a hit off that pipe, another weight lifted off my shoulders," she recalled. "I didn't want to be in the real world because it hurt so much.

"That lasted until Thanksgiving '99. I'd been out for a couple of months—I left school in February '99, during my junior year."

Describing her typical day during this period, she told us, "Basically I'd wake up, smoke some weed, watch TV. I didn't have a job, so I had all the time in the world."

"I started taking pain pills"—her doctor had prescribed them for an injury—"and I kind of got hooked on the pain pills. Eventually I was using harder drugs. Cocaine, crack. I was a habitual drinker. It depended on who was around, who had what. I really messed up my life.

"I could easily have graduated, gotten my degree, gone to college, and I had to settle for a GED—because of my sexuality?," she asked incredulously. "But I had to quit. I would have regretted staying." She left school when she was seventeen.

"I took the easy way out. I could have gone to court, taken my family through it, all my friends, everybody, but I took the easy way out."

Now nineteen, she has begun to turn her life around. She lives with her girlfriend and their daughter.

"I would hate to have her go through that or to treat somebody that way," she reflected.

VI. COPING WITH HARASSMENT AND VIOLENCE

Discrimination, harassment, and violence take a tremendous toll on youth. "It weighs on you like a ton of bricks," Lavonn G. explained.[182] "I was so angry that I'd been tolerating this behavior, that I was trying to accept it," Beth G. told us, referring to several months of repeated verbal threats and other harassing behavior. "I realized, it's affecting me at school; it's pushing me out of classes."[183]

With many experiencing such abuses on a daily basis, lesbian, gay, bisexual, and transgender youth are more likely than their heterosexual peers to use alcohol or other drugs, engage in risky sexual behaviors, or run away from home. In addition, although most lesbian, gay, bisexual, and transgender youth never consider or attempt suicide, a disproportionate number do.

These youth are remarkably resilient. In interview after interview, we spoke with youth who had survived persistent harassment and severe acts of violence. In many cases, they had taken action to change their circumstances and enable themselves to thrive—seeking assistance from helpful school counselors, demanding protection from administrators, forming gay-straight alliances, switching schools, or even bringing litigation against their school districts.

But their resilience in the face of formidable obstacles does not change the fact that they should not be subjected to these abuses in the first place. These risks to health and well-being flow directly from the state's failure to protect them from physical and mental violence, ensure their right to an education without discrimination, and secure other civil and political rights to which they are entitled.

Depression

Writing for PFLAG's Respect All Youth Project, Ann Thompson Cook notes that lesbian and gay youth "often invest tremendous energy in coping with society's negativity and discrimination. Lacking healthy adult [role] models, skills and support systems, many conclude that they have no hope of ever becoming happy and productive."[184] When Ritch Savin-Williams studied the effect of harassment and abuse on lesbian, gay, and bisexual youth, his findings matched what we heard from the youth we interviewed: he concluded that verbal and

---

[182]Human Rights Watch interview, Austin, Texas, March 23, 2000.

[183]Human Rights Watch interview, Boston, Massachusetts, May 8, 2000.

[184]Ann Thompson Cook, *Who Is Killing Whom?*, Issue Paper 1 (Washington, D.C.: Respect All Youth Project, PFLAG, 1998), p. 2.

physical abuse was common in the lives of lesbian, gay, and bisexual youth and was a source of stress that was "detrimental to their mental health."[185]

Many youth described experiencing sleeplessness, excessive sleep, loss of appetite, feelings of hopelessness, and other classic signs of depression. For example, Alex M., a Georgia sophomore, told us that continual harassment took him "to the point where I couldn't deal with it anymore. I found myself laying out of [skipping] school. I'd get up, but when it just got down to it I couldn't get myself to school. It was just I couldn't deal with it any more. I laid around the house all day." He missed fifty-six days of school during the first half of the school year. He explained, "It was mentally and physically stressful for me to go to that school. I remember going home and waking up in the morning just dreading it. Dreading the fact that I would have to go back to that school."[186]

In fact, youth told us that they were affected by harassment and violence even if it was not directed at them personally. "It feels really frustrating to see that," said Lore F., a 1999 high school graduate. "It feels like being backed into a corner. I think maybe for me it feels like that because I know the person who's doing it doesn't understand that they're hurting someone. It just reminds me of stuff—I just get upset. It makes me want to cry."[187]

Alcohol and Drug Use

"Drinking is a huge one," said Gwen B., describing the ways youth cope with discrimination and harassment.[188] "When I drink, I drink to pass out. I don't care where I go, I just drink to pass out," Blue S. told us. Asked why she drank, she said, "It just felt so good to feel half normal."[189]

"A lot of kids I used to hang out with when I was going through that not-out phase turned to drugs," reported Marina D.[190] "That's very important," Lavonn R. said of youth turning to drugs as a way of dealing with isolation and stigma. "I feel that's why a lot of gay adolescents turn to drugs. It's simply because when you get to the point where there's no one else there to listen to you, to be your friend, you'll turn to anybody. So it's like, 'Come on, hang out with us, we have marijuana.' So

---

[185]R.C. Savin-Williams, "Verbal and Physical Abuse as Stressors in the Lives of Lesbian, Gay Male, and Bisexual Youths: Associations with School Problems," *Journal of Consulting and Clinical Psychology,* vol. 62 (1994), p. 262.

[186]Human Rights Watch interview, Atlanta, Georgia, March 1, 2000.

[187]Human Rights Watch interview, San Francisco, California, January 25, 2000.

[188]Human Rights Watch interview, Greenfield, Massachusetts, May 31, 2000.

[189]Human Rights Watch interview, Greenfield, Massachusetts, May 31, 2000.

[190]Human Rights Watch interview, Greenfield, Massachusetts, May 31, 2000.

that's how I started going down that route, experiencing a lot of things fourteen and fifteen-year-olds shouldn't."

As with many older youth from rural or suburban areas, Lavonn moved to a large urban area in search of an accepting community:

> By the time I was seventeen, I was in my own apartment. By seventeen I had just come out. It's a whole new different world for you, without mommies, daddies, supervision. You just go wild. . . . I felt I was an adult and a big girl now. That led me into more drugs. When adolescents, teenagers, come into the city, with all the gay clubs, you have the feeling of acceptance. It's like a family; everybody wants that. I got that popularity. Drugs, a lot of everything, a lot of boys. It was fun, but I did a lot of things I should not have done. I've brought myself through a lot of problems. Drug addiction. I've been clean for three months now. If somebody had been there for me when I was younger, maybe I would have got to avoid a lot of problems.[191]

The 1999 Massachusetts Youth Risk Behavior Survey found that youth who identified themselves as lesbian, gay, or bisexual or who reported same-sex sexual experiences had higher rates of drug use than their peers. According to the survey, sexual minority youth—those who have identified themselves as lesbian, gay, or bisexual or who have had any same-sex sexual contact—had higher lifetime rates of marijuana use (70 percent compared to 49 percent of all other youth), cocaine (29 percent compared to 9 percent), methamphetamine (30 percent compared to 7 percent), and injected drugs (18 percent compared to 2 percent).[192]

---

[191]Human Rights Watch interview, Austin, Texas, March 23, 2000.

[192]See Massachusetts Department of Education, *1999 Massachusetts Youth Risk Behavior Survey* (Boston: Massachusetts Department of Education, 2000), chapter 4, www.doe.mass.edu/lss/yrbs99/ (accessed on April 3, 2001). See also Robert H. DuRant, Daniel P. Krowchuk, and Sara H. Sinal, "Victimization, Use of Violence, and Drug Use Among Male Adolescents Who Engage in Same-Sex Sexual Behavior," *Journal of Pediatrics,* vol. 133 (1998), p. 113.

The connection between victimization and alcohol or drug use is illustrated by another finding from the 1999 Massachusetts Youth Risk Behavior Survey. The survey found that, for girls, recent alcohol consumption was strongly associated with dating violence and unwanted sexual contact. Girls who reported recent alcohol use were also significantly more likely to report having ever been hurt by a date and having experienced sexual contact against their will. See *1999 Massachusetts Youth Risk Behavior Survey,* chapter 3. See also Karen M. Jordan, "Substance Abuse Among Gay, Lesbian, Bisexual, Transgender, and

Risky Sexual Behaviors

Faced with the stresses caused by routine harassment, violence, and ostracization, youth who are lesbian, gay, bisexual, or transgender may engage in unprotected sex or other risky sexual behaviors. Often lacking positive sources of peer support and outlets for socialization, they may downplay or disregard health concerns out of a desire for companionship and intimacy.

For these reasons, sexually active youth who are lesbian, gay, bisexual, and transgender are at increased risk for sexually transmitted diseases. This increased risk extends to HIV infection, transmitted most commonly among adolescents through sexual activity.

Gay and bisexual boys and young men are at the greatest risk for sexually transmitted diseases, including HIV. A study of gay and bisexual boys and young men in San Francisco and Berkeley, California, found that 33 percent had engaged in unprotected sex within the past six months; in New York, according to another study, 28 percent of young gay and bisexual males reported having unprotected sex in the last year.[193] A Minnesota study of gay and bisexual males between the ages of thirteen and twenty-one found that nearly one-quarter reported that they had had a sexually transmitted disease; the San Francisco study found that almost a third reported contracting at least one sexually transmitted disease.[194]

Caitlin Ryan and Donna Futterman observe that "the pervasiveness of AIDS within the gay community has resulted in feelings of futility among many young gay males; they may believe that HIV infection is inevitable and thus that prevention is useless."[195] Through June 2000, male-to-male sexual contact

---

Questioning Adolescents," *School Psychology Review,* vol. 29 (2000), p. 201; F. Shifrin and M. Solis, "Chemical Dependency in Gay and Lesbian Youth," *Journal of Chemical Dependency Treatment,* vol. 5 (1992), p. 67.

[193]*See* G.F. Lemp, A.M. Hirozawa, and D. Givertz, "Seroprevalence of HIV and Risk Behaviors Among Homosexual and Bisexual Men: The San Francisco/Berkeley Young Men's Survey," *Journal of the American Medical Association,* vol. 272 (1994), p. 449; I.H. Meyer and L. Dean, "Patterns of Sexual Behavior and Risk Taking Among Young New York City Gay Men," vol. 7 (1995 supplement), p. 13.

[194]*See* Gary Remafedi, "Predictors of Unprotected Intercourse Among Gay and Bisexual Youth: Knowledge, Beliefs, and Behavior," *Pediatrics,* vol. 94 (1994), p. 163; G.F. Lemp et al., "Seroprevalence of HIV and Risk Behaviors," p. 449.

[195]Caitlin Ryan and Donna Futterman, "Lesbian and Gay Youth: Care and Counseling," *Adolescent Medicine,* vol. 8 (1997), p. 313.

accounted for 34 percent of reported AIDS cases among thirteen to nineteen-year-old males, according to the Centers for Disease Control and Prevention.[196]

In addition, girls and boys may engage in risky sexual activity with partners of the opposite sex. "Everyone thought I was a freak—I tried to show off, always had a boyfriend to prove I was okay," said Kellsie N. "In tenth grade I got pregnant."[197] She dropped out of high school during her pregnancy and eventually received a General Educational Development diploma.

Kellsie's experience is not unusual. Asked if they had been pregnant or had gotten someone pregnant, 31.6 percent of sexually active students who either identified as gay, lesbian, or bisexual or have had same-sex sexual experiences replied that they had. Only 11.8 percent of all other students reported the same behavior. As Emery S. Hetrick and A. Damien Martin suggested in 1987, "Some young lesbians, out of a need to hide their sexual orientations, may indulge in heterosexual acting out, ranging from simple experimentation to heterosexual promiscuity. They report feeling that their families can more easily accept an unwanted pregnancy rather than a homosexual daughter."[198] More recent studies have offered similar rationales for risky sexual behavior by both girls and boys with members of the opposite sex.

Runaway, Homeless, and "Throwaway" Youth

Lesbian, gay, bisexual, and transgender youth who are subjected to harassment and violence may also end up living on the street in disproportionate numbers—often because they have been forced out of their homes or out of the foster care system after their sexual orientation is discovered.[199] In a national

---

[196]See Centers for Disease Control and Prevention, *HIV/AIDS Surveillance Report,* vol. 12 (2000), table 13.

[197]Human Rights Watch interview, Austin, Texas, March 15, 2000.

[198]Emery S. Hetrick and A. Damien Martin, "Developmental Issues and Their Resolution for Gay and Lesbian Adolescents," *Journal of Homosexuality,* vol. 14 (1987), p. 29.

[199]Half of the fifty-four lesbian and gay youth in the child welfare system interviewed by Dr. Gerald P. Mallon reported that they had spent periods of time living on the streets in preference to the hostile environment they found in child welfare settings. Three of the fifty-four told him that they were expelled from their homes when their parents discovered their sexual orientation. Others left their homes because family members subjected them to physical violence. One New York child welfare advocate told Dr. Mallon, "We just keep seeing kids getting beaten up and thrown out of their houses, kids getting beaten up by their fathers for being gay, or young lesbians getting sexually abused by male relatives trying to change them so they won't be gay." Gerald P. Mallon, *We Don't Exactly Get the Welcome*

survey of community-based agencies providing services to runaway, homeless, and other youth in high-risk situations, 6 percent of the youth served by the agencies identified themselves as gay or lesbian, a figure which almost certainly underestimates the proportion of lesbian, gay, bisexual, and transgender individuals in the street youth population.[200] As the National Network for Youth points out:

> Gay and lesbian youth are largely an invisible population, the majority of whom are dealing with rejection and unacceptance of their sexual orientation by family, friends and society in general. Because homosexuality is considered a social taboo, few gay and lesbian youth will openly discuss their sexual orientation with service providers.[201]

Large urban areas with sizable gay communities have larger proportions of street youth who identify themselves as lesbian, gay, bisexual, or transgender, perhaps because youth in these areas are less reluctant to identify themselves and perhaps because lesbian, gay, bisexual, and transgender street youth choose to come to these areas.[202] In Houston, Los Angeles, and New York, for example, studies of

---

Wagon: The Experiences of Gay and Lesbian Adolescents in Child Welfare Systems (New York: Columbia University Press, 1998), pp. 111, 50-51, 98.

[200]*See* National Network of Runaway and Youth Services (now the National Network for Youth), *To Whom Do They Belong? Runaway, Homeless and Other Youth in High-Risk Situations in the 1990s* (Washington, D.C.: National Network of Runaway and Youth Services, 1991), p. 5. In several other studies of shelter care facilities and street locations where homeless youth are known to congregate, 3 to 10 percent of youth reported their sexual orientation as lesbian, gay, or bisexual. *See, for example,* M. Greenblatt and M.J. Robertson, "Homeless Adolescents: Lifestyle, Survival Strategies, and Sexual Behaviors," *Hospital and Community Psychiatry,* vol. 44 (1993), p. 1177.

[201]National Network of Runaway and Youth Services, *To Whom Do They Belong,* p. 5. The unwillingness of some service providers to acknowledge that they serve youth who are lesbian, gay, bisexual, or transgender undoubtedly reinforces the reluctance of many youth to discuss their sexual orientation. Dr. Mallon recounts that one staff member at a New York social services agency told him, "We don't have any residents who are gay or lesbian. We have over a hundred adolescents in our programs and I know all of them and none of them are gay or lesbian!" Mallon, *Welcome Wagon,* p. 7.

[202]One youth services director suggests, "These cities are places where gay youth believe they will find acceptance and nurturing, but instead they tend to experience exploitation and homelessness." Gabe Kruks, "Gay and Lesbian Homeless/Street Youth: Special Issues and Concerns," *Journal of Adolescent Health,* vol. 12 (1991), p. 516. Among homeless youth as a whole, however, approximately 75 percent remain in their original communities, suggesting that "migration" of lesbian, gay, bisexual, and transgender youth

homeless youth have found that between 16 and 38 percent identified as lesbian, gay, or bisexual.[203] Once on the street, these youth are at increased risk for infection with HIV or other sexually transmitted diseases because significant numbers engage in "survival sex," trading sex for food and shelter.[204]

Suicide

As noted, most lesbian, gay, bisexual, or transgender youth never consider suicide. A recent analysis of nationally representative data of U.S. students in the seventh through the twelfth grades found, for example, that 84.5 percent of boys and 71.7 percent of girls who reported same-sex attractions or relationships had never attempted suicide and had never had suicidal thoughts.

But several youth reported to us that the harassment and violence they endured led them to consider suicide. For instance, Vega S., a sixteen-year-old lesbian in the Los Angeles school district, told us:

> At my old school, it was a lot of name calling. There was a lot of that, "pussyeater" and "dyke" and stuff. I used to ditch classes because of that reason, or I'd always be late. I would always be outside getting into trouble because I didn't want to go to class. People would just start saying stuff to me, or they would make it look like they wanted to throw

---

to the large cities is less significant than is often assumed. *See* J.A. Farrow et al., "Health and Health Needs of Homeless and Runaway Youth: A Position Paper of the Society for Adolescent Medicine," *Journal of Adolescent Health,* vol. 13 (1992), p. 717.

[203] A study of inner-city homeless youth aged eleven to twenty-three found that one-quarter reported that they were lesbian, gay, or bisexual. Sixteen percent of runaways between the ages of ten and twenty-four at one medical clinic in Los Angeles identified themselves as lesbian, gay, or bisexual, compared to 8 percent of nonrunaway youth at the clinic. And in a study of homeless young men between the ages of fifteen and twenty at a Covenant House medical clinic in New York, 25 percent reported being gay or bisexual. *See* N.H. Busen and B. Beech, "A Collaborative Model for Community-Based Health Care Screening of Homeless Adolescents," *Journal of Professional Nursing,* vol. 13 (1998), p. 316; G.L. Yates et al. "A Risk-Profile Comparison of Runaway and Non-Runaway Youth," *American Journal of Public Health,* vol. 78 (1988), p. 820; R.L. Stricof et al., "HIV Seroprevalence in a Facility for Runaway and Homeless Adolescents," *American Journal of Public Health,* vol. 81 (1991 supplement), p. 50.

[204] *See* Madlyn C. Morreale and Allison J. Boyle, "HIV Prevention for Two Populations of Youth in High-Risk Situations—Homeless Youth and Sexual Minority Youth: An Introduction to the Published Literature," *Issue Brief 5* (Washington, D.C.: National Network for Youth, n.d.), p. 13.

up. It got to the point where I didn't want to live anymore. I tried to kill myself.[205]

Luke G., a high school football player, recounted, "I had to hide who I was. I had to have perfect grades, do all the sports, be popular—and I did, but I couldn't handle the pressure; I felt suicidal. I went into therapy and talked about the pressure but not the cause."[206]

An analysis of the 1995 Massachusetts Youth Risk Behavior Survey data found that gay, lesbian, bisexual, and questioning youth are more than three times as likely as other students to report a suicide attempt.[207] An analysis of Minnesota junior and senior public high school students found that 28.1 percent of gay or bisexual boys and 20.5 percent of lesbian or bisexual girls reported that they had attempted suicide, as compared to 4.2 percent of heterosexual boys and 14.5 percent of heterosexual girls.[208]

Oregon's 1997 Youth Risk Behavior Survey did not ask students about their sexual orientation, but it did include a question asking them whether they had been harassed in the previous thirty days because they were *perceived* to be lesbian, gay, or bisexual. The 2 percent of youth who said that they had been harassed for this reason were four times more likely than their non-harassed peers to report that they had attempted suicide. Boys harassed because of the perception that they were gay or bisexual were six times more likely than their non-harassed peers to attempt suicide.[209]

---

[205]Human Rights Watch interview, Long Beach, California, October 13, 2000.

[206]Human Rights Watch interview, Austin, Texas, March 15, 2000.

[207]Robert Garofalo et al., "Sexual Orientation and Risk of Suicide Attempts Among a Representative Sample of Youth," *Archives of Pediatrics and Adolescent Medicine,* vol. 153 (1999), p. 487.

[208]Gary Remafedi et al., "The Relationship Between Suicide Risk and Sexual Orientation: Results of a Population-Based Study," *American Journal of Public Health,* vol. 88 (1998), p. 57. The study compared 212 boys and 182 girls who identified themselves as gay, lesbian, or bisexual to an equal number of heterosexual boys and girls.

[209]*See* Oregon Department of Human Services, "Suicidal Behavior, a Survey of Oregon High School Students, 1997," available at www.ohd.hr.state.or.us/chs/teensuic/teensuic.htm (accessed on April 23, 2001).

A 1998 study based on nationally representative data found that youth who report attractions to or relationships with persons of the same sex were more than twice as likely as their heterosexual counterparts to attempt suicide.[210]

---

[210]Stephen T. Russell and Kara Joyner, "Adolescent Sexual Orientation and Suicide Risk: Evidence from a National Study" (paper presented at the annual meeting of the American Sociological Association, San Francisco, California, August 1998), p. 8.

Eric C., California

Eric C. told Human Rights Watch, "I was involved in gangs until '97 or '98. The way a gang works, it's like a family there. . . . The guy I was under, I came out and told him. I told a lot of people. A lot."

Even though some members of his gang went to his school, he said, "When I came out, no one had much of a problem. The thing is, the boss, the guy above the one I ran under, he had a really big problem with me being gay." But the members of his section "had no problem whatsoever."

He explained his motivation for staying in the gang: "I had protection. They told me, if anybody fucked around with me, they were there for me."

Even so, he recalled that he wasn't always treated the same as other gang members. "I was never called to any guy fights," he said. "I was always told to stand back and watch. Whenever there were girl fights, I was always called. I was, like, just 'cause I'm gay doesn't mean I can't fight a guy."

Eventually, the gang boss' opposition to his membership in the gang resulted in his being targeted by other members because he was gay. "Things became really unsafe for me. I had people at school telling me a guy on the outside was looking for me," he said.

"Things got so bad, I told my mother what I was going through. She went berserk, called the police, went down to the school, talked to the assistant principal asking them to transfer me to another school."

When he and his mother went to the assistant principal to complete the transfer paperwork, "she thought I was dropping out of school," Eric told us. "She pulled out the dropout programs for me. When my mom repeated that we were looking for another school, she told us, 'He's obviously going to drop out,' even though I was a B-average student." The administrator did not look at his school records until Eric and his mother insisted that he would not accept placement in a dropout program. "Then she pulled out my transcripts. There everything was. I was a B-average student."

Although Eric was able to transfer, the district placed him at a school across town. "It's really far from here, about a forty-five minute bus ride. It has a good reputation with gay students, a really open atmosphere. No violence or fights at all for the last seven years. There were other high schools, but the school district was concerned that I wouldn't be safe."

In addition to the distance, Eric, who is Asian, noted that another downside to his new school was that "the majority of students are Caucasian. At most schools in San Francisco, the majority are Asian, African American, Latino, then Caucasian." At the same time, Eric told us that he appreciated the openness of the school. "I felt, like, a completely different atmosphere." At his old school, he said, "there was no GSA [gay-straight alliance], no resources I could go to. I just came out. There was nothing there."

He describes his new school as "completely different." He told us, "The kids are really open. All of the gay students there were really open with themselves, and there were a lot of gay kids there. The straight kids don't see the gay kids as a problem. Like, in my leadership class I talked about some problems I was having with my boyfriend. The other kids just acted like it was completely normal."

VII. TEACHERS AND ADMINISTRATORS

In virtually every case where lesbian, gay, bisexual, and transgender youth reported that their school experience has been positive, they attributed that fact to the presence of supportive teachers.

"It's wonderful here," said Erin B., contrasting her current school with the one she had attended the previous year, when she was in the seventh grade. She explained, "My science and English teachers are so nice. If someone says 'fag' or 'dyke,' they stop them. My teachers are really good about stopping homophobic words from being spread. There was one girl who used to give me complete hell. She'd tell me I'm fruity, stuff like that. The teacher took her into the hall and talked to her. My teachers are really cool."[211]

Most students do not receive such support from teachers or administrators, however.

"The teachers are a real mix. There are some who have put themselves on the line," Katrina Avila of the Boston Alliance of Gay, Lesbian, Bisexual, and Trangendered Youth told Human Rights Watch. "In cases of physical violence it's rare for teachers not to intervene. But teachers are not responding to comments."[212]

In some cases, in fact, "the teachers go along with the people that are making fun of other students," Paul M., a New Jersey senior, told us. "They should put a stop to it. Instead, it's like they're on the side of the person doing the harassment. It's not fair. I don't think that's right."[213]

David Buckel, a staff attorney with the Lambda Legal Defense and Education Fund, reports that he sees two typical responses from administrators. "The first response is that boys will be boys . . . . There's a notion that a boy should be fighting back as a man," he says. "Second, you'll hear the response that if you're going to be gay, you have to expect this kind of abuse, because you'll face it for the rest of your life."[214]

And, as discussed earlier in this report, harassment against young lesbians and bisexual girls often goes unrecognized.

---

[211]Human Rights Watch interview, Atlanta, Georgia, March 2, 2000.

[212]Human Rights Watch interview with Katrina Avila, director, Boston Alliance of Gay, Lesbian, Bisexual, and Transgendered Youth (BAGLY), May 8, 2000. BAGLY is a youth-led, adult supported social support organization for gay youth.

[213]Human Rights Watch interview, Bergen County, New Jersey, October 31, 1999.

[214]Human Rights Watch interview with David Buckel, senior staff attorney, Lambda Legal Defense and Education Fund, New York, New York, October 27, 1998.

Even teachers who are themselves lesbian, gay, bisexual, or transgender admitted to us that they did not always stand up for students who were being harassed. In every one of the seven states we visited, we spoke with teachers who were reluctant to be open about their sexual orientation at school because they feared losing their jobs. A teacher from a rural county near Macon, Georgia, told Human Rights Watch, "I'm out to my principal. I'm out, but he told me that if the parents found out, he didn't need that kind of shit in his life, and he'd hang me out to dry."[215]

We heard these fears expressed most often in states which do not provide protection from discrimination in employment on the basis of sexual orientation. Even in states with such protection, however, many teachers told us that they did not feel that they could be open about their sexual orientation. This fear kept many of the lesbian and gay teachers we interviewed from intervening to protect students from harassment and from educating their peers about the harassment, discrimination, and violence the lesbian, gay, bisexual, and transgender students face at school. But their fear also conveys the message to the gay youth that even adults in positions of authority face discrimination if they are publicly identified as gay or lesbian.

"Some teachers are very supportive, but they won't come out. They won't risk their jobs," said Alex Night of Lambda GLBT Community Services in El Paso, Texas. "We've had teachers who everybody knows are gay, and when a gay student gets harassed or beaten up, they won't do anything. And we've had straight teachers who stand up for the students."[216]

These fears affect both the teachers themselves and the students in their schools. Lesbian, gay, bisexual, and transgender youth consistently identified adult role models as an important source of support for them. In particular, many students told us that they thought their school experiences would have been better if they had a teacher who was openly gay. "It would almost be a perfect remedy," remarked Chance M., a Massachusetts senior, "making people face what they're afraid of."[217]

Official Inaction

The most common response to harassment, according to the students we interviewed, is no response. "Nothing. Nothing at all," Lavonn R. replied when

---

[215]Human Rights Watch interview, Macon, Georgia, December 17, 1999.
[216]Human Rights Watch interview with Alex Night, Lambda GLBT Community Services, El Paso, Texas, March 22, 2000.
[217]Human Rights Watch interview, Barnstable County, Massachusetts, May 10, 2000.

he was asked what teachers did when he was harassed in front of them. "I can't remember even once where a teacher stood up for me and helped me."[218]

"I'd see teachers walking down the hallway. They'd see something and not say anything," Chance M. told a Human Rights Watch researcher.[219] "I would think the teachers would be able to hear the comments," said James L., a fifteen-year-old in the Los Angeles area. "They just don't do anything."[220]

"What concerns me most is that teachers don't interject when they hear those comments," a counselor in West Texas remarked. "It's nothing for kids to call each other 'faggot.' Nothing is done."[221]

Many students felt that teachers and administrators do not respond because they believe that antigay comments are not harmful. Gabriel D., a sixteen-year-old in the San Francisco Bay area, commented, "There was this underlying tone that boys will be boys or kids will be kids, but that's wrong."[222]

Alex M. described the lengths he went to in order to get the school administration to address his complaint. "I reported it," he said. "I took a folder, wrote down dates and times every time I was harassed. I took it down to the principal. He said, 'Son, you have too much time on your hands to worry about these folks. I have more important things to do than worry about what happened two weeks ago.' I told him, 'I wanted to give you an idea of what goes on, the day-to-day harassment.' He took the folder away from me and threw it in the trash. That was my freshman year, first semester. After that I realized [the school] wasn't going to do anything."[223]

Frustrated by the prevalence of antigay comments and the lack of attention paid to them by their coworkers, several teachers told us that they do the best they can to address such harassment. "I would hear so many slurs everywhere I go. I can't do anything in the hallways because it's just too pervasive, but in my class I don't let it go on," a Georgia teacher stated.[224] A teacher in West Texas told us, "I'll tell my students, 'I don't want any putdowns on anybody on anything here. Here no one's going to be calling anybody a fag, a hick, a nerd, nothing like that.' I kind of make it a safe room that way."[225]

[218]Human Rights Watch interview, Austin, Texas, March 23, 2000.
[219]Human Rights Watch interview, Barnstable County, Massachusetts, May 10, 2000.
[220]Human Rights Watch interview, Los Angeles, California, January 19, 2000.
[221]Human Rights Watch interview, Lubbock, Texas, March 20, 2000.
[222]Human Rights Watch interview, San Francisco, California, January 28, 2000.
[223]Human Rights Watch interview, Atlanta, Georgia, March 1, 2000.
[224]Human Rights Watch interview, Atlanta, Georgia, December 14, 1999.
[225]Human Rights Watch interview, Lubbock, Texas, March 20, 2000.

Matt P. told us that the one openly lesbian teacher in his small New Hampshire school had a similar policy. "Her room was a safe zone," he reported. "But if there was something outside that she heard, she wouldn't say anything. But she wasn't in a position to say anything. She wasn't a full teacher at that point."[226]

Teachers may fail to respond to harassment because they lack the training to do so. Students sense the teachers' discomfort and unwillingness to intervene. "Teachers are given no direction on what to say to students," observed Sabrina L.[227] When we asked teachers about the training they received in preparation for teaching, most responded that their teacher training programs did not address harassment and discrimination based on sexual orientation or gender identity.

Inexperienced teachers may be particularly ill-equipped to address antigay harassment. "The younger teachers aren't quick to respond," Ron P. notes. "I think the younger teachers are scared to speak up to the students. The older teachers are open minded. The younger teachers are still trying to be friends with the students—you can't do that."[228]

But others felt that incoming teachers were more likely to be receptive to the needs of lesbian, gay, bisexual, and transgender youth. "I don't think we have a horrible school system, but I don't think it's going to take place with the teachers already teaching in the school system," a Georgia teacher offered.[229]

The teachers and youth with whom we spoke emphasized that most students would appreciate efforts to rein in harassment. "If a model was in place, something designed to stop violence and take advantage of what teachers always refer to as 'teachable moments,' there are lots of kids that would embrace it," says the Georgia teacher.[230]

In the absence of clear school district policies and lacking relevant training to fall back on, some teachers seem to be happy to let youth settle matters for themselves. Dylan N. told us that, on one occasion, the teacher walked out of the room when other students were throwing things at him.[231] A counselor in Georgia described another case of a student who was harassed because his classmates thought he was gay. "The whole administration knew what was going on," the counselor said, telling us that the principal referred the student to him. "He was having problems at lunch. The kids he was sitting with helped him out. I told him

---

[226]Human Rights Watch interview, Salem, Massachusetts, May 23, 2000.

[227]Human Rights Watch interview, Los Angeles, California, October 18, 1999.

[228]Human Rights Watch interview, Lubbock, Texas, March 21, 2000.

[229]Human Rights Watch interview, Atlanta, Georgia, December 18, 1999.

[230]Human Rights Watch interview, Atlanta, Georgia, December 18, 1999.

[231]Human Rights Watch interview, Atlanta, Georgia, December 15, 1999.

to tell the staff on duty when something happened, and he IDed [identified] a group of guys." The counselor told us that official intervention proved to be unnecessary. "Really the kids dealt with it—they got up in their face, told them to lay off, put some peer pressure on them. He didn't have a problem after that. He got a reputation of being a fighter. Word got out that he was not a kid to mess with."[232]

We heard numerous accounts of teachers and administrators who refused to act to protect lesbian, gay, bisexual, and transgender students out of the belief that they get what they deserve. Dempsey H. told us that when he went to the principal to complain of constant harassment, "He said, 'You chose this lifestyle; you need to carry all the baggage that comes with it.'"[233]

In Alex M.'s case, "They knew what was going on, but they wouldn't help," the sophomore told us. "I told this teacher, 'I've been experiencing harassment from some students at school.' He's like, 'Well, did you tell them you're gay?' I'm like, 'Yeah, the whole school knows.' So he says, 'Maybe you should've kept it to yourself.' They're telling me it's my fault. I was responsible for the harassment. The vice-principal said the same thing. He told me that I should have kept my sexuality to myself, that way they wouldn't have anything to talk about."[234]

Carol Petrucci, director of a Houston group for lesbian, gay, bisexual, and transgender youth, described a similar case involving a boy who openly identifies as gay at school. "The harassment began to get physical. The assistant principal told him that if he didn't walk around telling people he's gay, there wouldn't be any problems."[235] Stephen Scarborough, an attorney with the Lambda Legal Defense and Education Fund in Atlanta, sees a similar dynamic in virtually all of the cases he receives. It is the student being harassed because of his or her actual or perceived sexual orientation or gender identity who is blamed for the situation. If a concerned parent repeatedly complains to the administration about the harassment, the official response is often to transfer the student rather than address the problem and punish the perpetrators.[236]

Sometimes the refusal to protect lesbian, gay, bisexual, and transgender students from abuse stems from a perceived conflict with their personal beliefs.

---

[232]Human Rights Watch interview, Atlanta, Georgia, December 14, 1999.

[233]Human Rights Watch interview, Lubbock, Texas, March 21, 2000.

[234]Human Rights Watch interview, Atlanta, Georgia, March 1, 2000.

[235]Human Rights Watch interview with Carol Petrucci, director, Houston Area Teenage Coalition of Homosexuals (HATCH), Houston, Texas, March 17, 2000.

[236]Human Rights Watch interview with Steve Scarborough, staff attorney, Lambda Legal Defense and Education Fund, Atlanta, Georgia, December 14, 1999.

"One teacher said to me, 'I don't believe in that. I'm going to pray for you,'"
Dempsey H. told us.[237]

Participation in Acts of Harassment and Discrimination

Even more disturbing were the accounts we heard of teachers and
administrators who actually took part in harassing students because of their actual
or perceived sexual orientation or gender identity. It is disappointing, but not
surprising, to hear such reports. In a 1998 study of school counselors serving
kindergarten through twelfth grade, those surveyed assessed the attitudes of faculty,
students, and administrators as negative to intolerant.[238]

At the extreme, we heard several accounts of teachers and administrators who
actively targeted youth. Thomas B., a sixteen-year-old Arkansas sophomore, wrote
to Human Rights Watch to report that he had started receiving handwritten notes
in his locker at the end of his freshman year. When he showed the notes to several
teachers, his art teacher recognized the handwriting as that of a substitute teacher's.

The principal did not investigate the substitute's behavior. Instead, Thomas
relates:

My art teacher explained what had happened, and showed the principal
the notes. The principal asked the art teacher to leave, which she did.
I was alone in front of the administrators. I was terrified.

After talking a little bit about what happened, the principal began to ask
me questions such as, "Are you openly gay?" "How do you know
you're gay?" and the like. I responded as best I could, it was hard to
think straight. She then asked if I have been harassed by other students
at the school because of my orientation. When I said yes, she acted as
if it were my own fault for being harassed because I am open about my
sexuality. I felt horrible, and started to cry. They had me leave the
room for a while for them to talk.

I was called back around ten minutes later. They said they had to call
my mother because I was, "complaining about a staff member." This
made me feel worse, and cry even more. I didn't know what my mother

---

[237]Human Rights Watch interview, Lubbock, Texas, March 21, 2000.
[238]*See* J.H. Fontaine, "Evidencing a Need: School Counselors' Experiences with Gay
and Lesbian Students," *Professional School Counseling,* vol. 1 (1998), p. 8.

would do, she isn't very open about this type of thing. I wanted to run away and say, "forget it," but I couldn't bring myself to do it. After that, the principal suggested that I go see a therapist. With that I hit rock bottom, I've never been so sad, scared, and angry at the same time. She wanted me to see a therapist because of my sexuality![239]

Alex M. also experienced negative reactions from several of his teachers. "These two, I could tell they were very homophobic," he told us. "They know that it's according to the school rules, here in the Atlanta public school system, that they can't do anything harmful to me. Me being homosexual can't affect my grade in any way. But every time they see me coming down the hall, they make these physical gestures, like they roll their eyes or sigh. . . . And I had this world history teacher, he'd be like, 'oh, faggot this,' 'faggot that.' One time he told me I was going to hell."[240]

We heard several other accounts of teachers who responded with references to their own religious beliefs when they learned that one of their students was lesbian, gay, bisexual, or transgender. One teacher told Chauncey T. that he should expect to go to hell. "She told me devout Christian stuff, like if the Bible is the divine word of God, then gay people have to come to terms with the fact they can't go to heaven," he said. "She'd say she can't believe a sin so strong would strike someone so young."[241]

Leslie H., a sixteen-year-old whose mother is a lesbian, told us, "One of my teachers was like, 'Yeah, you know it's right for a man and a woman to be together. It's not right what your mother and other gay or lesbian people do.'"[242]

Transgender students are particularly targeted. "One teacher told the class that I'd had a sex change operation, but I hadn't," said Gerald A. "He was misinformed. It was rude of him."[243]

"They're harassed by their peers and the staff," said Vitaly, a staff attorney with Legal Services for Children in San Francisco. "There's name calling. The 'he/she' thing. Refusal by staff to use proper pronouns, even after names are

[239]E-mail message to Human Rights Watch from Thomas B., March 20, 1999.
[240]Human Rights Watch interview, Atlanta, Georgia, March 1, 2000.
[241]Human Rights Watch interview, Atlanta, Georgia, March 3, 2000.
[242]Human Rights Watch interview, Dallas, Texas, March 27, 2000.
[243]Human Rights Watch interview, San Francisco, California, October 27, 1999.

legally changed. Ridicule by the substitute teacher. In one case, physical harassment—a student pushed and shoved by a teacher."[244]

A Georgia teacher spoke to us about another case involving a transgender youth who was harassed by staff. "Right now we have a transgender student—he believes he's a boy," the teacher told us. "The students don't give him as much problems as the adults do." Teachers and administrators persistently refer to the student as "she" and use his female name in front of students. "I didn't know about the student until a counselor just automatically outed him to me. The counselor said, 'We can't refer to him as "he" because somebody might sue.' I'm like, you idiots, you can't be sued for calling somebody by the pronoun they want you to use."[245]

The same is true of other students who may not identify as transgender but who transgress gender stereotypes. Another Georgia teacher reported to us that a coworker would comment that one student "needs to dress more like a girl."[246] A counselor in Texas told us about one junior high school student she knew several years ago. "He had longer hair, wore pinks and purples; he would powder his nose in class. He had a circle of friends. The teachers had difficulty with him. They would do things to embarrass him in class. They'd tell him to put stuff away and quit acting like a girl. They'd say other rude things to him," she told us.[247]

More often, youth and adults report that some teachers and administrators make comments that generally present lesbian, gay, bisexual, and transgender individuals in a negative light. For example, one Georgia teacher told us, "Once I heard one of my coworkers, the science teacher, say, 'Stop that! What are you, a bunch of homosexuals?'"[248]

Jerome B., sixteen, had a similar experience. "Yeah, it was kind of all right 'til you got to the coaches and stuff," Jerome B. told us. "They be calling some of the gay guys 'girls' or 'sissies,' saying we scared to play football. Me and three friends of mine who are gay, we went through that." Asked how the coach singled his three friends and him out for this treatment, Jerome replied, "Coach just assumed I was gay. He picked right. I mean, I'm kind of out. All my friends know, but not the whole school. It's not any of their business."[249]

---

[244]Human Rights Watch interview with Vitaly, staff attorney, Legal Services for Children, San Francisco, California, January 24, 2000.

[245]Human Rights Watch interview, Atlanta, Georgia, December 14, 1999.

[246]Human Rights Watch interview, Atlanta, Georgia, December 18, 1999.

[247]Human Rights Watch interview, Lubbock, Texas, March 20, 2000.

[248]Human Rights Watch interview, Atlanta, Georgia, December 14, 1999.

[249]Human Rights Watch interview, Los Angeles, California, January 20, 2000.

"Once in health class, my freshman year, the teacher made some gay joke. I caught it and I wasn't pleased. It was when we got to something on homosexuality. He skimmed over it and made a joke," said Manny V. "In a health class—how can you do that?"[250]

And in many instances, youth and adults reported hearing remarks by administrators and teachers that were not directed at any particular student but were hurtful nonetheless. A Kansas City teacher told us, "These two male teachers in my building come up, and they're saying these little gay comments. They had no idea. 'That's so gay,' they say. They don't realize what effect it has. The teachers just don't know what's going on."[251]

Such comments have an effect on students' emotional well-being even if they are not intended to be hurtful and even if they are not directed at a particular student. As Melanie S., a Massachusetts sophomore, told us, "When I was going through the stage of trying to identify myself, school played a major part because I spend two-thirds of my day there. It's one thing to see kids talking about being gay in a negative sense. It's another thing to see an adult, a person you respect, talking negatively. Once you see a role model degrading you, it tears you apart."[252]

[250]Human Rights Watch interview, Los Angeles County, California, October 21, 1999.
[251]Human Rights Watch interview, Kansas City, Missouri, March 28, 2000.
[252]Human Rights Watch interview, Salem, Massachusetts, May 23, 2000.

Wendy Weaver, teacher, Utah

Wendy Weaver was pensive when we spoke with her on May 22, 2000, in Salem, Utah. That morning, her high school had held its annual awards assembly during which awards and trophies were handed out to individuals and teams for extracurricular activities. As a coach, she was used to being involved in the assembly, cheering the accomplishments of her players. Since 1982 she had lead the girls' volleyball team to four state championships and numerous winning seasons. But this year, in the wake of the school district's refusal to allow her to continue to coach because of her sexual orientation, Wendy Weaver was a spectator.

"I was well known and liked at school—both as a teacher and a coach. I didn't think it would make a difference when [my partner] and I bought a house and moved in together. Then during the summer vacation, this student called me at home. She asked me if I was gay. I knew that people knew—my ex-husband had told people in our community—I just said, 'Yes.'

"Then I got a call from the principal saying we need to talk. The school district issued a memo—really a gag order—saying I could not speak to anyone associated with the school district about my personal life. At first I didn't know what to do. But the more I thought about it the more I realized it was crazy, it was impossible to comply with. I couldn't even talk to [my partner] because our children attend school in the district. I even asked them to modify the order so that it was less broad, but they refused. They also told me I wouldn't be coaching again.

"At first I didn't know what to do. I spoke with lots of lawyers about employment discrimination but they said they couldn't help me because there is no protection from discrimination based on sexual orientation. Finally we met with the ACLU of Utah and they agreed to take the case.

"It's been hard. All the publicity. The charges of immorality. We were worried about the impact of going public on our kids. But I got a lot of quiet support—people saying, 'I don't agree with your lifestyle but . . . .

"It was important for me to fight this. The students don't understand their rights—they are so traumatized that they never even think of organizing. Maybe this has helped some of them."

The Pressures Faced by Lesbian, Gay, Bisexual, and Transgender Teachers and Staff

In an unsigned article published in the *Advocate* in April 2000, a Massachusetts teacher wrote, "You don't know me, and I can't tell you who I am. . . . I'm afraid that if I come out as a gay man in a forum this public, I will risk losing my job."[253]

A 1998 study of thirty-four gay and lesbian teachers from across the United States found that only nine had disclosed their sexual orientation to their current or former principals. While this study is by no means comprehensive or necessarily representative of gay, lesbian, bisexual, or transgender teachers nationally, it reinforces the impression that many teachers are not comfortable being identified as gay or lesbian to their supervisors.[254]

The failure of states to protect lesbian, gay, bisexual, and transgender teachers from job discrimination has several ramifications for lesbian, gay, bisexual, and transgender youth. At worst, teachers and counselors, regardless of their sexual orientation or sexual identity, may refuse to intervene to stop harassment of the gay students out of fear that they will then be, correctly or incorrectly, perceived to be gay themselves or to be "promoting homosexuality." Furthermore, school districts lose input from a knowledgeable group of adults who could potentially educate their peers on what lesbian, gay, bisexual, and transgender youth are experiencing and help them devise intervention strategies. Finally, discrimination against adults based on their sexual orientation or gender identity is readily apparent to the youth themselves. Abusive youth justify their harassment by pointing to societal and governmental support for discrimination, and abused youth get the message that even adults in positions of authority can be attacked because of who they are.

The Lack of Job Security

We repeatedly heard school employees make remarks similar to those of the *Advocate* columnist or the Georgia teacher quoted at the beginning of this chapter.

"I couldn't put a pink triangle up," another teacher in Georgia told us, referring to the common symbol of gay pride. "I'm out when I walk out the door,"

---

[253]Anonymous, "Teaching from the Closet," *Advocate,* April 11, 2000, p. 9.

[254]Sixty-five percent of those questioned had come out to one or more fellow teachers, however. *See* Gail K. Bliss and Mary B. Harris, "Experiences of Gay and Lesbian Teachers and Parents with Coming Out in a School Setting," *Journal of Gay and Lesbian Social Services,* vol. 8 (1998), p. 18.

he added. Asked what it would take for him to be out at school as well, he replied, "If I had the knowledge that I'd keep my job, I imagine I would be out."[255]

Many school employees told us that they were out selectively but risked losing their jobs if knowledge of their sexual orientation or gender identity were more widespread. A counselor in West Texas told us that her immediate supervisor knows that she is a lesbian. "[He] doesn't have a problem with me, with the fact that I'm a lesbian," she said. She does not intend to disclose her sexual orientation to her regional director. "I have a feeling that if [he] figured out what the rainbow sticker on my car was, there'd be a way I wouldn't be employed any more."[256]

Most states do not prohibit discrimination in employment on the basis of sexual orientation or gender identity. Eleven states and the District of Columbia protect employees from discrimination on the basis of sexual orientation. Only Minnesota and the District of Columbia also provide protection from discrimination in employment on the basis of gender identity.[257] In addition, local measures may protect teachers and administrators in individual cities or counties. In California, for example, Berkeley, Brisbane, Daly City, Laguna Beach, Long Beach, Pacifica, Santa Barbara County, and the city and county of Santa Cruz prohibit discrimination in public employment on the basis of sexual orientation. In Utah, similar measures were in force in Salt Lake City and Salt Lake County.[258]

At the federal level, the Employment Nondiscrimination Act (ENDA), which would have prohibited employment discrimination on the basis of sexual orientation and which was introduced by Sen. James M. Jeffords and Rep. Christopher Shays, was narrowly defeated on the same day that the Defense of Marriage Act was passed overwhelmingly.[259] Two attempts to reintroduce ENDA

---

[255]Human Rights Watch interview, Atlanta, Georgia, December 14, 1999.

[256]Human Rights Watch interview, Lubbock, Texas, March 20, 2000.

[257]The jurisdictions that prohibit discrimination in employment on the basis of sexual orientation are California, Connecticut, the District of Columbia, Hawaii, Massachusetts, Minnesota, Nevada, New Hampshire, New Jersey, Rhode Island, Vermont, and Wisconsin. *See* National Gay and Lesbian Task Force, "GLBT Civil Rights Laws in the United States," April 2000, www.ngltf.org/downloads/civilmap0400.pdf (accessed on January 29, 2001). *See also* Chapter XI, "Right to Nondiscrimination and Equal Protection of the Laws" section, "State Protection from Discrimination" subsection.

[258]*See* Wayne van der Meide, *Legislating Equality: A Review of Laws Affecting Gay, Lesbian, Bisexual, and Transgendered People in the United States* (Washington, D.C.: Policy Institute of the National Gay and Lesbian Task Force, 2000).

[259] The Employment Nondiscrimination Act was defeated 49-50, and the Defense of Marriage Act, which passed 85-14 on September 10, 1996. The Defense of Marriage Act allows states to refuse to recognize same-sex marriages from other jurisdictions, arguably

since 1996 have been defeated, as the bill has died in committee without coming
to a vote in either house of Congress. Federal employees, excluding members of
the military, are protected from employment discrimination on the basis of sexual
orientation by executive order, although the measure protects virtually no teachers,
nearly all of whom are employed by state or local governments.[260]

The lack of legal protection against discrimination in employment on the basis
of sexual orientation leaves teachers and administrators open to attack if they are
supportive of lesbian, gay, bisexual, and transgender students. The Lambda Legal
Defense and Education Fund notes, "One tactic is to target educators who attempt
to incorporate gay content into class instruction—for example, by referring to
sexual orientation discrimination issues in diversity classes, or by including
discussions about historical figures who were also lesbian or gay."[261]   In
Michigan's Plymouth-Canton School District, for example, two gay teachers were
ordered to take down a bulletin board for gay history month four days after they
had put it up. Lambda reports that similar displays had been posted in previous
years by staff members who were not gay; the administration expressed no
concerns over the bulletin board at that time.[262]

In states with laws that criminalize private sexual conduct between consenting
adults, teachers and administrators reported that they felt an increased sense of
vulnerability. "We had a sodomy law. When I started work, I signed a thing
saying that I'd uphold the laws of the State of Georgia," noted one teacher. "I feel
I can go further in terms of being out since the repeal of the sodomy statute."[263]

Teachers could often point to specific examples that indicated to them that
their school was hostile or unwelcoming to lesbian, gay, bisexual, and transgender
employees. "I know of a teacher who asked if she could have a safe room," a West
Texas teacher told us. A "safe room" is one in which the teacher will not permit

---

in violation of the Full Faith and Credit Clause of the U.S. Constitution, which provides,
"Full Faith and Credit shall be given in each State to the public Acts, Records, and judicial
Proceedings of every other State." U.S. Constitution, art. IV, § 1. *See* Robert L. Cordell II,
"Same-Sex Marriage: The Fundamental Right of Marriage and an Examination of Conflict
of Laws and the Full Faith and Credit Clause," *Columbia Human Rights Law Review,* vol.
26 (1994), p. 247.

[260]*See* Executive Order No. 13,087, 63 Fed. Reg. 30,097 (1998). This executive order
remained in force as of April 2001.

[261]Myron Dean Quon, "Teachers Under Fire: Educators Caught in the Cross-Hairs of
the Radical Right," *Lambda Update,* Fall 2000, p. 8.

[262]*See* ibid., p. 9.

[263]Human Rights Watch interview, Atlanta, Georgia, December 14, 1999.

harassment. "She was told, 'We don't do that here.'"[264] A teacher outside Boston told Human Rights Watch of the difficulties she and her partner had when their daughter was born. She took off a total of six days from work, telling the school that she was taking care of family members. Her partner also worked in the same school district. "Word got back to me to cut it out. They were saying, 'We know what she's doing and we don't want to know what she's doing.' I'd spent ten years in that school system."[265]

"[D]iscussions about homosexuality continue to evoke a high level of discomfort, and as such, administration and school boards sanction a policy of 'official invisibility,'" writes Dr. Gerald Mallon.[266] Reflecting this unspoken policy, many school employees echoed the Georgia teacher's statement that he was out as soon as he left school grounds. "I'm not openly gay in my profession, but people see me with my friends all the time," a teacher in West Texas said. "It's a nonsubject. That's the best way to describe it."[267]

Youth understand the pressures that lesbian, gay, bisexual, and transgender teachers face. Matt P. told us that at his New Hampshire school, "There was one teacher who was gay and out. She was quiet for her own sake." Melanie S., a student in Massachusetts, said, "I know a teacher, a guidance counselor; she's not out, but she's out to me and the people in the GSA. . . . She didn't come out. She wanted to wait three years, some sort of thing so she couldn't be fired."[268]

Students at a youth group expressed a similar recognition of the risks lesbian, gay, bisexual, and transgender teachers run if they choose to be open about their sexual orientation or gender identity. "In my school, there's this one gay teacher. Everybody knows, but he's never said anything," remarked Javier R. "That's his job, man," replied Paul M. "That's his way of paying the bills. He's scared." "That's his personal life. What he does at school shouldn't be about that," Miguel S. agreed.

Despite their recognition of these pressures, youth expressed disappointment in lesbian, gay, bisexual, and transgender teachers who would not provide them

---

[264]Human Rights Watch interview, Lubbock, Texas, March 20, 2000.

[265]Human Rights Watch interview, Boston, Massachusetts, May 8, 2000.

[266]Gerald P. Mallon, "It's Like Opening Pandora's Box: Addressing the Needs of Gay and Lesbian Adolescents Within Educational Systems," *The Council for Children with Behavioral Disorders Monograph: Highlights from the National Symposium on Understanding Individual Differences* (Reston, Virginia: Council for Children with Behavioral Disorders, n.d.), p. 2.

[267]Human Rights Watch interview, Lubbock, Texas, March 20, 2000.

[268]Human Rights Watch interviews, Salem, Massachusetts, May 24, 2000.

with support privately. Before our conversation turned to a different topic, Paul M. added, "Teachers should help us out if they're gay, one-on-one. There are some who won't even talk to us."[269]

As a result of these pressures, some lesbian, gay, bisexual, and transgender teachers are hesitant to offer support to students who suffer harassment based on their actual or perceived sexual orientation or gender identity. Katrina Avila of the Boston Alliance of Gay, Lesbian, Bisexual, and Transgender Youth observed, "In some schools, we've seen straight teachers push for it because teachers who weren't out wouldn't push."[270]

Asked about the potential impact of federal employment nondiscrimination legislation, Gail Goodman replied, "Huge. It would make a huge difference, especially to teachers."[271] A Michigan teacher told us, "Frankly, the role model thing won't change until gay teachers are protected from discrimination."[272]

But others were less optimistic. Asked what it would take to make it safe for teachers to be out, the Georgia teacher replied, "For some, never. Especially for the older teachers, it's just not going to happen."[273] Brenda Barron, the Gay, Lesbian, Straight Education Network's assistant field director for southern organizing, remarked, "Its passage would have a small impact, but I don't think the closet doors will fly open," she said. "There needs to be a lot of education, training, and visibility first . . . . The fear will still be there unless there's a dialogue."[274]

Harassment of Teachers by Students

Lesbian, gay, bisexual, and transgender teachers who are open about their sexual orientation or gender identity also risk becoming targets themselves for harassment and violence. In some cases, teachers are being harassed by their peers and in other cases by students. If the harassment goes unaddressed, regardless of

---

[269]Human Rights Watch interview, Bergen County, New Jersey, October 31, 1999 (group discussion with six youth).

[270]Human Rights Watch interview with Katrina Avila, director, Boston Alliance of Gay, Lesbian, Bisexual, and Transgender Youth, Boston, Massachusetts, May 8, 2000.

[271]Human Rights Watch interview with Gail Goodman, executive director, Out Youth, Austin, Texas, March 3, 2000.

[272]Human Rights Watch telephone interview, November 20, 2000.

[273]Human Rights Watch interview with Brenda Barron, assistant field director for southern organizing, GLSEN, Atlanta, Georgia, December 14, 1999.

[274]Human Rights Watch interview, Atlanta, Georgia, December 14, 1999.

who is doing the harassment, the lesbian, gay, bisexual and transgender students get a clear message that even adults cannot protect themselves from bias attacks.

"This one teacher we had was getting harassment from students," Alex M. said, referring to a teacher whom the students suspected of being gay. "He couldn't do anything. Students know by law the teachers can't touch them. I'm not sure where he is now, but he left because of the harassment."[275]

Chance M. reported, "We had a gay man, a substitute teacher. People would throw things at him. He was much older, but he had the guts to wear a rainbow chain. I got nervous being seen with him, but I talked to him. I remember him almost breaking down telling me that he had stuff thrown at him."[276]

In some cases, students actually end up defending the teachers, a role reversal that both underscores the vulnerability of gay-identified adults and the lack of a coherent policy for addressing bias-based harassment in the school system.

Clayton Vetter, who taught at Skyline High School in Salt Lake City, revealed that he was gay at a press conference organized to challenge a bill which would have severely restricted speech by teachers outside the classroom. He coached the debate team and after being publicly identified heard from a student on the debate team that a group of football players were planning to beat him up. They planned to use bars of soap in socks which they thought would break bones but not leave bruises. It was his student who confronted the players and told them that Vetter had never done anything to deserve being attacked. Vetter reports that the student was then challenged about whether he had ever been touched by Vetter. Vetter expressed concern, saying, "My students were scrutinized by other students and were treated as suspect just because of their association with me. It felt wrong that I couldn't protect them and yet they were put in the position of defending me." Vetter eventually left teaching. Although he was not fired, he felt immense pressure after being identified as gay. "I had to be the best debate coach ever," he told us.[277]

The Benefits of Openness

Most of the youth with whom we spoke agreed with Chance M., the student who described having an openly lesbian, gay, bisexual, or transgender teacher as "the perfect remedy."[278]   For students to trust that they will not suffer

---

[275]Human Rights Watch interview, Atlanta, Georgia, March 1, 2000.

[276]Human Rights Watch interview, Barnstable County, Massachusetts, May 10, 2000.

[277]Human Rights Watch interview with Clayton Vetter, Salt Lake City, Utah, May 23, 2000.

[278]Human Rights Watch interview, Barnstable County, Massachusetts, May 10, 2000.

discrimination based on their sexual orientation or gender identity, they need to see that adults too are protected from harassment and discrimination. When students perceive, as they often do, that teachers are gay, lesbian, or bisexual, but also perceive that it is not safe for them to be open about their identity, the youth again receive a message that how they identify is unacceptable.

"It definitely helps to have teachers who are out," said Erin B. "You know you're not alone. You see how people treat a teacher. So if you're not out, I would look to see how the students treat the teachers, and that would affect whether I'd be out."[279] "I think there should be more gay teachers," said Greg Z., citing similar reasons.[280]

Having a teacher who is openly lesbian, gay, bisexual, or transgender does not help only students who are themselves lesbian, gay, bisexual, and transgender. A 2000 study found that having a personal acquaintance who is gay, lesbian, or bisexual is linked to holding fewer negative attitudes toward lesbian, gay, and bisexual individuals.[281]

Supportive Teachers

Students repeatedly told us that having even just one adult in the school system who supported them was critical to them surviving the otherwise hostile atmosphere. Teachers need not be lesbian, gay, bisexual, or transgender to be supportive of students, of course. Greg Z. said, "My French teacher is my mentor. She knows about me. Young gay men need that moral and emotional support."[282] The same can be said of young lesbians and bisexual girls.

Youth told us that small things, such as a few words of acknowledgment, a gesture, or the tone of a teacher's voice, were immensely helpful to them. Melanie S., a Massachusetts sophomore, described her reaction after a teacher mentioned having gay acquaintances:

When I was in eighth grade, one teacher said, "I know gay people; I know a gay couple." She didn't have a negative attitude. She only talked about it real quick. I suppose she was even scared to talk about it. I heard that word. Just hearing that word, not even in a positive

---

[279]Human Rights Watch interview, Atlanta, Georgia, March 2, 2000.

[280]Human Rights Watch interview, Atlanta, Georgia, December 18, 1999.

[281]*See* Annie L. Cotton-Houston and Bradley M. White, "Anti-Homosexual Attitudes in College Students: Predictors and Classroom Interventions," *Journal of Homosexuality,* vol. 38 (2000), p. 127.

[282]Human Rights Watch interview, Atlanta, Georgia, December 18, 1999.

sense, just not in a negative sense, it was astounding. It made my month.[283]

Similarly, Lauren M. told us, "I went to the gay prom and wrote about it for class. My English teacher wrote on my paper, 'That sounds like a really wonderful thing—I'm glad you went.' Another teacher never addressed it directly, but he said hi to a girl I brought to the theater banquet. He spent time talking with her."[284]

Ron P. told us that it made a difference to him that with the exception of one teacher, he generally heard positive things from his teachers on gay issues. "My freshman year, we were having a discussion of homosexuality in class," he recounted. "The teacher was very supportive of homosexuality, though the class wasn't."[285]

And Burke D. spoke of his principal's reaction when he attended his prom with his boyfriend. "The administration didn't know about it in advance. When we got there, the principal came over to us. There were a lot of bewildered looks, but he was graceful about it. I was incredibly nervous. He asked to be introduced. He showed approval. That made a big difference. He took us over to the line for pictures. That's when people decided it was okay."[286]

While it is clear that students benefit from being supported by teachers and school officials, what was striking was how little support most students expected. Most students are so accustomed to being denigrated or ignored by their teachers that even a gesture as neutral as allowing a student to stay in a classroom during lunch to escape harassment was seen as significant. "I needed a safe place to stay during lunch—my English teacher would let me stay in her classroom and read. It saved my life," explained Nikki L., a fourteen-year-old lesbian who eventually left school in favor of independent study.[287]

---

[283]Human Rights Watch interview, Salem, Massachusetts, May 23, 2000.

[284]Human Rights Watch interview, Austin, Texas, March 15, 2000.

[285]Human Rights Watch interview, Lubbock, Texas, March 21, 2000.

[286]Human Rights Watch interview, Decatur, Georgia, December 15, 1999.

[287]Human Rights Watch interview, San Francisco, California, November 18, 1999.

Nikki L., California

"Everyone thinks I have a problem. They blame me, they blame my mom. They want me to be quiet. But I'm a lesbian. I feel like I've always known it. But I didn't get into trouble 'til seventh grade. I told a friend. Next thing I know, everyone seems to know. I got yelled at—on the playground, in gym, in the hall, in classes.

"Only one teacher ever did anything. Miss [Johnson], my English teacher—I love her—she made them stop it. I felt safe with her. I would go to her room for lunch and recess. She made me feel safe. She liked my poetry—encouraged me to write.

"But everywhere else was bad. I tried to defend myself. I'm little but I'm tough. When kids hit me, I hit back. I got suspended twice. Three days each. A group of boys tried to beat me up, but I kicked them. I was just defending myself, but the vice-principal thinks I have a reputation. He calls me a 'hard ass.' I'm tough. I'm not gonna let anyone just push me around and hit me.

"But I got really sick of going to school. I would tell my mom I was feeling sick so I didn't have to go to school. Finally she called the school. The principal said I needed to document three incidents before they would do anything. There were about twenty to thirty kids, mostly boys, who harassed me. My grades dropped.

"Then one day I was walking home and some kids threw a brick at me. It hit me in the head. They were calling me a 'fucking dyke.' I sorta lost consciousness and my head was bleeding. That did it. I decided to never go back to school. I'm too scared.

"Now I do independent study. My grades are back up. It's good. I don't have many friends. They are all a lot older than me. But that's okay—I like older people. They don't care if I am a dyke.

"I just wish they had suspended the guys who hit me. Adults don't pay attention. They should. Especially when kids act out."

VIII. SCHOOL COUNSELORS

As the first school officials to whom students may turn for information on issues related to sexual orientation and gender identity, school counselors have a special role in providing support to lesbian, gay, bisexual, transgender, and questioning youth. We heard from several students who credited their school counselors with providing them with guidance and support at critical points in their lives.

Unfortunately, too many youth hear misinformation and perceive bias from their school counselors. In large part, the failure of many counselors to serve lesbian, gay, bisexual, and transgender youth stems from a lack of training. To correct this problem, school districts should provide specialized training for school counselors on issues related to sexual orientation and gender identity.

Even when counselors are prepared to address the needs of these youth, many students will not approach them for information on lesbian, gay, bisexual, and transgender issues unless they understand that their conversations are confidential. Confidentiality is an important aspect of any counseling relationship, mandated by the ethical codes of the American School Counselor Association, the American Counseling Association, the National Board for Certified Counselors, and other professional associations. For youth grappling with issues of sexual orientation or gender identity and social stigmatization, harassment, and violence, confidentiality is critical. Counselors should always advise students of the parameters of counselor-student confidentiality.

We heard several cases of counselors who disclosed youths' sexual orientation to their parents, violating professional standards and potentially placing the youth at risk of rejection, abandonment, or violence by parents or guardians or local communities.

The Value of Supportive Counselors
"Unlike their heterosexual peers, lesbian and gay adolescents are the only social minority who must learn to manage a stigmatized identity without active support and modeling from parents and family," Caitlin Ryan and Donna Futterman note.[288] School counselors are well-positioned to help youth who are coping with social stigma, feelings of isolation, and the effects of harassment.

---

[288]Caitlin Ryan and Donna Futterman, "Lesbian and Gay Youth: Care and Counseling," *Adolescent Medicine: State of the Art Reviews,* vol. 8 (1997), p. 213. *See also* Michael Radkowsky and Lawrence J. Siegel, "The Gay Adolescent: Stressors, Adaptations, and Psychosocial Interventions," *Clinical Psychology Review,* vol. 17 (1997), p. 191.

We heard from several youth who told us that they greatly appreciated the support of the school counselors. "We do have really good counselors," said Jenna I. "My counselor is great. I couldn't ask for somebody more supportive." She noted that a district superintendent's order has resulted in training on lesbian, gay, bisexual, and transgender issues for all counselors.[289]

Similarly, Kimberly G. told us that she had often talked to her counselor about being a lesbian in high school. "I had a great counselor; he was always there for me," she said.[290]

And Andy S. told us that she learned about Out Youth, an Austin group for lesbian, gay, bisexual, and transgender youth, from her counselor. "I was going to the counselor lady. That's not why I was going, but that subject came up, that I was gay, and she gave me a pamphlet."[291]

Asked what lesbian, gay, bisexual, and transgender students need, Kimberly G. replied, "Good counseling. There should definitely be more counselors."[292]

Misinformation and Bias

But many more youth spoke to us about negative experiences with school counselors. "A lot try to be very understanding, but most have kids of their own and when you tell them they freak out," Dahlia P. observed. "They don't want their own kids exposed to gay people."[293] When Dempsey H. went to talk to one of his school counselors about the issues he faced as a gay youth, he reported, "She told me she was biased and could no longer speak to me on this topic."[294] Philip G. recounted that when he asked teachers at his school to make donations so that students could attend a youth lobby day in Sacramento, a guidance counselor replied, "I'm not going to donate to that. Is it for that gay thing?"[295] In fact, a 1992 study of school counselors found that two out of three of those surveyed had negative attitudes about gay and lesbian youth.[296]

---

[289]Human Rights Watch interview, Orange County, California, October 21, 1999.

[290]Human Rights Watch interview, Austin, Texas, March 15, 2000.

[291]Human Rights Watch interview, Austin, Texas, March 15, 2000.

[292]Human Rights Watch interview, Austin, Texas, March 15, 2000.

[293]Human Rights Watch interview, Austin, Texas, March 15, 2000.

[294]Human Rights Watch interview, Lubbock, Texas, March 21, 2000.

[295]Human Rights Watch interview, Los Angeles, California, October 20, 1999.

[296]See J.T. Sears, "Educators, Homosexuality, and Homosexual Students: Are Personal Feelings Related to Professional Beliefs?," *Journal of Homosexuality,* vols. 3/4 (1992), p. 29.

The Need for Training

In particular, youth expressed concerns about the training their counselors received on lesbian, gay, bisexual, and transgender issues. Erin B. remarked of her school's counselors, "They seem to be nice, but a lot aren't educated on gay issues. Once I went in to get advice about a friend of mine who was taking pills. Everything turned into about me being gay. I got no advice about my friend. That made me mad."[297]

Our interviews with counselors confirmed that students' concerns were well-founded. "I haven't found a way to ask if sexual orientation is an issue," said one counselor in Georgia, who is gay himself. He explained, "I don't do a lot of pushing. If they need help, I get them the help they need. Let the professional deal with it."[298]

When Manny V. went to speak to a school counselor about the isolation and depression he felt, he reports that he left with his needs unaddressed:

> Here if you ask for a counselor, they'll send in a student who's got some counselor training. Some of the student counselors have issues of their own. They'd say things to other students. What you tell them would leak out. When I went to talk with the student counselor, she didn't say much. She just shrugged her shoulders and acted supportive. Finally I asked if I could call in a friend of mine to talk to instead. I asked to see the school psychologist. I never got an appointment. I was not helped out at all.[299]

"I've heard about kids getting harassed for being gay," a second counselor told us. "This came to the attention of another counselor. The student was harassed because he was effeminate. In fact, the counselor thought he was a girl at first. The counselor didn't deal with the issue in the best way. She changed his schedule after talking with the other students, when the abuse continued. To me, that's punishing the kid."[300]

As a result, it is not surprising that the 1992 study of school counselors also found that most lesbian, gay, and bisexual students saw their counselors as ill-informed, unconcerned, and uncomfortable with talking to them about their sexual

---

[297]Human Rights Watch interview, Atlanta, Georgia, March 2, 2000.
[298]Human Rights Watch interview, Atlanta, Georgia, December 14, 1999.
[299]Human Rights Watch interview, Los Angeles County, California, October 21, 1999.
[300]Human Rights Watch interview, Atlanta, Georgia, December 14, 1999.

orientation.[301] Such impressions are reinforced by the fact that many students report that school counselors provide them only with career planning assistance rather than comprehensive school counseling.[302]

In recognition of the fact that school counselors can be an important source of support for lesbian, gay, bisexual, and transgender youth, the American School Health Association recommends that "every school district should provide access to professional counseling by specially trained personnel for students who may be concerned about sexual orientation."[303]

Providing such support begins with an awareness by counselors of the language they use. For example, "the assumption must not be made that males only date females or that sexual feelings only happen across gender," note two researchers.[304]

More generally, counselors should be familiar with the issues their lesbian, gay, bisexual, and transgender students face and be able to refer them to appropriate resources.[305] "We need to have educational programs on diversity and sexuality," said Dempsey H. "I think all counselors should have to go through that kind of workshop to let them know what it is. It's a sexuality, not just something we're doing to get attention."[306]

"What would help?" Eric C. pondered. "I don't really know. You can't tell all gay students to come out until you have better resources, counselors. . . .

---

[301]*See* Sears, "Educators, Homosexuality, and Homosexual Students," p. 29.

[302]The American School Counselor Association defines the school counselor's role as including the development of "comprehensive school counseling programs that promote and enhance student learning," noting that school counselors "are specialists in human behavior and relationships who provide assistance to students" by, among other means, meeting with students "individually and in small groups to help them resolve and cope constructively with their problems and developmental concerns." American School Counselor Association, "The Role of the Professional School Counselor," June 1999, www.schoolcounselor.org/role.htm (accessed on November 30, 2000).

[303]American School Health Association, "Gay and Lesbian Youth in School," 1997, in *Compendium of Resolutions* (Kent, Ohio: American School Health Association, August 1998), www.ashaweb.org/resolutions1.html (accessed on June 12, 2000).

[304]Amy L. Reynolds and Michael J. Koski, "Lesbian, Gay, and Bisexual Teens and the School Counselor: Building Alliances," *The High School Journal,* vol. 77 (1993-94), p. 90.

[305]*See also* American Psychological Association, Guidelines for Psychotherapy with Lesbian, Gay, and Bisexual Clients, Guideline 11, www.apa.org/pi/lgbc/publications/guidelines (accessed on January 23, 2001).

[306]Human Rights Watch interview, Lubbock, Texas, March 21, 2000.

Counselors need to be able to tell them where they can go for help. Where to go to meet people just like them."[307]

As a counselor at San Francisco's Lavender Youth Recreation and Information Center emphasized, training should include a component directed to the needs of transgender youth. "We need even more sociological training dealing with young trans people, the issues young trans people are going to face. Issues that come up for young trans people include depression and suicide based on feeling like you're one way yet physically being another."[308]

And because youth are grappling with issues of sexual orientation and gender identity in the fourth or fifth grade, elementary school counselors must be prepared to address these issues in age-appropriate ways. "Some of us realize that we're gay in elementary school, but we don't get the information we need until high school," said Philip G.[309]

"Having someone at school to talk to would really help," said Javier R., "maybe a special counselor." [310] Similarly, Sabrina L. told us, "We need them to be proactive. We're not given the resources and information we need."[311] Eric C. explained that he needed more than what he could get from a peer support group. "I wanted to talk to a professional, but I didn't see anybody like that" at the youth group he attended. "I wanted to talk to somebody who knows what they're doing, somebody who doesn't just fluke things out."[312]

But schools should recognize that some students will not be willing to approach their counselors for information about sexual orientation or gender identity. Noting that his school has a peer hotline, Dempsey H. suggested, "I think all schools should have those. Students may not feel comfortable going to the school counselor and saying they're gay."[313]

The Importance of Confidentiality

"Confidentiality is critical in clinical work with sexual minority youth and their parents and families," write Michael W. Bahr, Barbara Brish, and James M. Croteau, noting that "confidentiality has a seminal role in assisting these

[307]Human Rights Watch interview, San Francisco, California, January 27, 2000.
[308]Human Rights Watch interview, San Francisco, California, January 28, 2000.
[309]Human Rights Watch interview, Los Angeles, California, October 18, 1999.
[310]Human Rights Watch interview, Bergen County, New Jersey, October 31, 1999.
[311]Human Rights Watch interview, Los Angeles, California, October 18, 1999.
[312]Human Rights Watch interview, San Francisco, California, January 27, 2000.
[313]Human Rights Watch interview, Lubbock, Texas, March 21, 2000.

individuals in accessing support through counseling relationships with school staff or an eventual referral to a community resource."[314]

All schools should establish and implement policies providing confidentiality in discussions between counselors and students. Counselors should always advise students of the existence of counselor-student confidentiality and its limits. Counselors should refer to the ethical standards of the American School Counselor Association, the American Counseling Association, the National Board for Certified Counselors, and the National Association of Social Workers for authoritative guidance in determining when confidentiality should be breached. In those limited cases in which confidentiality cannot be maintained, counselors should take care to ensure that they disclose only the minimum that is necessary to protect the youth or others.

Ethical Obligations

As Caitlin Ryan and Donna Futterman note, "Virtually every health profession is bound by a code of ethics that mandates client confidentiality, which is also governed by state medical records laws, federal funding statutes, and the right to privacy."[315]

The American School Counselor Association recognizes that students have "the right to privacy and confidentiality," which "must not be abridged by the counselor except where there is clear and present danger to the student and/or other persons."[316] The ethical codes of the American Counseling Association and the National Board for Certified Counselors contain similar guarantees of confidentiality.[317]

---

[314]Michael W. Bahr, Barbara Brish, and James M. Croteau, "Addressing Sexual Orientation and Professional Ethics in the Training of School Psychologists in School and University Settings," *School Psychology Review,* vol. 29 (2000), p. 222.

[315]Ryan and Futterman, "Lesbian and Gay Youth," p. 240.

[316]American School Counselor, "Position Statement: The Professional School Counselor and Confidentiality," 1999, www.schoolcounselor.org/ethics/index.htm (accessed on December 14, 2000). *See also* American School Counselor Association, Ethical Standards for School Counselors, June 25, 1998, www.schoolcounselor.org/ethics/standards.htm (accessed on November 30, 2000).

[317]*See* American Counseling Association Code of Ethics, section B, www.counseling.org/resources/codeofethics.htm (accessed on November 30, 2000); American Counseling Association Standards of Practice, section B, www.counseling.org/resources/codeofethics.htm (accessed on November 30, 2000); National Board for Certified Counselors Code of Ethics, October 31, 1997, sections B.4-B.8, www.nbcc.org/ethics/nbcc-code.htm (accessed on November 30, 2000).

School counselors may be social workers, psychologists, or members of other professions with their own ethical obligations. For example, the National Association of Social Workers' Standards for the Practice of Social Work with Adolescents calls upon social workers to maintain confidentiality in their professional relationship with youth.[318]

And the National Education Association (NEA) calls on all of its members, whether or not they are counselors, to refrain from disclosing "information about students obtained in the course of professional service unless disclosure serves a compelling professional purpose or is required by law."[319] With regard to students who are lesbian, gay, bisexual, or transgender or who are questioning their sexual orientation or gender identity, the NEA recommends that school personnel "[r]espect the confidentiality of students who confide the fact or suspicion of their homosexual orientation or who ask for assistance in this matter."[320]

Youth are often not aware that they have the right to expect confidentiality from health professionals. A 1993 study of high school students in Massachusetts found, for example, that over half had never discussed confidentiality with their health providers; two-thirds did not know that they had the right to confidential care.[321]

The right to confidentiality varies from profession to profession and from state to state. In particular, many states have "duty to warn" provisions that require health professionals to notify others when a client is at risk of harming himself or herself or others.

The need to protect youth from harm to themselves while maintaining confidentiality may present dilemmas for counselors. A Georgia counselor described one such case to us. "I had a ninth grader, he admitted some suicide ideation to me. He said, 'The kids are calling me a wimp and some other things I can't say.' I explained that we'd have to call his dad and take him in for an

---

[318]*See* National Association of Social Workers, Standards for the Practice of Social Work with Adolescents, April 1993, Standard 9, www.naswdc.org/practice/standards/adolescents.htm (accessed on November 16, 2000). *See also* Code of Ethics of the National Association of Social Workers, 1999, Ethical Standard 1.07(c), www.naswdc.org/Code/ethics.htm (accessed on November 16, 2000).

[319]National Education Association, Code of Ethics of the Education Profession, 1975, Principle I-8, www.nea.org/aboutnea/code.html (accessed on June 12, 2000).

[320]National Education Association, "Teaching and Counseling Gay and Lesbian Students," Human and Civil Rights Action Sheet (Washington, D.C.: NEA, 1994).

[321]*See* T.L. Cheng et al., "Confidentiality in Health Care: A Survey of Knowledge, Perceptions, and Attitudes Among High School Students," *Journal of the American Medical Association,* vol. 269 (1993), p. 1404.

assessment. You have to call the family in every case. The protocol calls for preventive intervention, some immediate intervention."[322]

"Outing" Students

We heard a number of instances in which counselors not only failed to discuss confidentiality with students but also disclosed their sexual orientation to their parents. Gail Goodman spoke to us about one case:

I took a call from one sixteen-year-old who came out to his counselor. The only other person he'd told was his friend in California. The counselor said, "I can't help you with that." After he left, the counselor called his mother to make sure she knew. The youth went home that night not knowing that he'd been outed to his parents. Sitting around the dinner table, his mother said to him, "I got a call from the school counselor today. We're not going to have any gay kids in this family." His father took him outside and beat him up.

People at the school found out and started harassing him. He became suicidal. Ultimately he was able to move in with a family in [a different city] and finish school there.

Goodman notes, "School counseling is my background. As a mental health professional, you have a duty to your client. You don't out a kid no matter what the school policy says."[323]

"Confidentiality needs to be heavily touched on for those working with trans youth. I've known people who were outed by counselors or teachers, those who they go to for support. They've been outed to the rest of the school community," another counselor told us. "It means that gender issues become the defining factor of who they are among their peers in school. Suddenly they're walking around and everybody knows them as 'oh, that transsexual person.'"[324]

The practice of "outing" students to their parents or guardians runs counter to the recommendation of the American Academy of Pediatrics, which advises that "[t]he gay or lesbian adolescent should be allowed to decide when and to whom to

---

[322]Human Rights Watch interview, Atlanta, Georgia, December 14, 1999.
[323]Human Rights Watch interview with Gail Goodman, executive director, Out Youth, Austin, Texas, March 14, 2000.
[324]Human Rights Watch interview, San Francisco, California, January 28, 2000.

disclose his/her sexual identity."[325] Disclosure under these circumstances also violates the ethical codes of the American School Counselor Association, the American Counseling Association, the National Board for Certified Counselors, and the National Association for Social Workers, all of which require confidentiality to be preserved unless disclosure is required to prevent "clear and imminent danger" or a similar level of harm.

In the case Goodman describes, disclosure of the student's sexual orientation was not only unnecessary to protect the student or others from any clear, imminent danger, it also put the youth at risk of harm. Caitlin Ryan and Donna Futterman advise:

> Providers should be aware that the decision to disclose one's lesbian or gay identity, particularly to parents, may have long-term consequences. Most adolescents are dependent on parents for financial and emotional support. Although coming out can reduce stress and increase communication and intimacy in relationships, disclosure during adolescence may result in abandonment, rejection, or violence when parents abruptly learn or discover that their child is lesbian or gay.[326]

In addition, such actions violate the youth's basic right to privacy. "It's not like you can tell one person and have them keep it a secret," Dahlia P. notes. "I told a few and then everybody found out."[327]

Confidentiality is particularly important for youth who are survivors of assault, including sexual abuse and hate crimes. "Family and peer support are important resources for recovering from trauma; in many cases, an adolescent victim may not have 'come out' previously to parents or peers," caution Caitlin Ryan and Donna Futterman. "Parents may react to the assault with anger and 'blame the victim' if the adolescent's sexual orientation is initially disclosed as a result of the incident."[328]

Reflecting the importance of confidentiality, school policies should include a prohibition on disclosing students' sexual orientation or gender identity to their classmates, parents or guardians, or local communities.

---

[325] American Academy of Pediatrics, Statement on Homosexuality and Adolescence (1993), in Ryan and Futterman, "Lesbian and Gay Youth," p. 368.

[326] Ryan and Futterman, "Lesbian and Gay Youth," p. 220.

[327] Human Rights Watch interview, Austin, Texas, March 15, 2000.

[328] Ryan and Futterman, "Lesbian and Gay Youth," p. 249.

Alix M., midwestern United States

"Beginning in middle school, I became really depressed. At first I didn't know why. Didn't have a clue. But I knew it wasn't okay to be gay. No one was out at my middle school, but I heard lots of slurs all the time. Lots of homophobic comments. I was scared. Scared to be a lesbian. Scared to be out at school. Scared of being so alone. My grades started to fall. A counselor talked to me about my grades. I had always been a good student. But she didn't give me any opening to talk about sexuality. I needed to get information.

"Now I am a senior in high school. It's better now for me. But public spaces are the worst. I hear things all the time. The halls have a very male macho feeling—very sexist. I also had one teacher who would say 'that's so gay' instead of saying 'that's so stupid.'

"I had read about GSAs [gay-straight alliances] and wanted to start one. I began thinking about it my sophomore year. I did research on the Internet. I knew I needed to find a teacher to support the club. I was a little nervous. There are no out teachers. I asked fifteen teachers if they would be the faculty sponsor. They all said no. One really cool teacher just told me she couldn't deal with people's reaction. Finally, this one teacher said she would be the sponsor.

"The GSA began through word of mouth. We meet once a week, read books, watch videos, talk about the coming out process. I feel support now for the first time. And I know other kids like me have somewhere to go for support. It's no longer just me.

"Yeah, there has been some negative response. When we introduced the GSA to the faculty, one teacher went off, said we were all sinning, but other teachers defended us. Someone put graffiti on my car. Everyone once in a while I wonder what people are going to do to me, but mostly I just deal with it.

"I'm doing a lot better. I've become a strong individual. I've conquered my fears. I don't fear anything."

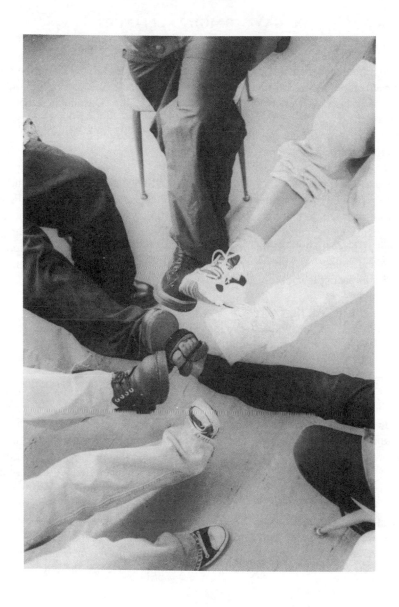

IX. GAY-STRAIGHT ALLIANCES

Many lesbian, gay, bisexual, transgender, and questioning students have formed school clubs, often known as gay-straight alliances, to provide each other with peer support, seek information about issues related to sexual orientation and gender identity, and ensure that schools respect their rights. Despite these benefits, many of the youth we interviewed had to overcome opposition from school administrators, the local school board, and the community before they could start gay-straight alliances at their schools.

Not all lesbian, gay, bisexual, and transgender students will join a gay-straight alliance. Nevertheless, schools should be facilitating such groups when students wish to form them. As a matter of federal law, in fact, school districts are obligated to permit such groups to have access to school grounds on the same terms as other noncurricular student groups. By facilitating the operation of gay-straight alliances on equal terms with other student groups, schools help secure the internationally recognized rights of youth to freedom of expression, freedom of association, freedom of peaceful assembly, and access to information.

The Benefits to Youth

Students told us that these groups can be tremendously helpful for lesbian, gay, bisexual, and transgender youth. "It was an outlet," Sam P. said of the gay-straight alliance he helped form. "We could talk about safer sex ed and get basic information people would be afraid to get in class."[329]

"Our GSA started again last year with a new advisor. We held a safe schools workshop. It was a wicked good experience. We talked about gay issues, what we can do to improve schools, things like that," Melanie S., a Massachusetts sophomore, told us. "We have a case in our main entrance with a large rainbow flag. We have lots of fliers posted telling students where you can go, giving information on programs like NAGLY [the North Shore Alliance of Gay and Lesbian Youth]. . . We're going to try to put up pictures of us at Youth Pride. None of our flyers have gotten ripped down. We're not asking for complete understanding, just acceptance."[330]

Karen M. Jordan, a DePaul University professor, suggests, "These groups offer age-appropriate opportunities for socialization and for meeting other gay, lesbian, bisexual, transgender, questioning, or supportive teens, thereby providing

---

[329]Human Rights Watch interview, Austin, Texas, March 15, 2000.
[330]Human Rights Watch interview, Salem, Massachusetts, May 24, 2000.

social support and furnishing opportunities for developing social skills."[331] As the authors of a 1999 study note, "A sense of community is naturally important, but for marginalized populations, it is imperative."[332]

Many of the youth we interviewed suggested that more schools assist students in forming gay-straight alliances. "We should have GSAs in schools, just like we have FCAs—that's the Fellowship of Christian Athletes," said Dempsey H. "I think GSAs should be supported and put in as standard in schools."[333] Dahlia P. told us that a gay-straight alliance would have made her school experience better. "They have 4-H clubs, cheerleaders, football, but they don't have an LGBT club," she said.[334]

Gay-straight alliances are not the solution for all schools, particularly if schools take no other steps to foster respect for all students and to protect youth from harassment and violence. "Before you create a GSA, you need a program" to give students information about sexuality, Manny V. suggested. "Offer a program like a separate course on sexuality, perhaps that kind of course. You might broaden the sexuality area of the health class. Make sure it's worth credits [toward graduation]."[335]

"It's one thing to be out and go to a youth group. It's another thing to step out in front of the student body," a counselor notes. "GSAs, yeah, I don't see them as the first step. Maybe if the goal is creating an incident? But I'd start with other ways that have support built in."[336]

And a Georgia teacher cautions, "I tell them it's not an overnight process. It may not happen while you're at the school. And the thing to be most cognizant of for all the good you can do for others, don't do harm to yourself. You don't have to actually become a martyr."[337]

As Dahlia P. emphasized, however, gay-straight alliances can provide crucial support to otherwise isolated students. "I felt so alone. There was no one there for

---

[331]Karen M. Jordan, "Substance Abuse Among Gay, Lesbian, Bisexual, Transgender, and Questioning Adolescents," *School Psychology Review,* vol. 29 (2000), p. 204.

[332]Andrea A. Nesmith, David L. Burton, and T.J. Cosgrove, "Gay, Lesbian, and Bisexual Youth and Young Adults: Social Support in Their Own Words," *Journal of Homosexuality,* vol. 37 (1999), p. 106.

[333]Human Rights Watch interview, Lubbock, Texas, March 21, 2000.

[334]Human Rights Watch interview, Austin, Texas, March 15, 2000.

[335]Human Rights Watch interview, Los Angeles County, California, October 21, 1999.

[336]Human Rights Watch interview, Atlanta, Georgia, December 14, 1999.

[337]Human Rights Watch interview, Atlanta, Georgia, December 18, 1999.

me to turn to," she told us. A gay-straight alliance at her school "would have helped a lot," she said.[338]

Efforts to Suppress Gay-Straight Alliances

Despite these benefits, students who seek to form gay-straight alliances often face tremendous opposition from school officials and others. Alex M., a Georgia sophomore, told us, "My old school wouldn't let me form a GSA. I just remember that they told me that it was not necessary to the curriculum to have a GSA, so I wouldn't be able to form one. This happened this past semester."[339]

"We had complaints from parents," said Sabrina L., one of the organizers of the gay-straight alliance at her high school in Orange County, California. "They said we were 'promoting,' 'recruiting,' that kind of stuff." She also reported that her group was prevented from handing out health information.[340]

School districts have sometimes gone to extremes to block gay-straight alliances in their schools, as the experience of East High School students in Salt Lake City, Utah, shows. Students at East High School sought to form a gay-straight alliance known as the Rainbow Club in 1998. The purpose of the club, modeled on similar clubs that have formed throughout the United States, was to provide a safe space in which students could discuss issues facing lesbian, gay, bisexual, and transgender youth.

Under the 1984 federal Equal Access Act, all schools that receive federal funding must provide equal access to school resources to all noncurricular clubs. However, a 1995 school board policy, adopted in response to an earlier attempt by another group of students to form a gay-straight alliance at East High, prohibited all student groups or organizations "not directly related to the curriculum" to "organize or meet on school property" at any public secondary school in the Salt Lake City School District.[341]

---

[338]Human Rights Watch interview, Austin, Texas, March 15, 2000.

[339]Human Rights Watch interview, Atlanta, Georgia, March 1, 2000.

[340]Human Rights Watch interview, Los Angeles, California, October 18, 1999.

[341]A written policy issued by the school board in February 1996 declared that "limited open forums," as defined in the federal Equal Access Act, do not exist in district schools. Under the Equal Access Act, "[a] public secondary school has a limited open forum whenever such school grants an offering to or opportunity for one or more noncurriculum related student groups to meet on school premises during noninstructional time." 20 U.S.C. § 4071(b). The Equal Access Act further provides that:

It shall be unlawful for any public secondary school which receives Federal financial assistance and which has a limited open forum to deny equal access or a fair opportunity to, or discriminate against, any students who wish to conduct

Acting under this policy, the school district terminated forty-six clubs, including the Human Rights Club, the Native American Club, and the Polynesian Club at East High; the Black Student Union, the Latino Club, the Native American Club, and Students of the Orient at West High; Advancement of Hispanic Students, the Ethnic Alliance, and the Polynesian Club at Highland High. It classified other clubs, including a school community organization known as the Improvement Council at East, as "curriculum-related." The district also permitted some unapproved clubs to meet outside of class time on school grounds.[342]

The students filed a suit against the school district, arguing that, despite the blanket ban, some noncurricular clubs were still meeting with the support of the school and that an unwritten but active policy violated the students' constitutional right to freedom of speech because it restricted the expression of positive views of gays and lesbians. The students won a partial victory in October 1999, when a federal district judge found that the school district violated the Equal Access Act by denying access to the gay-straight alliance during the time that it allowed the Improvement Council at East to meet on school grounds.[343]

In a related case, a group of students at East High School started the People Recognizing Important Social Movements (PRISM) club, which it defined as curricular because it was a forum for discussing democracy, civil rights, equality, discrimination and diversity from the perspective of lesbians and gay men. The school administrator responsible for approving applications for clubs denied the students' application to start the club, ruling that it was not curriculum-related. These students also filed suit against the school district.[344]

In April 2000, a federal judge granted a preliminary injunction prohibiting the school district from denying PRISM access to school grounds on the same

---

a meeting within that limited open forum on the basis of the religious, political, philosophical, or other content of the speech at such meetings.

Ibid. § 4071(a).

[342]The Supreme Court has found that "a student group directly relates to a school's curriculum if the subject matter of the group is actually taught or will soon be taught, in a regularly offered course; if the subject matter of the group concerns the body of courses as a whole; if participation in the group is required for a particular course; or if participation in the group results in academic credit." *Board of Education of Westside Community Schools v. Mergens,* 496 U.S. 226, 239-40 (1990).

[343]*See East High Gay/Straight Alliance v. Board of Education of Salt Lake City School District,* 81 F. Supp. 2d 1166, 1197 (D. Utah 1999).

[344]*See East High School Prism Club v. Seidel,* 95 F. Supp. 2d 1239 (D. Utah 2000).

terms as other curriculum-related student clubs.[345] In September 2000, the Salt Lake City school board reversed its 1995 policy, allowing PRISM, the Rainbow Club, and other student noncurricular groups to meet on school grounds.

Salt Lake City is not the only school district that has attempted to block student gay-straight alliances. Settling another prolonged dispute in September 2000, California's Orange Unified School District agreed to recognize El Modena High School's Gay-Straight Alliance on the same terms as other student clubs. Students had applied in September 1999 to form the club to promote acceptance among gay and straight students. After delaying its decision for several months, the school board denied the students' application in December 1999, noting that it would consider a new application "for a tolerance club with an appropriate name and a mission statement that clearly states that sex, sexuality, [and] sex education will not be the subject of discussion in club meetings."[346] Under the settlement, the Gay-Straight Alliance was allowed to keep its name and have the same access to school facilities given all other student clubs, as the federal Equal Access Act requires, including the right to meet on school grounds, to use the school's public address system to announce club meetings, and to be featured in the school yearbook. The settlement also provided that students would be able to discuss antigay discrimination and harassment and other lesbian, gay, bisexual, and transgender issues.[347]

Not all school officials oppose students forming gay straight alliances. Sam P. told us that he experienced no opposition from his school's administration when he started a GSA in 1996. He said, "I got a lot of support from most of the administration. I started my GSA after finding out about the governor's commission in Massachusetts. . . . I went to my principal . . . . I told him what I wanted to do. I wanted to be active in school, and I came up with the idea of starting a GSA. He said, 'Great idea, let's do it.'" Not all of the teachers were as enthusiastic, however. "I had an English teacher who made a few comments before she knew I was heading it all up. We were having a discussion on gays in the

---

[345]Ibid., p. 1251.

[346]*Colin v. Orange Unified School District*, 83 F. Supp. 1135, 1140 (C.D. Cal. 2000). Several weeks before the school board considered the application, El Modena High School principal Nancy Murray told the student organizers that the name of their club was inappropriate, suggesting that they choose an alternative name such as the "Tolerance Club," the "Acceptance Club," or the "Alliance." Ibid., p. 1139.

[347]*See* Lambda Legal Defense and Education Fund, "Back to School: Protecting Students from Discrimination," www.lambdalegal.org/cgi-bin/pages/sections/back2school/gsas (accessed on February 16, 2001).

military, and she asked the class, 'How do you feel about the fag group on campus?' I said, 'I think my group is working pretty well.' She apologized; she said she thought that using that word would get students to respond. We talked about it, and we worked it out."[348]

---

[348]Human Rights Watch interview, Austin, Texas, March 15, 2000.

X. ACCESS TO INFORMATION

Schools play an important role in ensuring that youth have the freedom to seek, receive, and impart information, a right guaranteed by the International Covenant on Civil and Political Rights.[349] This right includes the right to have access to information about sexual orientation and gender identity.

In addition to supporting gay-straight alliances, which are addressed in the previous chapter, schools may provide students with access to information about sexual orientation and gender identity by including such information in health education classes and other parts of the curriculum, by making information available in school libraries, and by providing them with information about outside youth groups.

Health Education

Every state we visited requires its public schools to provide health education to their students. Accurate health information is critical for lesbian, gay, bisexual, and transgender youth because those who are victimized are more likely to engage in risky behaviors, including alcohol and drug abuse and unprotected sex. Despite this fact, youth repeatedly spoke of receiving limited, erroneous, and biased health information as it related to their sexual orientation or gender identity.

"In our health class, we didn't even touch on homosexuality at all. It's almost like forbidden ground. That would have eased a lot of people's minds," Lauren M. said.[350] "There needs to be more education, not just one awareness month or one day. Sex ed is a place to do that," the mother of thirteen-year-old Tod R. told us. "I read [Tod's] sex ed book. It's not homophobic—gay issues are just absent."[351] Both students and youth service providers working with lesbian, gay, bisexual and transgender youth called on health education classes to be inclusive. Their recommendations are consistent with 1990 and 1994 resolutions of the American School Health Association that call on schools to address sexual orientation as an aspect of sexuality in the health education curriculum.[352]

---

[349]*See* ICCPR, art. 19(1). For a fuller analysis of the right to freedom of expression in international law and the restrictions that may be placed on it, see Chapter XII, "Freedom of Expression" section.

[350]Human Rights Watch interview, Austin, Texas, March 15, 2000.

[351]Human Rights Watch telephone interview, February 8, 2000.

[352]*See* American School Health Association (ASHA), "Gay and Lesbian Youth in School" (1990) and "ASHA Supports Quality Sexuality Education" (1994), in *Compendium of Resolutions* (Kent, Ohio: ASHA, August 1998), www.ashaweb.org/resolutions.html

Nevertheless, most health education programs are not addressing the needs of lesbian, gay, bisexual, and transgender students. "When gay kids start hearing things about heterosexual sex, they tune it out," suggests Ralph Bowden, an attorney in Decatur, Georgia. "They don't get information."[353]

The missed opportunities—and resulting risks to youth—are not limited to sex education. Karen M. Jordan notes that "information initiatives, geared toward all youth (and adults as well), would educate them about the realities of gay and lesbian life and dispel myths."[354] Including as a matter of course information on issues relating to sexual orientation and gender identity helps to remove social stigma against lesbian, gay, bisexual, and transgender individuals. An inclusive approach to health education has the potential to reduce harassment and violence against lesbian, gay, bisexual, and transgender youth. Such an approach may also combat their sense of isolation, reduce depression and other mental health concerns, and reduce the health risks that result.

The denial of accurate, relevant health information to lesbian, gay, bisexual, and transgender youth is not only unwise, it is also discriminatory. "That's one of the biggest disservices that's being done to gay youth," Bowden says. "It means the school district is denying them access to information that their straight counterparts are receiving."[355]

In fact, legislation or policies in some states forbid teachers from providing their students with complete and unbiased health education. For example, South Carolina law requires high school students to receive "comprehensive health education." The statute provides, however, that health education "may not include a discussion of alternate sexual lifestyles from heterosexual relationships including, but not limited to, homosexual relationships except in the context of instruction concerning sexually transmitted diseases."[356] In Georgia, the Clayton County Board of Education's health education policy states, "When homosexuality is discussed in sex education classes it shall not be presented as an acceptable alternative lifestyle."[357] Arizona's health education standards prohibit the teaching

---

(accessed on March 21, 2001).

[353]Human Rights Watch interview with Ralph Bowden, attorney, Atlanta, Georgia, December 14, 1999.

[354]Karen M. Jordan, "Substance Abuse Among Gay, Lesbian, Bisexual, Transgender, and Questioning Adolescents," *School Psychology Review,* vol. 29 (2000), p. 203.

[355]Human Rights Watch interview with Ralph Bowden, December 14, 1999.

[356]S.C. Code Ann. §§ 59-32-30(A)(3), (5) (1999).

[357]Clayton County Board of Education, "Board Policy: Instruction, Health and Physical Education," August 12, 1991.

or "promotion of homosexuality" in the AIDS and sex education curriculum. Similarly, Utah's health core curriculum provides: "The following may NOT be taught: . . . . (2) The acceptance or advocacy of homosexuality as a desirable or healthy sexual adjustment or lifestyle . . . ."[358] In Oregon, an initiative on the November 2000 ballot would have prohibited public schools from "encouraging, promoting, or sanctioning homosexual or bisexual behavior." Voters rejected the measure by a narrow margin, with 47 percent casting their ballots in favor of enacting the prohibition.[359]

Such measures may even be permitted when state law prohibits discrimination based on sexual orientation. The Minnesota Human Rights Law contains the caveat that it does not "authorize or permit the promotion of homosexuality or bisexuality in education institutions or require the teaching in education institutions of homosexuality or bisexuality as an acceptable lifestyle."[360] Connecticut's human rights law contains a nearly identical provision.[361]

Especially when they are faced with hostile laws or policies, teachers and administrators are often uncertain about what information they can give students on lesbian, gay, bisexual, and transgender issues. The result is that the little information youth do get on these issues is frequently inaccurate or misleading. To compound the problem, the uncertainty and discomfort many educators feel when addressing these issues allows some teachers to express their personal prejudices without challenge. Dempsey H. told us, "My health teacher was like, 'There's a huge AIDS crisis in Lubbock; do you know why?,'" he said. "We said because it's a college town, there's lots of students here. He said, 'No, it's because there's a huge gay community here.'"[362] And Drew L. related that in a health class at his Louisiana high school, "We were talking about AIDS, and the teacher said the rate in the homosexual population was higher. He gave us some answer like, 'Generally homosexual men are less picky about who they choose to be with.'"[363]

---

[358]The Utah policy instructs that if students ask questions about gay issues, teachers are told to respond, "That's not what we're here to discuss" or "That's something you should talk with your parents about." Diane Urbani, "Classes on Sex Get Clear Limits," *Deseret News* (Salt Lake City), August 16, 1999.

[359]*See* Cable News Network, "Voter Results in Oregon," www.ccn.com/ELECTIONS/2000/results/OR/ (accessed on November 17, 2000).

[360]Minn. Stat. § 363.021(2) (1999).

[361]*See* Conn. Gen. Stat. § 46a-81r (1999).

[362]Human Rights Watch interview, Lubbock, Texas, March 21, 2000.

[363]Human Rights Watch interview, Dallas, Texas, March 27, 2000.

Other Classroom Instruction

Similarly, students rarely hear anything about issues relating to sexual orientation or gender identity elsewhere in the curriculum. If they do hear about someone who is lesbian, gay, bisexual, or transgender, it is almost invariably in a negative light.

"I think, yes, a few times issues were brought up with the topic of homosexuality," said Lavonn R. "Nothing positive."[364]

James L., a gay sophomore, said:

Nobody talks about it. Nobody really mentions gay or lesbian issues. Well, there was this article in the school paper, but even after I reread it I didn't get the point of the article. Something about gay people getting more visible in society. But I haven't had any teachers talk about it, except that my history teacher has a sign up for Project 10. It doesn't sound encouraging: the sign says something about the "loneliest" students. I'm not *lonely*. I just don't know anything about it. I don't know any teachers who are gay.

I would want people to feel comfortable talking about it, because, since people don't bring it up, people don't talk about it, they think it's just something strange, something weird. If you can make it so it's not like that, so it's seen as something you can talk about openly, that would change a lot.[365]

Lauren M. made a similar observation. "It's not even in the curriculum. It's like we're not even supposed to know about it. 'That's so gay' is the only thing we ever hear about it." She returned to the topic at the end of our interview when we asked her what recommendations she would make. "Gay education," she offered. "It's not even in the curriculum. Anything that would let people know. Hate crimes education. Let people know what's really going on. That would be really helpful."[366]

In 1990, the Association for Supervision and Curriculum Development adopted a resolution calling on its members to "develop policies, curriculum materials, and teaching strategies that do not discriminate on the basis of sexual

---

[364]Human Rights Watch interview, Austin, Texas, March 23, 2000.

[365]Human Rights Watch interview, Los Angeles, California, January 19, 2000.

[366]Human Rights Watch interview, Austin, Texas, March 15, 2000.

orientation."[367] Hilda F. Besner, a clinical psychologist, and Charlotte F. Spungin, an education specialist, note:

> Schools are natural forums for presenting information to students, and homosexuality should be included in the curriculum. Other subjects that affect minority groups are covered, so it seems logical that the subject of homosexuality be addressed. In addition to the usual curriculum, schools throughout the nation are used as forums for teaching about alcohol and drug abuse, race relations, child abuse, automobile safety, voting, gun safety, sex equity, AIDS, world hunger, and many other special interest topics. It is the rare school or community that addresses the needs of gay and lesbian students.[368]

Most of the students with whom we spoke agreed with these recommendations. "I'd like to see in the majority of schools some service or class having a focus on GLBT youth," said Tyrone V., seventeen. "I think it should be in every school."[369] Drew L., a Dallas freshman, urged teachers to "start in elementary school" with videotapes designed for the appropriate grade. After thinking a few minutes, however, he remarked, "Not a videotape, then they'd have to send out a letter, because then the parents would take their kids out of the class. It'd have to be something without getting permission. Something with no liability for teachers. Maybe they could have the parents sign a contract at the beginning of the year saying that the teachers can show educational videos."[370]

Nevertheless, most of the teachers we interviewed did not feel that they could bring up lesbian, gay, bisexual, and transgender issues in class. "My principal would faint," said a teacher in West Texas said when we asked him.[371] Others expressed uncertainty about how to go about introducing lesbian, gay, bisexual and transgender issues into their classroom discussions.

---

[367]Association for Supervision and Curriculum Development (ASCD), Resolution on Student Sexual Orientation (Alexandria, Virginia: ASCD, 1990), www.ascd.org/aboutascd/position.html (accessed on March 21, 2001).

[368]Hilda F. Besner and Charlotte J. Spungin, *Gay and Lesbian Students: Understanding Their Needs* (Washington, D.C.: Taylor & Francis, 1995), p. 99.

[369]Human Rights Watch interview, Long Beach, California, January 19, 2000.

[370]Human Rights Watch interview, Dallas, Texas, March 27, 2000.

[371]Human Rights Watch interview, Lubbock, Texas, March 20, 2000.

Lesbian, gay, bisexual, and transgender issues can readily be incorporated into existing school programs that address discrimination, civil rights, and minority groups.[372]

In addition, these issues can be raised in most subjects currently taught in U.S. public schools. For example, classes on the sciences, mathematics, literature, the arts, and other disciplines can note the contributions of lesbian, gay, bisexual, and transgender individuals. Social studies classes can include discussions of related current and historical issues.

Some teachers shared the strategies they used. "I bring up gay and lesbian issues in class," a Georgia teacher told us. "I'm a literature teacher, so there are many natural ways to do it. Each day I start out with a five-minute news article. I bring it in so I can control the topic. For instance, today's was on gender issues in sports, on Title IX noncompliance in the State of Georgia. So there were gay and lesbian issues in the news. If we read something by a gay or lesbian author, I'll tell them even if there's the remotest connection to the book."[373] The Gay, Lesbian, and Straight Education Network and teacher education specialists offer additional curriculum suggestions.[374]

Classroom discussions of lesbian, gay, bisexual, and transgender issues should not be confined to health education. Noting "the danger of medicalization," education researcher Arthur Lipkin cautions, "We run the risk of having [students] think that homosexuality is inevitably linked with deviance and illness. Even if the teacher is gay-friendly and the curriculum is accurate, placing the matter under the subject heading of 'health' or 'disease prevention' carries its own message."[375]

Integrating these issues into the curriculum is beneficial to youth who are struggling with issues of sexual orientation and gender identity in much the same

---

[372]Amnesty International USA; the Gay, Lesbian, and Straight Education Network; and the Human Rights Resource Center at the University of Minnesota have developed a series of classroom exercises that address lesbian, gay, bisexual, and transgender issues as human rights issues. *See* David M. Donahue, *Lesbian, Gay, Bisexual, and Transgender Rights: A Human Rights Perspective* (Minneapolis, Minnesota: Human Rights Resource Center, University of Minnesota, 2000).

[373]Human Rights Watch interview, Atlanta, Georgia, December 14, 1999.

[374]*See, for example,* Besner and Spungin, pp. 107-109; Virginia Casper and Steven B. Schultz, *Gay Parents/Straight Schools: Building Communication and Trust* (New York and London: Teachers College Press, 1999), pp. 155-65; Arthur Lipkin, "The Case for a Gay and Lesbian Curriculum," *The High School Journal,* vol. 77 (1993-94), p. 95; Dan Woog, *School's Out: The Impact of Gay and Lesbian Issues on America's Schools* (Los Angeles and New York: Alyson Books, 1995), pp. 333-60.

[375]Lipkin, "Gay and Lesbian Curriculum," p. 101.

way that access to accurate health information is. Classroom acknowledgment of these issues reduces the sense of isolation faced by youth who are lesbian, gay, bisexual, or transgender or who are questioning their sexual orientation or gender identity.

Adding these issues to the curriculum has the potential to benefit all students by increasing their awareness and tolerance of those who are different from them. A straight high school senior is quoted by Lipkin as saying, "The more we talk about homosexuality in class, the more comfortable I am with the idea, with gay people, with my own sexuality, and with my own male identity."[376]

Despite these potential benefits, school districts probably do not have to be warned to proceed with caution in incorporating these issues into the school curriculum. Cautions Lipkin, "It would be a mistake first to *require* all teachers to teach this subject, especially without proper training."[377]

It is clear, however, that lesbian, gay, bisexual, and transgender issues have a place in the general school curriculum, both because they are appropriately addressed within academic subjects currently taught and because their inclusion furthers the educational mission, as articulated in the Universal Declaration of Human Rights, of promoting "the full development of the human personality" and "the strengthening of respect for human rights and fundamental freedoms."[378]

"I know school is not meant to be therapy," Tod R.'s mother said. "But they should be building good citizenship."[379]

Libraries

"It's like gay people don't exist," Leslie H. said of her Dallas-area school's library.[380] Given the resistance of most schools even to raising lesbian, gay, bisexual, and transgender issues in the classroom, it is not surprising that most students told us that their school libraries had few or no resources on these issues.

"We really needed more resources," William H. commented. "There were two books on queer issues in the school library. I read them under the guise of doing a paper on homophobia. The paper basically gave me permission to read about homosexuality. By the end of one of the books, I was bawling, a big mess.

---

[376]Ibid., p. 98.

[377]Ibid., p. 105.

[378]Universal Decalaration of Human Rights, art. 26(2), G.A. Res. 217A (III), U.N. Doc. A/810, p. 71 (1948).

[379]Human Rights Watch telephone interview, February 8, 2000.

[380]Human Rights Watch interview, Dallas, Texas, March 27, 2000.

I thought to myself, 'Why am I crying?' Then I realized that the book was about me."[381]

"You can't find any information at school," offered Manny V., a 1999 graduate of a San Bernandino Valley high school in Los Angeles County.[382] And Philip G. said that in his Los Angeles school, "being gay there was never seen as positive. You would never find materials in the library, no books, no teachers who were out. There was no insinuation at all of a gay life."[383]

In schools where books and other materials on lesbian, gay, bisexual, and transgender issues are available, they are often there only because of the efforts of supportive teachers. Matt P. told us, "There were one or two books in the English room, not in the library. It wasn't part of the library. I think the English teacher had rescued them from somewhere. Two books. One about a guy who drowned, the other about a kid whose brother has AIDS. . . . Those were the resources. I know, because I was searching."[384] Similarly, a Georgia teacher said, "I bring in books from home. When I get caught someday, I will be fired. But this job isn't enough to worry about."[385]

Some students will never be comfortable using their school library as a source of information about issues related to sexual orientation or gender identity. "I think it's really hard to go to the library and get a book on gay life," said Paul M. "You'd be scared to go up to the counter to check it out."[386] "You cannot go to the library to check out books," the Georgia teacher stated. "It's too dangerous. People can see you, somebody has to check out the book to you, people can see your name on the card and tell you've checked the book out."[387]

The Internet allays some of these fears, although it presents different concerns. "Having the information available on line helps a lot," Paul M. noted.

"I agree," Steve D. said. "I wouldn't have come out as early to my parents if I hadn't been able to get information on line."[388]

[381]Human Rights Watch interview, San Francisco, California, January 27, 2000.

[382]Human Rights Watch interview, Los Angeles, California, October 18, 1999.

[383]Human Rights Watch interview, Los Angeles, California, October 20, 1999.

[384]Human Rights Watch interview, Salem, Massachusetts, May 23, 2000.

[385]Human Rights Watch interview, Atlanta, Georgia, December 14, 1999.

[386]Human Rights Watch interview, Bergen County, New Jersey, October 31, 1999 (group discussion).

[387]Human Rights Watch interview, Atlanta, Georgia, December 14, 1999.

[388]Human Rights Watch interview, Bergen County, New Jersey, October 31, 1999 (group discussion).

"If you're under eighteen, it's hard to meet people," Ron P. said. "Unless you have the Internet, then it's easy. The Internet is helpful, but it's also harmful. . . . It starts controlling your life when you're a gay teen, because that's all you have. You can lie so easily. You can become anything you want. A lot of older men have taken advantage of teenagers. Some kids aren't wise to that."[389]

It is in part for this reason that many schools restrict students' Internet access. It is also common, for example, to prevent youth from having access to pornographic websites. And the Children's Internet Protection Act, signed into law on December 21, 2000, requires public elementary and secondary schools and public libraries to block children's access to "inappropriate matter" and "materials harmful to minors" as a condition of federal funding programs intended to increase students' access to the Internet.[390]

But many schools that restrict students' Internet access block them from any site that discusses lesbian, gay, bisexual, and transgender issues.[391] For example, Sabrina L. reported that her school and most others in her school district used filtering software that prevents students from having access to material posted by gay rights groups.[392]

For those students who are willing to use library resources, schools can make access to such information easier for youth by ensuring that library holdings are catalogued and shelved so that students can find them with a minimum of difficulty. For example, cataloguing systems should use contemporary subject headings such as "lesbian" and "gay" rather than relying exclusively on outdated terminology such as "homosexual" or "homophile." Books on lesbian, gay, bisexual, and transgender issues should be kept in the same manner as other holdings, preferably on open shelves, rather than being kept in the librarian's office and made available only on request.

---

[389]Human Rights Watch interview, Lubbock, Texas, March 21, 2000.

[390]*See* Children's Internet Protection Act, H.R. 5666, 106th Cong., 2d sess., §§ 1732, 1711 (2000), *incorporated by reference into* Consolidated Appropriations Act, 2001, Pub. L. No. 106-554, § 1(a), 114 Stat. 2763 (2000).

[391]*See* John Spear, "How Filtering Software Impacts Our Schools," in Gay and Lesbian Alliance Against Defamation, *Access Denied, Version 2.0: The Continuing Threat Against Internet Access and Privacy and Its Impact on the Lesbian, Gay, Bisexual and Transgender Community* (New York: GLAAD, December 1999), pp. 16-19.

[392]Human Rights Watch interview, Orange County, California, October 21, 1999.

Outside Youth Groups

Another way that schools can help lesbian, gay, bisexual, and transgender students is by making information available to them about outside youth groups. "When I went there, I could feel safe—a lot less tension," said Manny V. "Students couldn't handle this stuff on their own. It's bigger than they are."[393]

"I feel much more comfortable here. It's pretty tight; it's really cool," said Leigh S. "It's really tight to be around people who don't care if you're gay. Nobody's going to pass judgment on you. Once you step out of the car and into school, it's a different world."[394]

---

[393]Human Rights Watch interview, Los Angeles County, California, October 21, 1999.
[394]Human Rights Watch interview, Austin, Texas, March 15, 2000.

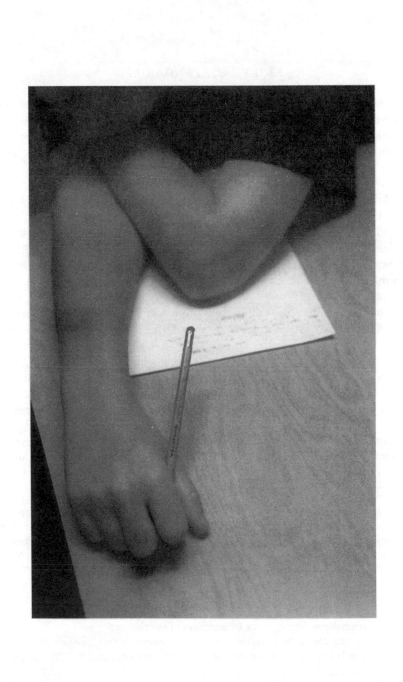

XI. LEGAL STANDARDS

International law establishes that every person, including youth, has the right to protection from physical and mental violence, the right to freedom from discrimination, the right to an education, and the rights to freedom of expression, association, and peaceful assembly.

The Right to Protection from Physical and Mental Violence

Article 24 of the International Covenant on Civil and Political Rights (ICCPR) guarantees the right of the child "to such measures of protection as are required by his status as a minor." The United States did not take any reservations to article 24 when it ratified the ICCPR in 1992. In addition, both the ICCPR and the Convention against Torture and Other Cruel, Inhuman or Degrading Treatment or Punishment, which the United States ratified in 1994, prohibit cruel, inhuman, or degrading treatment.[395]

To determine the scope of these provisions with regard to children under the age of eighteen, they should be read together with the Convention on the Rights of the Child, a treaty which the United States has signed but not yet ratified. Reflecting almost universal consensus on children's human rights, the convention recognizes that children are entitled to special care and assistance and that the best interests of the child must be a primary consideration in all actions concerning children. Under article 19 of the convention, youth have the right to protection from "all forms of physical or mental violence, injury or abuse, neglect or negligent treatment, maltreatment or exploitation including sexual abuse, while in the care of parent(s), legal guardian(s) or any other person who has the care of the child."[396]

---

[395]International Covenant on Civil and Political Rights (ICCPR), arts. 24, 7, *opened for signature* December 19, 1966, 999 U.N.T.S. 171 (entered into force March 23, 1976); Convention against Torture and Other Cruel, Inhuman or Degrading Treatment or Punishment, art. 16, *adopted* December 10, 1984, 1465 U.N.T.S. 85 (entered into force June 26, 1987). The United States did enter a reservation to article 7 of the ICCPR, noting:

That the United States considers itself bound by Article 7 to the extent that "cruel, inhuman or degrading treatment or punishment" means the cruel and unusual treatment or punishment prohibited by the Fifth, Eighth, and/or Fourteenth Amendments to the Constitution of the United States.

"U.S. Reservations, Declarations, and Understandings, International Covenant on Civil and Political Rights," *Congressional Record,* vol. 138 (daily edition, April 2, 1992), p. S4781-01.

[396]Convention on the Rights of the Child, arts. 3,19, *adopted* November 20, 1989, G.A. Res. 44/25, U.N. Doc. A/RES/44/25 (entered into force September 2, 1990).

Article 19 of the convention protects youth from private acts of violence and harassment as well as from acts committed by state agents. For example, the Committee on the Rights of the Child has relied on this provision to call for state action to address child abuse within the family.[397] By its terms, the provision is not limited to domestic violence; the state's obligation to protect extends to "all forms" of violence or neglect committed against a youth while the youth is in the care of another person. In fact, the committee's concluding observations on country reports have addressed problems of violence or threats of violence by youth against other youth in schools and other institutions.[398]

Because the United States has signed but not ratified the convention, it is not generally bound by the terms of the treaty. As a signatory, however, it has the obligation to refrain from actions which would defeat the treaty's object and purpose.[399]

---

[397]*See Concluding Observations of the Committee on the Rights of the Child: Japan,* paras. 19 and 40, Committee on the Rights of the Child, 18th sess., U.N. Doc. CRC/C/15/Add.90 (June 5, 1998); *Concluding Observations of the Committee on the Rights of the Child: Costa Rica,* paras. 9 and 16, Committee on the Rights of the Child, 4th sess., U.N. Doc. CRC/C/15/Add.11 (October 18, 1993); *Concluding Observations of the Committee on the Rights of the Child: Jordan,* paras. 15 and 23, Committee on the Rights of the Child, 6th sess., U.N. Doc. CRC/C/15/Add.21 (April 25, 1994). Established by the Convention on the Rights of the Child, the committee receives and comments on reports by states of the measures they have taken to comply with the convention. Its comments and general recommendations provide authoritative guidance on the scope of the rights established by the convention.

The Committee on the Elimination of Discrimination against Women has interpreted a similar provision of the Convention on the Elimination of All Forms of Discrimination against Women (CEDAW), *adopted* December 18, 1979, 1249 U.N.T.S. 13 (entered into force September 3, 1981), to extend to "all kinds of violence" against women, including private violence. *See General Recommendation No. 19, Violence against Women,* Committee on the Elimination of Discrimination against Women,, 11th sess., U.N. Doc. CEDAW/C/1992/L.1/Add.15 (1992).

[398]*See* Rachel Hodgkin and Peter Newell, *Implementation Handbook for the Convention on the Rights of the Child* (New York: UNICEF, 1998), p. 246.

[399]*See* Vienna Convention on the Law of Treaties, art. 18, *concluded* May 23, 1969, 1155 U.N.T.S. 331 (entered into force Jan. 27, 1980). Although the United States has not ratified the Vienna Convention on the Law of Treaties, it regards this convention as "the authoritative guide to current treaty law and practice." S. Exec. Doc. L., 92d Cong., 1st sess. (1971), p. 1. The International Court of Justice has recognized that the convention "may in many respects be considered as a codification of existing customary law." *Fisheries Jurisdiction Case (United Kingdom v. Iceland),* 1974 I.C.J. 3, 18; *see also Advisory Opinion*

The protection of children from violence, whether committed by state agents or at the hands of private individuals, is a key component of the principal object and purpose of the Convention on the Rights of the Child. Article 3(2) of the convention requires states to "undertake to ensure the child such protection and care as is necessary for his or her well-being . . . ." The preamble to the convention invokes "the dignity and worth of the human person," declares that youth should be "brought up in the spirit of the ideas proclaimed in the Charter of the United Nations, and in particular in the spirit of peace, dignity, tolerance, freedom, equality and solidarity," and emphasizes "the need for extending particular care to the child."[400]

Protection from violence is also an essential component in securing other rights protected by the convention. As this report documents, harassment and violence against gay, lesbian, bisexual, or transgender youth is a violation of their right to physical integrity. Additionally, the harassment and violence may deprive them of their right to an education on equal terms with their peers. Such harassment and violence may also have serious mental health consequences and infringe upon the right of youth to the enjoyment of the highest attainable standard of health.[401]

The obligation to protect requires more than having laws against harassment, assault, and child abuse on the books. When youth have been subjected to abuse and other forms of violence, the convention requires the state to "promote [their] physical and psychological recovery" in a setting that "fosters [their] health, peer-respect, and dignity."[402]

Human Rights Watch views the obligation to protect youth from violence, as delineated in article 19 of the Convention on the Rights of the Child, as one aspect of the "measures of protection . . . required by [one's] status as a minor" to which youth are entitled under article 24 of the ICCPR. This view is consistent with the Human Rights Committee's general comment on the scope of article 24, which

---

on Namibia, 1971 I.C.J. 16, 47. No international tribunal has explicitly found article 18 of the Vienna Convention to be a declaration of existing customary international law, however.

[400]An examination of the preamble is an appropriate means of identifying a treaty's object and purpose. *See Advisory Opinion on Reservations to the Convention on the Prevention and Punishment of the Crime of Genocide,* 1951 I.C.J. 15; *Austria v. Italy,* 4 Y.B. Eur. Conv. on H.R. 116, 138 (1961); *The Effect of Reservations on the Entry into Force of the American Convention on Human Rights (Arts. 74 and 75), Advisory Opinion OC-2/82 of September 24, 1982,* Inter-Am. Ct. H.R. (Ser.A) No. 2 (1982).

[401]*See* Convention on the Rights of the Child, arts. 28, 24(1).

[402]Ibid., art. 39.

notes that "every possible economic and social measure should be taken . . . to prevent [children] from being subjected to acts of violence and cruel and inhuman treatment" and calls for "measures of protection . . . aimed at removing all discrimination in any field."[403]

Under this interpretation of these provisions, the state's obligation to protect extends to private violence and harassment committed by one student against another when school officials know or should reasonably know of the risk of abuse. As discussed below, youth have the right to receive an education. Their right to be in school carries the reasonable expectation that school authorities will take steps to ensure their safety.[404]

U.S. Constitutional Standards

The U.S. Constitution prohibits states from depriving any "person of life, liberty, or property, without due process of law."[405] The U.S. Supreme Court has held that this provision, known as the Due Process Clause, imposes "no affirmative obligation on the State to provide the general public with adequate protective services." The court explained:

> [N]othing in the language of the Due Process Clause itself requires the State to protect the life, liberty, and property of its citizens against invasion by private actors. The Clause is phrased as a limitation on the State's power to act, not as a guarantee of certain minimal levels of safety and security. . . . Its purpose was to protect the people from the State, not to ensure that the State protected them from each other.[406]

---

[403]*General Comment 17, Rights of the Child (Art. 24)*, paras. 3, 5, Human Rights Committee, 35th sess., 1989.

[404]This conclusion is strengthened by the fact that most U.S. students have not only the right to attend school but also the duty to do so: Most U.S. states have compulsory attendance laws that obligate students to attend classes until the age of sixteen. *See* "Right to Education" section, below.

[405]U.S. Constitution, Amendment XIV, § 1. The Due Process Clause is part of the Fourteenth Amendment, one of three constitutional amendments enacted after the U.S. Civil War in order to protect the rights of newly freed slaves. The Fourteenth Amendment also provides that no state shall "deny to any person within its jurisdiction the equal protection of the laws." Ibid. For a discussion of this provision, known as the Equal Protection Clause, see "Right to Nondiscrimination and Equal Protection" section, below.

[406]*DeShaney v. Winnebago County Department of Social Services*, 489 U.S. 189, 195-96 (1989).

The Court has recognized, however, that the state may assume a duty to care for an individual in limited circumstances. For example, the state must provide adequate medical care to incarcerated or detained persons. Similarly, it must ensure the "reasonable safety" of involuntarily committed mental patients.[407]

However, it has been reluctant to extend the limited circumstances in which the state has a duty to protect individuals from private violence. In a 1989 case, for instance, the Court held that the state was not obligated to protect a four-year-old boy from violence at the hands of his father even though state authorities had received medical reports indicative of child abuse. In addition, the caseworker who visited the child's home had observed that the child had head injuries and reported her suspicions that the child was being physically abused.[408]

A school is arguably a custodial setting, and as such, it falls within the narrow limits of the constitutional duty to protect an individual from harm. Most courts have found, however, that school administrators are not constitutionally obligated to protect students from harm at the hands of other students.[409] In *Nabozny v.*

---

[407]*See Estelle v. Gamble,* 429 U.S. 97, 103-4 (1976) (duty to provide adequate medical care to incarcerated prisoners); *Revere v. Massachusetts General Hospital,* 463 U.S. 239, 244 (1983) (duty to provide medical care to suspects in police custody who have been injured during arrest); *Youngberg v. Romeo,* 457 U.S. 307, 314-25 (1982) (finding a duty to provide involuntarily committed mental patients with services necessary to ensure their "reasonable safety" from selves and others and suggesting an obligation to provide them with "adequate food, shelter, clothing, and medical care").

[408]*DeShaney,* 489 U.S. at 192-93. The Court's opinion noted, "In March 1984, Randy DeShaney beat 4-year-old Joshua so severely that he fell into a life-threatening coma. Emergency brain surgery revealed a series of hemorrhages caused by traumatic injuries to the head inflicted over a long period of time. Joshua did not die, but he suffered brain damage so severe that he is expected to spend the rest of his life confined to an institution for the profoundly retarded." Ibid., p. 193.

[409]Most U.S. courts have rejected arguments that compulsory school laws or a school's *in loco parentis* status create a custodial relationship that is sufficient to trigger a duty to protect. *See D.R. v. Middle Bucks Area Vocational Technical School,* 972 F.2d 1364, 1369-73 (3d Cir. 1992) (en banc), *cert. denied,*113 S. Ct. 1266 (1993); *Doe v. Hillsboro Independent School District,* 113 F.3d 1412, 1415 (5th Cir. 1997) (eighth-grade girl raped by school custodian); *Sargi v. Kent City Board of Education,* 70 F.3d 907, 911 (6th Cir. 1995) (bus driver did not seek medical attention for student who collapsed due to heart failure); *J.O. v. Alton Community Unit School District 11,* 909 F.2d 267, 272 (7th Cir. 1990) (students alleged that they were sexually assaulted by teacher); *Dorothy J. v. Little Rock School District,* 7 F.3d 729, 732 (8th Cir. 1993) (mentally retarded student sexually assaulted by another mentally retarded student in school shower); *Maldonado v. Josey,* 975 F.2d 727, 731-33 (10th Cir. 1992), *cert. denied,* 113 S. Ct. 1266 (1993); *Russell v. Fannin*

Podlesny, a case involving a Wisconsin student who was viciously and repeatedly harassed and physically assaulted because he is gay, a federal appellate court noted:

> However untenable it may be to suggest that under the Fourteenth Amendment a state can force a student to attend a school when school officials know that the student will be placed at risk of bodily harm, our court has concluded that local school administrations have no affirmative substantive due process duty to protect students.[410]

Despite the reluctance of the courts to expand the state's limited duty to provide protection from private violence, the court observed in *Nabozny* that the argument is not foreclosed to future litigants, noting:

> There is evidence to suggest that Nabozny informed school officials that he was at risk, and that the officials took no action—for years. Moreover, in some cases schools arguably serve as temporary custodians of children, limiting parents' ability to care for children, or children's ability to care for themselves. Many parents and students rely on schools to provide students with food, shelter, discipline, guidance, and medical care, in addition to an education, while the students are on campus. In this case, it seems that Alton High even fulfilled a police function by providing a "police liaison" officer. Depending upon the state law, a student may be compelled to attend school. In a small town the state law requirement may be tantamount to a requirement that the student attend specific schools. The extent of a school's control over a student also might vary with the student's age; schools control kindergarten students more than high school students. It may be,

---

County School District, 784 F. Supp. 1576, 1582-83 (N.D. Ga.), *aff'd without opinion,* 981 F.2d 1263 (11th Cir. 1992); *B.M.H. v. School Board of Chesapeake,* 833 F. Supp. 560, 569-70 (E.D. Va. 1993) (eighth-grade girl sexually assaulted by classmate after she had reported classmate's threat to rape her) .

[410]*Nabozny v. Podlesny,* 92 F.3d 446, 458-59 (7th Cir. 1996) (citing *J.O. v. Alton Community Unit School District 11,* 909 F.2d 267, 272-73 (7th Cir. 1990)). In *Alton Community,* the Seventh Circuit concluded that school administrators do not have a "special relationship" with students. In the absence of a "special relationship," a state actor has no duty under U.S. law to protect a potential victim.

therefore, that in some cases a school is in a custodial relationship with its students.[411]

Even if a due process challenge is not foreclosed, the protections it would afford fall well below the protection that international law affords to children under article 24 of the ICCPR and article 19 of the Convention on the Rights of the Child. In addition, students in the United States face formidable challenges in contending that their schools have an affirmative constitutional duty to offer protection. They are much more likely to succeed on other constitutional bases, particularly the denial of the equal protection of the laws. The Supreme Court observed in *DeShaney* that "the State may not, of course, selectively deny its protective services to certain disfavored minorities without violating the Equal Protection Clause."[412] In Nabozny, the student ultimately prevailed in his suit against the school district on this alternative constitutional ground.[413]

Federal Legislation
Even if the Due Process Clause of the U.S. Constitution does not require teachers and school administrators to protect students from violence, federal law obligates school officials to address some forms of harassment and violence. To a large extent, however, federal law offers lesbian, gay, bisexual, and transgender students only limited remedies for the harassment and violence many suffer at the hands of other students.

Constitutional Limitations
The first limitation results from the United States' federal structure. Congress' powers are limited to specific areas; powers not expressly granted by the Constitution are reserved to the states.[414] As an application of this constitutional principle, Congress does not have general authority to regulate crime or to legislate in other areas that are traditionally regulated by state or local government.[415]

---

[411]*Nabozny,* 92 F.3d at 459 n.13. The court did not consider these factors because the student did not challenge or attempt to distinguish the court's holding in *Alton Community.*

[412]*DeShaney,* 498 U.S. at 196 n.3.

[413]*See Nabozny,* 92 F.3d at 455-58. *See also* "The Right to Nondiscrimination and Equal Protection of the Laws," below.

[414]*See* U.S. Constitution, Amendment IX.

[415]*See, e.g., Cohens v. Virginia,* 19 U.S. (6 Wheat.) 264, 426 (1821) (Marshall, C.J.) (concluding that Congress "has no general right to punish murder committed within any of the States").

Congress does have explicit authority to enforce the Fourteenth Amendment, which guarantees that no state shall deprive any person of life, liberty, or property without due process of law or deny any person the equal protection of the laws.[416] When it acts under the remedial authority of the Fourteenth Amendment, Congress may legislate in areas that are within the states' traditional sphere of influence, and it may also regulate acts that are not in themselves unconstitutional. As interpreted by the courts, however, the Fourteenth Amendment prohibits only state action; it does not reach private conduct.[417]

To avoid the constitutional problems presented under the Fourteenth Amendment by attempts to regulate private action, Congress has often enacted civil rights laws under its authority to regulate interstate commerce.[418] The courts now generally uphold legislation regulating any activity that uses the channels of interstate commerce or has a substantial effect on commerce across state lines. As part of the Civil Rights Act of 1964, for example, Congress prohibited racial discrimination in public accommodations after concluding that such discrimination by hotels and restaurants had an adverse impact on interstate commerce.[419] Federal

---

[416]Section 5 of the Fourteenth Amendment gives Congress "power to enforce, by appropriate legislation," the provisions of the amendment.

[417]In 1883, the Supreme Court overturned the Civil Rights Act of 1875, 18 Stat. 336, which criminalized racially motivated interference by one private actor of another's "enjoyment of . . . inns, public conveyances on land or water, theatres, and other places of public amusement." The Court held:

> The wrongful act of an individual, unsupported by any such [state] authority, is simply a private wrong or a crime of that individual; an invasion of the rights of the injured party, it is true, whether they affect his person, his property, or his reputation: but if not sanctioned in some way by the State, or not done under State authority, his rights remain in full force, and may presumably be vindicated by resort to the laws of the State for redress.

Civil Rights Cases, 109 U.S. 3 (1883). *See also United States v. Morrison*, 529 U.S. 598, 624 (2000) (noting the "enduring vitality" of the *Civil Rights Cases*). *But see United States v. Guest*, 383 U.S. 745, 774 (1966) (Brennan, J., concurring in part and dissenting in part) (expressing the view that *Civil Rights Cases* were wrongly decided and that the Fourteenth Amendment permits Congress to prohibit actions by private individuals).

[418]The Commerce Clause gives Congress the power "To regulate Commerce with foreign Nations, and among the several States, and with the Indian Tribes." U.S. Constitution, art. I, § 8, cl. 3.

[419]*See* Civil Rights Act of 1964, Title II, Pub. L. No. 88-352, 78 Stat. 241 (codified as amended at 42 U.S.C. §§ 2000a-1 to 2000a-6 (2001)); *Heart of Atlanta Motel, Inc., v. United States*, 379 U.S. 241 (1964) (upholding Title II under the Commerce Clause); *Katzenbach v. McClung*, 379 U.S. 294 (1964) (same).

law also provides protection against private discrimination based on race, sex, religion, national origin, age, and disability in employment.[420]

In recent years, however, the Supreme Court has placed stricter limits on Congress' use of the Commerce Clause to make laws affecting noncommercial activity. In May 2000, the Court struck down a provision of the Violence Against Women Act of 1994 that allowed victims of gender-motivated crimes of violence to bring federal civil lawsuits against their attackers.[421]

Congress has also passed civil rights legislation under its spending power.[422] By placing conditions on state agencies' acceptance of federal funds, such laws attempt to ensure that taxpayers' money is not spent in a discriminatory manner. For example, the Civil Rights Act of 1964 included a provision banning racial discrimination "in any program or activity receiving Federal financial assistance."[423] Under a provision enacted as Title IX of the Education Amendments of 1972, schools that receive federal funds are prohibited from discriminating on the basis of sex.[424]

As with the Commerce Clause, the Spending Clause gives Congress considerable latitude to regulate state and even private activity. Often, in fact, the spending power allows Congress to achieve indirectly what it would be unable to do by direct regulation. The courts have held that Congressional authority to spend for the "general welfare" enables it to legislate over matters that are not authorized

---

[420]*See* 42 U.S.C. § 2000e-2 (2001) (prohibiting employment discrimination based on race, religion, sex, or national origin); 29 U.S.C. § 623(a) (2001) (age); 42 U.S.C. § 12112 (2001) (disability).

[421]*See Morrison,*529 U.S. at 601 (invalidating 42 U.S.C. § 13981 (2000)). The courts have upheld the Violence Against Women Act's federal criminal remedy to punish domestic violence occurring during interstate travel, *see* 18 U.S.C. § 2261(a)(1) (2001), reasoning that the provision permissibly regulates the use of "channels" of interstate commerce, in this case "the interstate transportation routes through which persons and goods move." *United States v. Lankford,* 196 F.3d 563, 571-72 (5th Cir. 1999) (citing other federal appellate cases upholding 18 U.S.C. § 2261(a)(1) under the Commerce Clause).

[422]The spending power is found in article I, section 8, of the U.S. Constitution, which provides: "The Congress shall have Power to lay and collect Taxes, Duties, Imposts and Excises, *to pay the Debts and provide for the common Defence and general Welfare of the United States . . .*" (emphasis added).

[423]Civil Rights Act of 1964, Title VI, § 601, Pub. L. No. 88-352, 78 Stat. 241 (codified as amended at 42 U.S.C. §§ 2000d to 2000d-4a (2001)).

[424]*See* Education Amendments of 1972, Pub. L. No. 92-318, Title IX, 86 Stat. 374 (codified as amended at 20 U.S.C. § 1681(a) (2000)).

by any of its other powers, and Congress may attach conditions to its funding even if the effect of the conditions is to regulate state or private conduct.[425]

Congressional Inaction

Even to the extent it is permitted to do so under the Constitution, Congress has not yet enacted measures to provide protection from violence and discrimination based on sexual orientation. In June 2000, the Senate passed a bill that would expand federal hate crimes legislation to include crimes based on real or perceived sexual orientation, gender, and disability; the House did not act on the proposed legislation.[426] On September 10, 1996, the Senate narrowly defeated the

---

[425]Since 1935, the Supreme Court has interpreted the Spending Clause to empower Congress "to authorize expenditure of public moneys for public purposes," a power which "is not limited by the direct grants of legislative power found in the Constitution." *United States v. Butler*, 297 U.S. 1, 66 (1936). *See, for example, South Dakota v. Dole*, 483 U.S. 203, 207 (1987) (noting that "objectives not thought to be within Article I's 'enumerated legislative fields' . . . may nevertheless be attained through use of the spending power and the conditional grant of federal funds"). *See generally* Albert J. Rosenthal, "Conditional Federal Spending and the Constitution," *Stanford Law Review*, vol. 39 (1987), p. 1103; Lynn A. Baker, "Conditional Federal Spending After *Lopez*," *Columbia Law Review*, vol. 95 (1995), p. 1911.

Congressional power under the Spending Clause is not unlimited because legislation enacted under the Spending Clause may not infringe on individual liberties or other constitutional rights. In 1984, for example, the Supreme Court invalidated legislation that prohibited editorializing by public radio stations that received federal funding from the Corporation for Public Broadcasting. *See Federal Communications Commission v. League of Women Voters*, 468 U.S. 364 (1984). In addition, the Supreme Court has suggested that Congress may not use its spending power in such a way that federal "pressure turns into compulsion" or to impose conditions that are "unrelated to the federal interest in particular national projects or programs." *Dole*, 483 U.S. at 211, 207.

[426]*See* Hate Crimes Prevention Act of 1999, S. 622 IS, 106th Cong., 1st Sess. (1999). Currently, federal law permits federal prosecution of a hate crime only if the crime was motivated by bias based on race, religion, national origin, or color and the perpetrator intended to prevent the victim from exercising a federally protected right. Federal law also covers a broader range of hate crimes, including those motivated by actual or perceived sexual orientation or gender, that are committed on federal property. *See* 18 U.S.C. § 245; Violent Crimes Control and Law Enforcement Act of 1994, § 280003(a), Pub. L. No. 103-322, 108 Stat. 2096 (codified at 28 U.S.C. § 994 note (2001)).

To satisfy the constitutional concerns outlined above, the hate crimes bill approved by the Senate would only apply to crimes in which the perpetrator or the victim traveled in interstate commerce, used the "facilities" of interstate commerce, or engaged in activity affecting interstate commerce. *See* S. 622 IS, sec. 4, § 245(c)(1).

proposed Employment Non-Discrimination Act, which would have prohibited employment based discrimination based on sexual orientation. Similar measures to prohibit employment discrimination on the basis of sexual orientation were introduced in both houses of Congress in 1997 and 1999 but never made it to a vote.[427] Congress has not considered any measures that would expressly extend protection to students who are harassed or discriminated against on the basis of their sexual orientation.

Limited Protection Under Title IX

Despite the lack of explicit protection from discrimination based on sexual orientation, students who are the victims of harassment and discrimination based on sexual orientation or gender identity have some protection under Title IX of the Education Amendments of 1972, which prohibits sex discrimination in federally funded educational programs.[428]

The federal courts have found that Title IX prohibits sexual harassment when the harassment creates a hostile environment or is used as a *quid pro quo,* such as a request for sexual relations in exchange for a grade.[429] Title IX protects both

---

[427]*See* Employment Non-Discrimination Act of 1999, H.R. 2355, 106th Cong., 1st Sess. (1999) (bill introduced by Rep. Christopher Shays); S. 1276, 106th Cong., 1st Sess. (1999) (parallel bill introduced by Sen. James M. Jeffords); Employment Non-Discrimination Act of 1997, H.R. 1858, 105th Cong., 1st Sess. (1997) (introduced by Rep. Shays); S. 869, 105th Cong., 1st Sess. (1997) (parallel bill introduced by Sen. Jeffords).

[428]*See* Education Amendments of 1972, Pub. L. No. 92-318, Title IX, 86 Stat. 374 (codified as amended at 20 U.S.C. § 1681(a) (2000)). The Office for Civil Right's policy guidance on Title IX states: "The 'educational program or activity' of a school includes all of the school's operations. This means that Title IX protects students in connection with all of the academic, educational, extra-curricular, athletic, and other programs of the school, whether they take place in the facilities of the school, on a school bus, at a class or training program sponsored by the school at another location, or elsewhere." U.S. Department of Education, Office for Civil Rights, "Sexual Harassment Guidance: Harassment of Students by School Employees, Other Students, or Third Parties," *Federal Register,* vol. 62 (March 13, 1997), p. 12034, 12038.

[429]In doing so, the courts drew on employment discrimination cases under Title VII of the Civil Rights Act of 1964, Pub. L. No. 88-352, 78 Stat. 241 (codified as amended at 42 U.S.C. §§ 2000e to 2000e-17 (2001)). These cases have concluded, "Without question, when a supervisor sexually harasses a subordinate because of the subordinate's sex, that supervisor 'discriminate[s]' on the basis of sex." *Meritor Savings Bank FSB v. Vinson,* 477 U.S. 57, 64 (1986). *See, for example, Franklin v. Gwinnett County Public Schools,* 503 U.S. 60, 75 (1992) ("We believe the same rule should apply when a teacher sexually harasses and abuses a student.").

male and female students from sexual harassment, and the harassed student and the perpetrator may be of the same sex.[430] In a 1999 decision, the Supreme Court confirmed that school districts may be liable under Title IX if they act with deliberate indifference to instances of student-on-student sexual harassment.[431]

The chief limitation of Title IX for lesbian, gay, bisexual, and transgender students is that the statute only protects against harassment that is based on sex. The U.S. Department of Education's Office for Civil Rights advises, for example, that "heckling comments made to students because of their sexual orientation, such as 'gay students are not welcome here,' does not constitute sexual harassment under Title IX."[432]

Nevertheless, harassment based upon sexual orientation is often sexualized in nature, as the following examples illustrate:

- A gay male student was subjected to years of verbal harassment and physical assaults that included a mock rape at the hands of male classmates.[433]
- Leslie H. told us that her classmates would "grab my breast area."[434]
- Gabriel D. reported that his harassers would mimic sexual acts.[435]
- A young lesbian may be subjected to a "campaign of sexually explicit graffiti" by other girls.[436]

---

[430]In the context of employment discrimination, the Supreme Court has found that workplace harassment can violate Title VII's prohibition against "discrimination . . . because of . . . sex" when the harasser and the harassed employee are of the same sex. *Oncale v. Sundowner Offshore Services, Inc.,* 523 U.S. 75, 80 (1998). At least two federal appeals courts have considered Title IX claims in which the alleged harasser and the harassed student were of the same sex. *See Kinman v. Omaha Public School District,* 94 F.3d 463 (8th Cir. 1996) (finding that sexual harassment between members of the same gender is actionable under Title IX); *Seamons v. Snow,* 84 F.3d 1226 (10th Cir. 1996) (dismissing suit on other grounds).

[431]*See Davis v. Monroe County Board of Education,* 526 U.S. 629 (1999).

[432]U.S. Department of Education, Office for Civil Rights and National Association of Attorneys General, *Protecting Students from Harassment and Hate Crime* (Washington, D.C.: U.S. Department of Education and Bias Crimes Task Force of the National Association of Attorneys General, 1999), p. 18.

[433]*See Nabozny v. Podlesny,* 92 F.3d 446, 451-52 (7th Cir. 1996).

[434]Human Rights Watch interview, Dallas, Texas, March 27, 2000.

[435]Human Rights Watch interview, San Francisco, California, January 28, 2000.

[436]U.S. Department of Education, Office for Civil Rights, "Sexual Harassment Guidance: Harassment of Students by School Employees, Other Students, or Third Parties," *Federal Register,* vol. 62 (March 13, 1997), p. 12039.

When harassment takes the form of mock rapes or threats of rape, sexual advances, or lewd sexual comments, it constitutes sexual harassment for Title IX purposes even though the harassment is directed at lesbian, gay, bisexual, and transgender students because of their sexual orientation.[437]

But even sexualized harassment may not be enough, as illustrated by a March 2001 employment discrimination case that underscores the need for explicit protections against discrimination based on sexual orientation. In that case, a gay employee demonstrated that he was subjected to "a panoply of markedly crude, demeaning, and sexually oriented activities." For example, "coworkers would insert their fingers into his anus through his clothing, grab his crotch, and caress his face and touch his body 'like they would do to a woman.'" Nevertheless, the federal appellate court dismissed his claim under Title VII of the Civil Rights Act of 1964, finding that the employee "did nothing to show . . . that the harassment was based on his gender."[438] As with Title IX, Title VII protects against discrimination based on sex but does not prohibit discrimination based on sexual orientation.

In addition, under Title IX, even if the student establishes that the harassment she suffered was based on sex, she must show that the harassment interferes with her access to an education.[439] The Office for Civil Rights notes:

---

[437]Similarly, school districts often treat lesbian, gay, bisexual, and transgender students differently in ways that may constitute discrimination based on sex. In *Nabozny v. Podlesny*, for example, the court found that a Wisconsin school did not address a gay student's complaints of harassment with the same diligence that it would have if the student had been female. *See* 92 F.3d 446, 455 (7th Cir. 1996). *See generally* "Right to Equal Protection and Nondiscrimination" section, below.

[438]*Rene v. MGM Grand Hotel, Inc.*, 243 F.3d 1206 (9th Cir. 2001).

[439]Under the Office for Civil Rights's guidelines, the sexual harassment must be "sufficiently severe, persistent or pervasive to limit a student's ability to participate in or benefit from an educational program or activity or to create a hostile or abusive educational environment." Office for Civil Rights, "Sexual Harassment Guidance," p. 10238. This standard should not be taken to require students to show physical or mental injury before they may invoke Title IX's protections. In the related context of employment discrimination, the Supreme Court has noted that the statute "takes a middle path between making actionable any conduct that is merely offensive and requiring the conduct to cause a tangible physical injury. . . . Title VII comes into play before the harassing conduct leads to a nervous breakdown." *Harris v. Forklift Systems, Inc.*, 510 U.S. 17, 21-22 (1993). The Office for Civil Rights's guidelines emphasize that the severity of the abuse is evaluated from both an objective perspective and the perspective of the student targeted for harassment. Office for Civil Rights, "Sexual Harassment Guidance," p. 12041.

[A] student's grades may go down or the student may be forced to withdraw from school because of the harassing behavior. A student may also suffer physical injuries and mental or emotional distress.

However, a hostile environment may exist even if there is no tangible injury to the student. For example, a student may have been able to keep up his or her grades and continue to attend school even though it was more difficult for him or her to do so because of the harassing behavior.[440]

A decision by the student or her parents to change schools can also support a finding that a hostile environment exists.[441]

Finally, the student must show that the school administrators knew of and were deliberately indifferent to the abuse.

Title IX requires the federal agencies that administer funding to provide administrative remedies for violations of the statute, including, in the most extreme cases, loss of funding. Students also have the option of bringing private actions against the school district.[442]

In January 1997, a gay high school student in Fayetteville, Arkansas, filed an administrative complaint under Title IX with the U.S. Department of Education's Office for Civil Rights, the first case of antigay harassment handled under the department's administrative procedures. The student alleged that he was harassed by several students throughout the previous two years, beginning when he was in the eighth grade. The harassment escalated into physical violence. One attack by a group of six youth left him with a broken nose and damaged kidneys, keeping him out of school for two months. When he was in the tenth grade, he dropped out of school.[443]

The Office for Civil Rights reached an agreement with the Fayetteville School District in June 1998. Under the terms of the agreement, the school district was

---

[440]Office for Civil Rights, "Sexual Harassment Guidance," p. 12041.

[441]*See Doe v. University of Illinois,* 138 F.3d 653, 655 (7th Cir. 1998); *Oona R.-S. V. McCaffrey,* 143 F.3d 473, 475 (9th Cir. 1998).

[442]*See Cannon v. University of Chicago,* 441 U.S. 677 (1979) (finding that Title IX is enforceable through an implied private right of action); *Franklin v. Gwinnett County Public Schools,* 503 U.S. 60 (1992) (private actions under Title IX may seek money damages in addition to injunctive relief); *Gebser v. Lago Vista Independent School District,* 524 U.S. 274 (1998); *Davis v. Monroe County Board of Education,* 526 U.S. 629 (1999).

[443]*See* Mitchell Zuckoff, "Making Men: The Boy Who Doesn't Fit In," *Boston Globe,* June 20, 1999; Mark Walsh, "District Agrees to Protect Gay Students," *Education Week,* July 8, 1998, p. 30.

required to change its policies to provide explicit protection against sexual harassment directed at gay and lesbian students, train its teachers, staff, and students, and file compliance reports with the Office of Civil Rights.[444]

State and Local Protection from Harassment

Only Massachusetts, Vermont, and Wisconsin expressly prohibit harassment against gay and lesbian students.[445] In addition, California and Connecticut prohibit discrimination in public schools on the basis of sexual orientation.[446]

Forty-four U.S. states provide for enhanced criminal penalties for hate crimes; twenty-five states and the District of Columbia define hate crimes to include crimes against a person on the basis of his or her sexual orientation, according to the National Gay and Lesbian Task Force.[447] In 2000, after blocking hate crimes legislation for more than a decade, the New York State Senate passed a hate crimes bill that includes sexual orientation; the measure went into effect in October 2000.[448]

Missouri's hate crimes law, signed on July 1, 1999, includes sexual orientation, gender, and disability, defining sexual orientation to include transgender individuals. California and Vermont are the only other states that explicitly define crimes motivated by hatred against transgender persons as hate

---

[444]See Commitment to Resolve, *Fayetteville Public Schools,* OCR Case No. 06971182 (June 8, 1998); Letter from Taylor D. August, director, Dallas Office, Office for Civil Rights, to David S. Buckel, staff attorney, Lambda Legal Defense and Education Fund, June 17, 1998.

[445]See 16 Vt. Stat. Ann. § 565 (2000); Mass. Regs. Code tit. 603, § 26.07 (2000); Wis. Admin. Code § PI 9.02(9) (2000).

[446]See Cal. Educ. Code § 220 (2000); Conn. Gen. Stat. § 10-15c (1999). The California measure does not explicitly list sexual orientation as a prohibited basis of discrimination, instead providing that "[n]o person shall be subjected to discrimination on the basis of sex, ethnic group identification, race, national origin, religion, color, mental or physical disability, *or any basis that is containing in the prohibition of hate crimes* set forth in subdivision (a) of Section 422.6 of the Penal Code . . . ." Cal. Educ. Code § 220 (2000) (emphasis added). Hate crimes based on sexual orientation are prohibited by the California Penal Code. See Cal. Penal Code § 422.6 (2000).

[447]See National Gay and Lesbian Task Force, "Hate Crimes Map," January 2001, www.ngltf.org/issues (accessed on February 7, 2001).

[448]See N.Y. Penal Law § 485.05. The State Assembly had passed a hate crimes bill every year since 1989, always including gays and lesbians in the list of protected groups. See Richard Pérez-Peña, "State Senate to Pass Bill on Hate Crime," *New York Times,* June 7, 2000, p. B1; "Attacking Hate Crimes," *New York Times,* June 9, 2000, p. A30 (editorial).

crimes. In addition, the bias crimes statutes for Minnesota and the District of Columbia may be interpreted to cover crimes motivated by a person's gender identity.[449]

The Right to Nondiscrimination and Equal Protection of the Laws

> All human beings are born free and equal in dignity and rights.
> —Universal Declaration of Human Rights, article 1

Article 26 of the ICCPR reaffirms that "all persons are equal before the law and are entitled without any discrimination to the equal protection of the law." The guarantees of equality before the law and the equal protection of the laws prevent

---

[449]The Missouri statute defines "sexual orientation" as "male or female heterosexuality, homosexuality or bisexuality by inclination, practice, identity or expression, *or having a self-image or identity not traditionally associated with one's gender.*" Mo. Rev. Stat. § 557.035 (1999) (emphasis added). California's bias crimes law defines gender as "the victim's actual sex or the defendant's perception of the victim's sex, and includes the defendant's perception of the victim's identity, appearance, or behavior, whether or not that identity, appearance, or behavior is different from that traditionally associated with the victim's sex at birth." Cal. Penal Code § 422.76 (2001). The Vermont statute covers "conduct [that] is maliciously motivated by the victim's actual or perceived . . . sexual orientation or gender identity." 13 Vt. Stat. Ann. § 1455 (2000).

Minnesota defines a "bias offense" as "conduct that would not constitute a crime and was committed because of the victim's or another's actual or perceived race, color, religion, sex, sexual orientation, disability as defined in section 363.01, age or national origin." Minn. Stat. § 611A.79 (2000). While the hate crimes law does not include gender identity and does not define these categories, the state human rights law defines "sexual orientation" as "having or perceived as having an emotional, physical, or sexual attachment to another person without regard to the sex of that person or having or being perceived as having an orientation for such attachment, *or having or being perceived as having a self-image or identity not traditionally associated with one's biological maleness or femaleness.*" Ibid. § 363.01(41a) (2000) (emphasis added).

And the District of Columbia's statute covers acts demonstrating prejudice based on "actual or perceived" sex, sexual orientation, and "personal appearance," among other categories. D.C. Code § 22-4001 (2000). Bias crime against transgender individuals is covered under the statute if it is based on perceived sex or sexual orientation. In addition, a federal district court has found that discrimination against transgender individuals may be unlawful under the district human rights law's prohibition of discrimination based on personal appearance. *See Underwood v. Archer Management Services, Inc.*, 857 F. Supp. 96, 98-99 (D.D.C. 1994).

a government from arbitrarily making distinctions among classes of persons in promulgating and enforcing its laws. As the Human Rights Committee, responsible for interpreting the obligations of the ICCPR, has concluded, article 26 "prohibits discrimination in law or in fact in any field regulated and protected by the public authorities," whether or not the legislation covers a right guaranteed in the covenant.[450]

In particular, under article 26, "the law shall prohibit any discrimination and guarantee to all persons equal and effective protection against discrimination on any ground such as race, colour, sex, language, religion, political or other opinion, national or social origin, property, birth, or other status."[451]

A related provision of the ICCPR provides that the state may not discriminate in securing the fundamental rights and liberties guaranteed in the convention. Article 2 of the ICCPR requires states parties to "respect and ensure to all individuals within its territory and subject to its jurisdiction the rights recognized in the present Covenant, without distinction of any kind, such as race, colour, sex, language, religion, political or other opinion, national or social origin, property, birth, or other status." Article 2 of the Convention on the Rights of the Child contains a similar provision.[452]

Neither the ICCPR nor the Convention on the Rights of the Child explicitly prohibits discrimination based on sexual orientation. Nevertheless, the examples in the nondiscrimination provisions of impermissible distinctions are not exclusive;

---

[450]*General Comment 18, Nondiscrimination,* para. 12, Human Rights Committee, 37th sess., 1989, in *Compilation of General Comments and General Recommendations Adopted by Human Rights Treaty Bodies,* U.N. Doc. HRI/GEN/1/Rev.1, p. 26 (1994).

[451]The Human Rights Committee understands article 26 to prohibit both discriminatory intent and discriminatory effect. It has concluded that "the term 'discrimination' as used in the Covenant should be understood to imply any distinction, exclusion, restriction or preference which is based on any ground such as race, colour, sex, language, religion, political or other opinion, national or social origin, property, birth or other status, *and which has the purpose or effect* of nullifying or impairing the recognition, enjoyment or exercise by all persons, on an equal footing, of all rights and freedoms." Ibid., para. 7 (emphasis added). *See also* CEDAW, art. 1, ("effect or purpose"); International Convention on the Elimination of All Forms of Racial Discrimination, art. 1(1) ("purpose or effect"), *opened for signature* March 7, 1966, 660 U.N.T.S. 195 (entered into force January 4, 1969).

[452]Article 2(1) of the Convention on the Rights of the Child provides, "States Parties shall respect and ensure the rights set forth in the present Convention to each child within their jurisdiction without discrimination of any kind irrespective of the child's or his or her parent's or legal guardian's race, colour, sex, language, religion, political or other opinion, national, ethnic or social origin, property, disability, birth or other status."

these treaties prohibit discrimination on any basis "such as" those listed. Each provision clarifies that the scope of the prohibition on discrimination covers more than the categories that are given:

- Article 26 provides that "the law shall prohibit *any* discrimination."
- Article 26 also requires legislation to protect "against discrimination on *any* ground."
- States must respect and ensure the rights recognized in the ICCPR "without distinction of *any* kind."
- States must respect and ensure the rights recognized in the Convention on the Rights of the Child "without discrimination of *any* kind."

These prohibitions on all forms of discrimination do not mean that every distinction is impermissible. As the Human Rights Committee has observed, "not every differentiation of treatment will constitute discrimination, if the criteria for such differentiation are reasonable and objective and if the aim is to achieve a purpose which is legitimate under the Covenant."[453]

A common theme of these provisions is the prohibition of distinctions on the basis of qualities that are inherent to individuality and humanity. Sexual orientation is such a quality, a deeply rooted and profoundly felt element of selfhood.

Even if the categories listed as impermissible bases for discrimination were the only grounds prohibited under these articles, sexual orientation would be covered by the provisions' reference to "other status." Although sexual orientation is only one aspect of a person's identity, individuals who are lesbian, gay, bisexual, or transgender are frequently viewed as a distinct class of persons. Lesbian, gay, bisexual, and transgender persons are often subjected to harassment, violence, and other discrimination solely because of their sexual orientation. In recognition of this fact, some state and local governments in the United States have enacted measures to protect against discrimination based on sexual orientation in employment, housing, access to public accommodations, education, and even marriage. Other U.S. state and local governments have taken measures intended to have the opposite effect by legislatively invalidating court decisions granting

---

[453]*General Comment 18, Nondiscrimination*, para. 13, Human Rights Committee, 37th sess., 1989.

lesbian, gay, bisexual, and transgender individuals access to civil rights or benefits on equal terms with heterosexuals.[454]

The Human Rights Committee has not settled the question of whether "other status" includes sexual orientation, and the Committee on the Rights of the Child has not specifically addressed the sexual orientation of youth or of their parents as a ground of discrimination.[455] Nevertheless, the interpretation that sexual orientation is covered as an "other status" is supported by the *travaux préparatoires* and the commentary of legal scholars, each of which is appropriately examined to determine the content of an international legal obligation.[456] With regard to the term's scope in the ICCPR, Manfred Nowak, a leading scholar on the history of the covenant and the scope of the rights it guarantees, notes, "In the final analysis, every conceivable distinction that cannot be objectively justified is an impermissible discrimination."[457] Similarly, the delegates who participated in the drafting of the Convention on the Rights of the Child understood the term to cover a broad range of distinctions.[458]

---

[454]*See* Chapter III, "Legal Developments" section. *See generally* Wayne van der Meide, *Legislating Equality: A Review of Laws Affecting Gay, Lesbian, Bisexual, and Transgendered People in the United States* (New York: The Policy Institute of the National Gay and Lesbian Task Force, 2000); Dan Hawes, *1999 Capital Gains and Losses: A State-by-State Review of Gay, Lesbian, Bisexual, Transgender, and HIV/AIDS-Related Legislation in 1999* (Washington, D.C.: National Gay and Lesbian Task Force, 1999).

[455]The Human Rights Committee declined to reach this issue in a 1992 case involving a challenge to Australia's sodomy laws because it concluded that the legislation violated the right to privacy under article 17 of the ICCPR. *See Views of the Human Rights Committee under article 5, paragraph 4, of the Optional Protocol to the International Covenant on Civil and Political Rights concerning Communication No. 488/1992: Australia*, para. 11, Human Rights Committee, 50th sess., U.N. Doc. CCPR/C/50/D/488/1992 (April 4, 1994).

[456]*See* Vienna Convention on the Law of Treaties, art. 32; Statute of the International Court of Justice, article 38(d).

[457]Manfred Nowak, *U.N. Covenant on Civil and Political Rights: CCPR Commentary* (Kehl am Rhein, Germany: N.P. Engel, 1993), p. 45.

[458]The working group that drafted the Convention on the Rights of the Child included "other status" after initially considering "any other distinction whatsoever" and "any other basis whatever." The U.S. representative to the 1981 working group submitted proposed text that included the phrase but did not offer an explanation of its meaning. At the 1989 working group, the representatives from Portugal, Italy, Sweden, Australia, the Netherlands, and the Federal Republic of Germany proposed that "other status" be included in the final text in order to make it consistent with the ICCPR and other international human rights instruments. The delegate from Sweden stated that "other status" would include aspects of family status, including the status of being born out of wedlock. The delegate from Senegal

The Human Rights Committee takes a third approach, interpreting the ICCPR's prohibition on discrimination based on sex to include a prohibition on discrimination on the basis of sexual orientation.[459] Although the committee did not explain its reasoning in reaching its decision, many cases of discrimination on the basis of sexual orientation also constitute discrimination on the basis of sex. This is particularly true of cases that involve same-sex relationships. For example, a female soldier dismissed under the U.S. Department of Defense's "don't ask, don't tell, don't pursue" policy after mentioning that she is dating another woman is discriminated against on the basis of sex as well as sexual orientation, because she would not be dismissed in the same circumstances if she were a man.

And sexual orientation discrimination may be viewed as sex discrimination even in the absence of a same-sex relationship. In a 1996 case, a federal appellate court found that a Wisconsin school district ignored a gay male student's complaints of harassment at the hands of male classmates when it would have responded to a similar complaint by a female student.[460] Arguably, every instance of sexual orientation discrimination is discrimination on the basis of sex—gay, lesbian, and bisexual persons are singled out for discrimination because of their attraction or potential attraction to a member of the same sex.

As a practical matter, it may be easier to interpret sex discrimination to include sexual orientation discrimination than it would be to enact legislation explicitly prohibiting discrimination on the basis of sexual orientation. In the United States, for example, Wisconsin's employment discrimination law includes sexual orientation discrimination within its prohibition on discrimination based on sex. The Oregon Court of Appeals has found that the state law banning discrimination based on sex also applies to discrimination based on sexual orientation.[461]

---

said that "other status" covered every possible status. *See Report of the 1981 open-ended Working Group on the Question of a Convention on the Rights of the Child,*para. 44, U.N. Commission on Human Rights, 38th sess., U.N. Doc. E/CN.4/L.1575 (February 17, 1981); *Report of the 1989 open-ended Working Group on the Question of a Convention on the Rights of the Child,* paras. 148, 166-67, U.N. Commission on Human Rights, 45th sess., U.N. Doc. E/CN.4/1989/48 (March 2, 1989).

[459]*Views of the Human Rights Committee under article 5, paragraph 4, of the Optional Protocol to the International Covenant on Civil and Political Rights concerning Communication No. 488/1992: Australia,* para. 8.7, Human Rights Committee, 50th sess., U.N. Doc. CCPR/C/50/D/488/1992 (April 4, 1994).

[460]*Nabozny v. Podlesny,*92 F.3d 446, 455 (7th Cir. 1996).

[461]*See* Wis. Stat. § 111.36(1)(d)(1) (1999); *Tanner v. Oregon Health Sciences University,* 971 P.2d 475 (Ore. Ct. App. 1998).

Youth are entitled to equality before the law, the equal protection of the laws, and protection from discrimination no less than adults are. The Human Rights Committee has reaffirmed that "as individuals, children benefit from all of the civil rights enunciated" in the ICCPR.[462] This principle applies to all youth, including those who identify as gay, lesbian, bisexual, or transgender; those who are perceived to fall within one of those groups; or those who are questioning their sexual orientation or gender identity.

U.S. Law

The U.S. Constitution guarantees all persons equal protection of the laws.[463] As the U.S. Supreme Court has noted, however, the right to equal protection "must co-exist with the practical necessity that most legislation classifies [people] for one purpose or another, with resulting disadvantage to various groups or persons."[464]

The courts require the state to show a compelling justification for laws that impose burdens on fundamental rights, such as the right to vote or to have access to the courts.[465] They also give heightened scrutiny to classifications based on race,

---

[462]*General Comment 17, Rights of the Child (Article 24),* para. 2, Human Rights Committee, 35th sess., 1989, in *Compilation of General Comments and General Recommendations Adopted by Human Rights Treaty Bodies,* U.N. Doc. HRI/GEN/1/Rev.1, p. 23 (1994).

[463]U.S. states are bound by the equal protection clause of the Fourteenth Amendment, which provides that "[n]o State shall . . . deny to any person within its jurisdiction the equal protection of the laws." U.S. Constitution, Amendment XIV, § 1. The federal courts have interpreted the due process clause of the Fifth Amendment to require the federal government to observe substantially similar norms of equal treatment. *See, for example, Bolling v. Sharpe,* 347 U.S. 497 (1954) (invalidating racial segregation in District of Columbia public schools under the due process clause of the Fifth Amendment). The due process clause provides that "[n]o person shall be deprived of life, liberty, or property, without due process of law." U.S. Constitution, Amendment V.

[464]*Romer v. Evans,* 517 U.S. 620, 631 (1996) (citing *Personnel Administrator of Massachusetts v. Feeney,* 442 U.S. 256, 271-72 (1979); *F.S. Royster Guano Co. v. Virginia,* 253 U.S. 412, 415 (1920)).

[465]In addition, U.S. courts accord some, but not all, intimate personal choices as fundamental rights, recognizing a "private realm of family life which the state cannot enter" without a compelling justification. *Prince v. Massachusetts,* 321 U.S. 158, 166 (1944) . For example, states may not enact laws that interfere with personal decisions to marry a person of the opposite sex, to have children, or not to have children. *See Loving v. Virginia,* 388 U.S. 1, 12 (1967) (invalidating law against racial intermarriage); *Skinner v. Oklahoma,* 316 U.S. 535 (1942) (invalidating state law providing for sterilization of certain repeat felons); *Cleveland Board of Education v. LaFleur,* 414 U.S. 632 (1974); *Griswold v. Connecticut,*

ancestry, sex, and illegitimacy.[466] All other classifications—including those based on sexual orientation—must meet the lesser standard of showing only that there is at least a rational basis for the discrimination.[467]

Even when the state distinguishes among people in ways that do not implicate fundamental rights or create "suspect" classifications, it cannot act out of prejudice or out of a desire to harm a politically unpopular group.[468] In *Romer v. Evans,* the U.S. Supreme Court overturned a Colorado state constitutional amendment that prohibited any legislative or judicial action protecting against discrimination on the basis of sexual orientation.[469] The Court held:

---

381 U.S. 479 (1965) (invalidating state statute criminalizing use of contraceptives); *Roe v. Wade,* 410 U.S. 113 (1973) (holding that only a compelling state interest can justify state regulation of a decision to end a pregnancy). But in *Bowers v. Hardwick,* 478 U.S. 186 (1986), the U.S. Supreme Court upheld Georgia's sodomy statute, holding that the U.S. Constitution does not protect consensual sexual relations between members of the same sex in the privacy of their home. (The Georgia Supreme Court overturned the state's sodomy law in 1998, finding that it violated the state constitution's guarantee of the right to privacy. *See Powell v. State,* 510 S.E.2d 18, 26 (Ga. 1998).)

[466]*See, e.g., McLaughlin v. Florida,* 379 U.S. 184, 191-92 (1964) (race); *Oyama v. California,* 332 U.S. 633 (1948) (ancestry); *J.E.B. v. Alabama ex rel. T.B.,* 511 U.S. 127, 136 (1994) (sex); *Lalli v. Lalli,* 439 U.S. 259, 265 (1978) (illegitimacy).

[467]Rational basis review is a deferential standard under which there is no constitutional violation if "there is any reasonably conceivable state of facts" that would provide a rational basis for the government's conduct. *FCC v. Beach Communications, Inc.,* 508 U.S. 307, 313 (1993).

[468]*See, for example, City of Cleburne v. Cleburne Living Center,* 473 U.S. 432 (1985) (invalidating a zoning ordinance that created barriers to opening a group home for the mentally retarded); *U.S. Department of Agriculture v. Moreno,* 413 U.S. 528 (1973) (invalidating federal legislation restricting food stamp eligibility to households in which all members were related after finding that the restriction was intended to prevent "hippies" and "hippie communes" from participating in the program); *Plyler v. Doe,* 457 U.S. 202 (1982) (invalidating Texas law denying a free public education to the children of undocumented immigrants).

[469]The amendment read:

No Protected Status Based on Homosexual, Lesbian, or Bisexual Orientation. Neither the State of Colorado, through any of its branches or departments, nor any of its agencies, political subdivisions, municipalities or school districts, shall enact, adopt or enforce any statute, regulation, ordinance or policy whereby homosexual, lesbian or bisexual orientation, conduct, practices or relationships shall constitute or otherwise be the basis of or entitle any person or class of persons to have or claim any minority status, quota preferences, protected status or claim of discrimination. This Section of the Constitution

We must conclude that Amendment 2 classifies homosexuals not to further a proper legislative end but to make them unequal to everyone else. This Colorado cannot do. A state cannot so deem a class of persons a stranger to its laws.[470]

Similarly, the federal court observed in *Nabozny*, "We are unable to garner any rational basis for permitting one student to assault another based on the victim's sexual orientation . . . ."[471]

State Protection from Discrimination

Eleven states and the District of Columbia have enacted legislation offering protection against discrimination in private employment on the basis of sexual orientation.[472]   Eighteen states and the District of Columbia prohibit such discrimination in public employment.[473] Minnesota and the District of Columbia are the only jurisdictions that explicitly prohibit discrimination in private employment on the basis of gender identity, although Iowa extends this protection to its state employees.[474]

Five of the seven states visited by Human Rights Watch for this report—Georgia, Kansas, New York, Texas, and Utah—do not expressly prohibit

---

shall be in all respects self executing.
Colorado Constitution, art. II, § 30b (adopted in a 1992 statewide referendum; invalidated by *Romer,* 517 U.S. at 635).

[470]*Romer,* 517 U.S. at 635.

[471]*Nabozny v. Podlesny,* 92 F.3d 446, 458 (7th Cir. 1996).

[472]The states with statutory prohibitions on sexual orientation discrimination in private employment are California, Connecticut, Hawaii, Massachusetts, Minnesota, Nevada, New Jersey, New Hampshire, Rhode Island, Vermont, and Wisconsin. *See* Cal. Gov't Code §§ 12920-21 (2000); Cal. Lab. Code § 1102.1 (2001); Conn. Gen. Stat. § 46a-81(c) (1999); Haw. Rev. Stat. § 378-2 (2000); Mass. Gen. L. ch. 151B, § 4 (1999); Minn. Stat. § 363.03 (1999); Nev. Rev. Stat. Ann. §§ 613.330, 610.020, 610.150 (2000); N.H. Rev. Stat. Ann. § 354-A:7(I) (1999); N.J. Stat. Ann. § 10:5-12 (2001); R.I. Gen Laws § 28-5-3 (2001); Vt. Stat. Ann., Title 21, § 495 (2000); Wis. Stat. Ann. § 111.36 (1999). *See also* D.C. Code §§ 1-2501 to 1-2557 (2000).

[473]In addition, a number of states have enacted legislation prohibiting state contractors from discriminating on the basis of sexual orientation. *See, for example,* Nev. Rev. Stat. Ann. § 338.125 (2000).

[474]*See* Wayne van der Meide, *Legislating Equality* (Washington, D.C.: The Policy Institute of the National Gay and Lesbian Task Force, 2000), pp. 4-5.

discrimination in private employment on the basis of sexual orientation.[475] For example, New York's Human Rights Law recognizes as a civil right the "opportunity to obtain employment without discrimination because of age, race, creed, color, national origin, sex or marital status" but excludes express reference to sexual orientation.[476] New York also guarantees the opportunity to obtain education without discrimination but excludes sexual orientation from the list of protected grounds.[477]

The Right to Freedom of Expression

International law guarantees all persons, including children and adolescents, the right to freedom of expression. Guaranteed in both the ICCPR and the Convention on the Rights of the Child, this right encompasses the "freedom to seek, receive, and impart information and ideas of all kinds."[478] As the European Court of Human Rights has observed, "[f]reedom of expression constitutes one of the essential foundations of a democratic society and one of the basic conditions for its progress and for each individual's self-fulfilment."[479]

The Human Rights Committee has observed that "as individuals, children benefit from all of the civil rights enunciated in" the ICCPR.[480] Consistent with this view, the state may not show less respect to the right of children and adolescents to freedom of expression. The Convention on the Rights of the Child

---

[475]See Ga. Code Ann. § 45-19-29 (1999) (unlawful practice to discriminate in employment because of race, color, religion, national origin, sex, disability, or age); Kan. Stat. Ann. §§ 44-1001, 44-1002, 44-1009(a), 44-1113 (1999) (prohibiting discrimination in employment because of race, religion, color, sex, disability, national origin, ancestry, or age); N.Y. Exec. Law § 291(1) (1999) (no employment discrimination on basis of age, race, creed, color, national origin, sex, or marital status); Tex. Labor Code § 21.125 (2000) (covering race, color, sex, national origin, religion, age, and disability); Utah Code Ann. § 34A-5-106 (2000) (prohibiting discrimination in employment based on race, color, sex, "pregnancy, childbirth, or pregnancy related conditions," age "if the individual is 40 years of age or older," religion, national origin, and disability).

[476]N.Y. Exec. Law § 291(1).

[477]Ibid. § 291(2).

[478]ICCPR, art. 19(2); Convention on the Rights of the Child, art. 13(1).

[479]Zana v. Turkey, 1997-VII Eur. Ct. H.R. 2533, para. 51(i) (1997).

[480]General Comment 17, Rights of the Child (Article 24), para. 2, Human Rights Committee, 35th sess., 1989, in Compilation of General Comments and General Recommendations Adopted by Human Rights Treaty Bodies, U.N. Doc. HRI/GEN/1/Rev.1, p. 23 (1994).

reinforces this conclusion by guaranteeing the right of youth to freedom of expression in terms that are identical to those of article 19 of the ICCPR.[481]

With its tradition of strong protections on speech, the United States should be receptive to the view that youth are entitled to freedom of expression. In fact, the U.S. delegate who participated in the drafting of the Convention on the Rights of the Child observed that "the protection of children's civil and political rights was of fundamental importance to his country, particularly because the 'child,' as defined in the draft Convention, included adolescents who had often acquired the skills needed to participate fully and effectively in society."[482]

Permissible Restrictions on Free Expression

The state may only limit freedom of expression insofar as necessary for the protection of the rights or reputations of others, national security or public order, or public health or morals.[483] Under both conventions, these limitations must be strictly construed.

The Protection of Public Morals

Those who attempt to restrict expression relating to sexual orientation and gender identity often claim that they do so out of a need to protect public morals. This justification is invoked with particular frequency when youth may be the recipients of expression with lesbian, gay, bisexual, or transgender content.

"Public morals" is not defined in the ICCPR or the Convention on the Rights of the Child. The Human Rights Committee has stated that "public morals differ widely. There is no universally applicable common standard. Consequently, in

---

[481]*Compare* Convention on the Rights of the Child, art. 13(1), (2), *with* ICCPR, art. 19(2), (3).

[482]*Report of the 1987 open-ended Working Group on the Question of a Convention on the Rights of the Child,* para. 112, U.N. Commission on Human Rights, 43d sess., U.N. Doc. E/CN.4/1987/25 (March 9, 1987). The U.S. delegate also spoke against the "paternalistic flavour" of a proposed amendment that would have restricted children's and adolescent's right to freedom of expression for their "spiritual and moral well-being." *See Report of the 1989 open-ended Working Group on the Question of a Convention on the Rights of the Child,* para. 272, U.N. Commission on Human Rights, 45th sess., U.N. Doc. E/CN.4/1989/48 (March 2, 1989).

[483]*See* ICCPR, art. 19; Convention on the Rights of the Child, art. 13. These provisions also require that any limitations be expressly provided for by law.

this respect, a certain margin of discretion must be accorded to the responsible national authorities."[484]

Applying this standard, the Human Rights Committee has shown deference to state restrictions on expression with lesbian, gay, bisexual, or transgender content. In a 1980 case that challenged a state-owned broadcaster's decision to censor programs with gay content, the Human Rights Committee concluded:

> The Committee finds that it cannot question the decision of the responsible organs of the Finnish Broadcasting Corporation that radio and TV are not the appropriate forums to discuss issues related to homosexuality, as far as a programme could be judged as encouraging homosexual behaviour. . . . As far as radio and TV programmes are concerned, the audience cannot be controlled. In particular, harmful effects on minors cannot be excluded.[485]

Articulated in a case decided more than twenty years ago, the view that a television or radio program with gay content "encourag[es] homosexual behaviour" and has "harmful effects on minors" is based on an understanding of sexual orientation that has been rejected by the major health and medical health

---

[484] *Views of the Human Rights Committee under article 5(4) of the Optional Protocol to the International Covenant on Civil and Political Rights concerning Communication No. R.14/61*, para. 10.3, Human Rights Committee, in *Report of the Human Rights Committee*, U.N. General Assembly, 37th sess., U.N. Doc. A/37/40, Supp. No. 40 (1982), pp. 161-165.

[485] Ibid., para. 10.4. Similarly, the European Court of Human Rights concluded in 1971 that the "protection of the morals of the young" justified British authorities' seizure of *The Little Red Schoolbook*. Aimed at youth between twelve and eighteen years of age, the book contained a twenty-six page section on sex that discussed topics such as masturbation, pornography, contraception, abortion, and homosexuality. *The Handyside Case*, 24 Eur. Ct. H.R. (ser. A) (1971). In May 2000, the European Court of Human Rights upheld a decision by Hungary's Constitutional Court that denied registration to a gay rights group because the group did not restrict its membership to adults. The European Court of Human Rights stated:
> The conditions for registration that the applicant association should exclude minors from membership pursued the legitimate aims of the protection of morals and the rights and freedoms of others. The Court finds that the interference was proportionate to the aims pursued and could, therefore, reasonably be regarded as necessary in a democratic society.

Decision as to the admissibility of Application No. 35419/97 (Szivárvány v. Hungary), slip opinion, p. 1 (Eur. Ct. H.R. May 17, 2000).

professions. In the United States, the American Academy of Pediatrics, the American Counseling Association, the American Psychological Association, the National School of Social Psychologists, and the National Association of Social Workers have all taken the position that homosexuality is not a mental disorder.[486] In addition, there is no merit to the notion that lesbian, gay, bisexual, and transgender role models "cause" youth to become gay, lesbian, bisexual, or transgender.[487]

The Finnish Broadcasting case should be viewed in light of the Human Rights Committee's recent concluding observations to country reports, in which the committee has increasingly called upon states to protect people from discrimination on the basis of sexual orientation.[488] Nevertheless, the committee has not addressed issues of sexual orientation and gender identity as they relate to youth, meaning

---

[486]*See Just the Facts About Sexual Orientation and Youth: A Primer for Principals, Educators, and School Personnel* (New York: GLSEN, 1999), p. 5.

[487]In fact, studies of children raised by gay and lesbian parents conclude that they are no more likely to be gay, lesbian, bisexual, or transgender than the children of straight parents are. *See* Charlotte Patterson, "Children of Lesbian and Gay Parents," *Child Development*, vol. 63 (1992), p. 1025; Susan Golombok et al., "Children in Lesbian and Single-Parent Households: Psychosexual and Psychiatric Appraisal," *Journal of Child Psychology and Psychiatry*, vol. 24 (1983), pp. 551, 564; Frederick W. Bozett, "Children of Gay Fathers," *Gay and Lesbian Parents* (1987), pp. 39, 47.

[488]For example, in its concluding observations on the country reports submitted by China (for Hong Kong), Trinidad and Tobago,and the United Kingdom (for the Crown Dependencies), the committee called for prohibitions on discrimination based on sexual orientation. *See Concluding Observations of the Human Rights Committee (Hong Kong): China*, para. 15, Human Rights Committee, 67th sess., U.N. Doc. CCPR/C/79/Add.117 (November 4, 1999); *Concluding Observations of the Human Rights Committee: Trinidad and Tobago*, para. 11, Human Rights Committee, 70th sess., U.N. Doc. CCPR/CO/70/TTO (November 3, 2000); *Concluding Observations of the Human Rights Committee (Crown Dependencies): United Kingdom of Great Britain and Northern Ireland*, para. 14, Human Rights Committee, 68th sess., U.N. Doc. CCPR/C/79/Add.119 (March 27, 2000). The committee called on Austria to remove discriminatory provisions setting the age of consent for sexual relations between men at a higher age than that for sexual relations between men and women. *Concluding Observations of the Human Rights Committee: Austria*, para. 13, Human Rights Committee, 64th sess., U.N. Doc. CCPR/C/79/Add.103 (November 19, 1998). And it has urged Chile to abolish its law criminalizing sodomy "as between adults," noting that Chile's sodomy laws violate the right to privacy and "may reinforce attitudes of discrimination between persons on the basis of sexual orientation." *Concluding Observations of the Human Rights Committee: Chile*, para. 20, Human Rights Committee, 65th sess., U.N. Doc. CCPR/C/79/Add.104 (March 30, 1999).

that it has not revisited its finding in the Finnish Broadcasting case that restrictions on airing programs with gay content might be appropriate in order to avoid "harmful effects on minors."[489]

In recent years, national courts have closely scrutinized attempts to limit expression with lesbian, gay, bisexual, or transgender content, even when the target audience includes youth. In 1997, the Israeli Supreme Court overturned a decision by the Ministry of Education to ban a television program on gay youth. In July 2000, it held its first hearing in a case challenging the Israeli film board's decision to declare *Edge of Seventeen,* a film about a gay teenager, off limits to viewers under the age of eighteen.[490]

Even under the Finnish Broadcasting case's standard for evaluating restrictions based on the protection of public morals, it is difficult to justify restrictions on the freedom of expression of lesbian, gay, bisexual, and transgender students in the United States. Gay characters regularly appear in movies and television shows seen by teenagers. The federal Equal Access Act allows students to form gay-straight alliances on equal terms with other school noncurricular groups; some states, notably Massachusetts, require schools to assist their students in forming gay-straight alliances. Four states explicitly provide that lesbian, gay, bisexual, and transgender students may not be discriminated against in school.

More fundamentally, it is troubling that the Finnish Broadcasting case's test for public morals effectively permits a group of persons to be singled out for restrictions on expression on the basis of prejudice. As several members of the Human Rights Committee observed in the Finnish Broadcasting Corporation case, restrictions on speech should not be applied "as to perpetuate prejudice or promote intolerance. It is of special importance to protect freedom of expression as regards minority views, including those that offend, shock or disturb the majority."[491]

---

[489]*Views of the Human Rights Committee under article 5(4) of the Optional Protocol to the International Covenant on Civil and Political Rights concerning Communication No. R.14/61,* para. 10.3, Human Rights Committee, in *Report of the Human Rights Committee,* U.N. General Assembly, 37th sess., U.N. Doc. A/37/40, Supp. No. 40 (1982), pp. 161-165.

[490]*See The Society for the Protection of Personal Rights v. Minister of Education,* 51(5) Piskei Din 822 (Israel 1997); *The Society for Protection of Personal Rights for GLBT and others v. Board of Film Review,* No. 4902/00, heard by the Israeli Supreme Court on July 27, 2000. *See generally* Alon Harel, "The Rise and Fall of the Israeli Gay Legal Movement," *Columbia Human Rights Law Review,* vol. 31 (2000), p. 443.

[491]Individual opinion by committee members Opsahl, Lallah, and Tarnopolsky in Communication No. R.14/16, para. 10.3, in *Views of the Human Rights Committee under article 5(4) of the Optional Protocol to the International Covenant on Civil and Political Rights concerning Communication No. R.14/61,* Human Rights Committee, in *Report of the*

This view comports with the requirements of both the ICCPR and the Convention on the Rights of the Child that the rights recognized in the conventions be ensured without discrimination.[492] This concern is particularly appropriate where it is expression of youth that would be restricted. As one U.S. appellate court has noted, "Under the guise of beneficent concern for the welfare of school children, school authorities, albeit unwillingly, might permit prejudices of the community to prevail."[493]

Finally, the deferential approach of the majority in the Finnish Broadcasting case should be evaluated in light of the fact that silence on gay issues has not protected lesbian, gay, bisexual, and transgender youth. Instead, as this report demonstrates, these youth are subjected to harassment, violence, and other forms of discrimination in great numbers across the country. As a result, many abuse drugs or alcohol, skip school and eventually drop out altogether, or attempt suicide.

The Protection of Public Order

Freedom of expression may also be restricted for the protection of public order. For example, the right to free expression does not extend to defamatory speech or speech that incites to violence.[494] International law also permits restrictions on speech that is racist or otherwise "constitutes incitement to discrimination."[495]

Human Rights Committee, U.N. General Assembly, 37th sess., U.N. Doc. A/37/40, Supp. No. 40 (1982), pp. 161-165.

[492]*See* ICCPR, art. 2(1); Convention on the Rights of the Child, art. 2(1).

[493]*James v. Board of Education of Central District No. 1,* 461 F.2d 566, 575 (2d Cir. 1972).

[494]Defamatory speech may be restricted under article 19(3)(a) of the ICCPR, which permits restrictions "[f]or respect of the rights or reputations of others." Incitement to violence is prohibited under article 20(2) of the convention. *See also Glimmerveen and Hagenbeek v. Netherlands,* App. Nos. 8348/78 and 8406/78. 18 Eur. Comm'n H.R. Dec. and Rep. 187 (1979) (rejecting a complaint from Dutch politicians convicted for distributing leaflets advocating racial discrimination and the removal of Surinamers, Turks, and other "guest workers" from the Netherlands) Under U.S. law, speech that "is directed to inciting or producing imminent lawless action and is likely to incite or produce such action" may be proscribed. *See Brandenburg v. Ohio,* 395 U.S. 444, 447 (1969).

[495]*See* ICCPR, art. 20(2). The United States entered a reservation to article 20, providing "[t]hat Article 20 does not authorize or require legislation or other action by the United States that would restrict the right of free speech and association protected by the Constitution and laws of the United States." "U.S. Reservations, Declarations, and Understandings, International Covenant on Civil and Political Rights," *Congressional*

In the school context, this exception would permit restrictions on speech that interferes with school discipline. As with all restrictions on expression, however, this exception should be applied only to the extent that it is provided for by law, serves to protect the public order, and is necessary for attaining this purpose.[496] Students' speech should not be subjected to arbitrary or unlimited restrictions.

As a final matter, restrictions for the protection of public order should not be imposed discriminatorily. As noted above, limitations on expression that ostensibly ensure school discipline but single out lesbian, gay, bisexual, and transgender students for restrictions run afoul of the nondiscrimination provisions of the ICCPR and the Convention on the Rights of the Child.

The First Amendment and the Equal Access Act

The U.S. Constitution provides strong protection for the freedom of expression. Under the First Amendment, "Congress shall make no law . . . abridging the freedom of speech . . . ."[497]

There is no question that this constitutional right extends to youth. In a case involving high school students, the Supreme Court held that "[i]n the absence of constitutionally valid reasons to regulate their speech, students are entitled to freedom of expression"; they do not "shed their constitutional rights at the schoolhouse gate."[498]

In the university context, the First Amendment forbids an institution to deny a group recognition on the ground that the group's purpose conflicts with the university's philosophy. For example, a federal appeals court found that Texas A

Record, vol. 138 (daily edition, April 2, 1992), p. S4781-01.

[496]See *General Comment 10, Freedom of Expression (Article 19),* para. 4, Human Rights Committee, 19th sess., 1983, in *Compilation of General Comments and General Recommendations Adopted by Human Rights Treaty Bodies,* U.N. Doc. HRI/GEN/1/Rev.1, p. 11 (1994); Manfred Nowak, *U.N. Covenant on Civil and Political Rights: CCPR Commentary* (Kehl am Rhein, Germany: N.P. Engel, 1993), p. 350. In particular, Nowak notes that "[i]nterference [with free expression] based solely on an administrative provision or a vague statutory authorization violates Art. 19." Ibid., p. 351. *See also Silver & Others v. United Kingdom,* 61 Eur. Ct. H.R. (ser. A), at 21 (1983); *Olsson v. Sweden,* 130 Eur. Ct. H.R. (ser. A), at 30 (1988).

[497]U.S. Constitution, Amendment I. Under the Due Process Clause of the Fourteenth Amendment, the First Amendment applies to state governments as well as Congress. *See Gitlow v. New York,* 268 U.S. 652, 666 (1925). As noted, the Due Process Clause provides, "nor shall any State deprive any person of life, liberty, or property, without due process of law . . . ." U.S. Constitution, Amendment XIV, § 1.

[498]*Tinker v. Des Moines Independent School District,* 393 U.S. 503, 505-6 (1969).

& M University could not constitutionally deny recognition to a gay student support group on this basis.[499]

Students who wish to form gay-straight alliances also benefit from the federal Equal Access Act. Enacted to protect the rights of student Bible study groups to meet on school property, the act requires public secondary schools to provide access to gay-straight alliances or other groups for lesbian, gay, bisexual, or transgender students equal to the access that is offered other student groups.[500]

The Equal Access Act should be interpreted in a manner that is consistent with international law.[501] Noncurricular school clubs are important vehicles for securing the internationally recognized rights of youth to freedom of expression, freedom of association, freedom of peaceful assembly, and access to information. The nondiscrimination principle of the ICCPR supports the conclusion that, when a public school generally permits students to form extracurricular groups, it may not arbitrarily deny that privilege to disfavored groups of youth.

As noted above, state constitutions and statutes may afford greater protection than that offered by the federal constitution; the First Amendment delineates the minimum level of protection that the federal and state governments are required to observe. In Massachusetts, students are explicitly guaranteed the right to freedom of expression: under Massachusetts law, "[t]he right of students to freedom of expression shall not be abridged, provided that such right shall not cause any disruption or disorder within the school."[502] Similarly, the California Supreme Court has stated that the state's constitution provides greater protection to freedom of speech than the U.S. Constitution.[503]

---

[499] See Gay Student Services v. Texas A & M University, 737 F.2d 1317, 1327 (5th Cir. 1984), cert. denied and appeal dismissed, 471 U.S. 1001 (1985).

[500] See 20 U.S.C. § 4071 (2001). For a discussion of successful student efforts to secure recognition of gay-straight alliances in their high schools, see Chapter IX, "Efforts to Suppress Gay-Straight Alliances" section.

[501] When interpreting statutes, the courts follow the principle that "an Act of Congress ought never to be construed to violate the law of nations if any other possible construction remains . . . ." Murray v. Schooner Charming Betsy, 6 U.S. (2 Cranch) 64, 118 (1804) (Marshall, C.J.).

[502] Mass. Gen. L. ch. 71, § 82 (1999). For the full text of the statute, see Appendix E.

[503] See Robins v. Pruneyard Shopping Center, 592 P.2d 341 (Cal. 1979), aff'd, 447 U.S. 74 (1980). See also Committee to Defend Reproductive Rights v. Myers, 625 P.2d 779, 783 (Cal. 1981) (noting that the California Supreme Court has "on numerous occasions construed the California Constitution as providing greater protection than that afforded by parallel provisions of the United States Constitution.").

A second question is whether teachers and administrators can be fired or disciplined for expression that takes place outside of the classroom. Under the First Amendment, speech made outside of a school-sponsored activity may not be restricted unless the school district can show that the speech "would materially and substantially interfere with the requirements of appropriate discipline in the operation of the school."[504] A school district must show severe disruption to justify dismissing or disciplining an employee because of his or her speech.

In evaluating restrictions placed on teachers and other public employees, the courts first examine whether the employees' speech or actions address a matter of public concern—a test that is easy to meet when the school district takes action that "transmute[s] what should [be] a private issue into a matter of public concern."[505] In *Weaver,* the federal district court noted, in fact, that "the recent public debate concerning the sexual orientation of a candidate for Utah state legislature supports a conclusion that, in Utah at least, questions on this topic are almost always construed as matters of public concern."[506]

Teachers do not enjoy the same protections for speech in the classroom, however. In general, the government may determine "what is and is not expressed when it is the speaker or when it enlists private entities to convey its own message."[507] Nevertheless, the Lambda Legal Defense and Education Fund distinguishes school efforts to restrict expressions of intolerance from attempts to silence teachers who are out:

> As we see it, a teacher who comes out actually helps promote *tolerance.* Although an "out" teacher on campus may cause some heated discussion, the result of such speech is the promotion of tolerance: this teacher shows that teachers can be gay and be role models. Further, the removal of a teacher would not be countenanced because her race or religion caused some consternation on campus. In the same vein, a

---

[504]*Tinker v. Des Moines Independent School District,* 393 U.S. 503, 509 (1969).

[505]*Weaver v. Nebo School District,* 29 F. Supp. 2d 1279, 1284 (D. Utah 1998).

[506]Ibid., p. 1284, n. 3. In addition, some issues are considered "inherently of public concern"; racial discrimination is one such example. *See Connick v. Myers,* 461 U.S. 138, 148 n.8 (1983). Citing *Connick,* Justice Brennan commented in a 1985 case, "I think it impossible not to note that a similar public debate is currently ongoing regarding the rights of homosexuals." *Rowland v. Mad River Local School District, Montgomery County, Ohio,* 470 U.S. 1009, 1012 (1985) (Brennan, J., dissenting from denial of certiorari), *denying cert. to* 730 F.2d 444 (6th Cir. 1984).

[507]*Rosenberger v. Rector and Visitors of the University of Virginia,* 515 U.S. 819, 833 (1995).

teacher should not be . . . forced to hide her sexual orientation because of homophobia.[508]

The Use of Sodomy Laws as Justification for Restrictions on Freedom of Expression

Fifteen states criminalize consensual sexual relations between adults of the same sex, classifying these acts as "sodomy," "sexual misconduct," "unnatural intercourse," or "crimes against nature." In 1986, the Supreme Court upheld Georgia's sodomy law, ruling that laws prohibiting private consensual sex between adults do not violate the U.S. Constitution.[509]

More recently, the national trend has been to overturn such laws. The Georgia Supreme Court struck down the state's sodomy law in 1998, concluding that the provision violated the state constitution. State courts in Arkansas, Kentucky, Michigan, Montana, Tennessee, and Texas have also invalidated state sodomy laws on state constitutional grounds. Defying this trend, Louisiana's highest court upheld the state's "crimes against nature" statute in July 2000.[510]

Despite the national trend, public officials have invoked these laws as a justification for their refusal to recognize lesbian, gay, bisexual, and transgender student groups on college and university campuses. In what is perhaps the most extreme example of this effort, the Alabama legislature prohibited the use of public funds or public facilities "to, directly or indirectly, sanction, recognize, or support

---

[508]Myron Dean Quon, "Public Teachers' Right to Be Open Regarding Their Sexual Orientation Under Federal and California Law" (Lambda Legal Defense and Education Fund, February 22, 1999), http://www.lambdalegal.org/cgi-bin/pages/documents/record?record=382 (accessed on April 23, 2001).

[509]See Bowers v. Hardwick, 478 U.S. 186 (1986).

[510]See Powell v. State, 510 S.E.2d 18, 26 (Ga. 1998) (finding that law "manifestly infringes" on right to privacy under Georgia Constitution); Picado v. Jegley, No. CV 99-7048, slip opinion at 8 (Ark. Cir. Ct. March 23, 2001) (finding sodomy statute "unconstitutional under the Arkansas Constitution on right to privacy grounds"); Commonwealth v. Wasson, 842 S.W.2d 487, 491-92 (Ky. 1992) (concluding that state law prohibiting "deviate sexual intercourse with another person of the same sex" violated rights of privacy and equal protection under Kentucky Constitution); Michigan Organization for Human Rights v. Kelly, No. 88-815820-CZ (Mich. Cir. Ct. 1990) (trial court finding that state law violated Michigan privacy rights); Gryczan v. State, 942 P.2d 112 (Mont. 1997); Campbell v. Sundquist, 926 S.W.2d 250 (Tenn. Ct. App. 1996); Lawrence v. State of Texas, Nos. 14-99-00109-Cr and 14-99-00111-CR, 2000 Tex. App. LEXIS 3760 (Tex. Ct. App. June 8, 2000); State of Louisiana v. Smith, No. 99-0606, 2000 La. LEXIS 1911 (La. July 6, 2000) (upholding state statute).

the activities or existence of any organization or group that fosters or promotes a lifestyle or actions prohibited by the sodomy and sexual misconduct laws."[511] A federal district court struck down the statute as a violation of the First Amendment.[512]

In addition, some school administrators have used the sodomy laws as a basis for directing lesbian, gay, bisexual, and transgender teachers at high schools and middle schools not to disclose their sexual orientation. Even when school administrators have not made such threats, the existence of state sodomy laws and the lack of employment discrimination protection for lesbian, gay, bisexual, and transgender employees has a chilling effect on teachers.

The Human Rights Committee, the treaty body charged with receiving individual complaints of violations of the ICCPR, concluded in 1992 that Tasmania's sodomy law amounted to an arbitrary interference with privacy, in violation of article 17 of the ICCPR.[513] The European Court of Human Rights has found that sodomy laws "constitute[] a continuing interference" with the right to respect for one's private life under the analogous provision of the Convention for the Protection of Human Rights and Fundamental Freedoms, a regional human rights treaty.[514]

---

[511] Ala. Code § 16-1-28(a) (2000). While the statute was pending before the state legislature, the Alabama attorney general issued an opinion advising that "an organization that professes to be comprised of homosexuals and/or lesbians may not receive state funding or use state-supported facilities to foster or promote those illegal, sexually deviate activities defined in the sodomy and sexual misconduct laws." See Gay Lesbian Bisexual Alliance v. Sessions, 917 F. Supp. 1548, 1550-51 (M.D. Ala. 1996), aff'd sub nom. Gay Lesbian Bisexual Alliance v. Prior, 110 F.3d 1543 (11th Cir. 1997)

[512] See id. at 1557. See also Gay Student Services v. Texas A & M University, 737 F.2d 1317, 1319 (5th Cir. 1984); Gay Lib v. University of Missouri, 558 F.2d 848 (8th Cir. 1977); Gay Alliance of Students v. Matthews, 544 F.2d 162 (1976); Gay Students Organization of the University of New Hampshire v. Bonner, 509 F.2d 652 (1st Cir. 1974).

[513] Views of the Human Rights Committee under article 5, paragraph 4 of the Optional Protocol to the International Covenant on Civil and Political Rights concerning Communication No. 488/1992: Australia, para. 9, Human Rights Committee, 50th sess., U.N. Doc. CCPR/C/50/D/488/1992 (April 4, 1994). Article 17(1) of the ICCPR provides:

No one shall be subjected to arbitrary or unlawful interference with his privacy, family, home or correspondence, nor to unlawful attacks on his honour and reputation.

[514] See Dudgeon Case, para. 41 (Eur. Ct. H.R. September 23, 1981); Norris Case, para. 38 (Eur. Ct. H.R. October 26, 1988); Modinos v. Cyprus, para. 24 (Eur. Ct. H.R. March 25, 1993). Under the European convention. "[e]veryone has the right to respect for his private and family life, his home and his correspondence." Convention for the Protection of Human

The Human Rights Committee has specifically noted that the existence of sodomy laws in the United States is a "serious infringement of private life" and has "consequences . . . for [the] enjoyment of other human rights without discrimination."[515]

The United States did not enter a reservation to Article 17 when it ratified the ICCPR. Although its instrument of ratification provided that this article and most other provisions of the ICCPR are not "self-executing," meaning that they are not enforceable in federal or state courts until implemented through domestic legislation, the United States explicitly recognized that the federal and state governments have a responsibility to implement the terms of the covenant.[516]

These facts lead Human Rights Watch to renew our call for the repeal of state laws criminalizing private consensual conduct between adults of the same sex to bring the United States into conformity with international law.[517]

Rights and Fundamental Freedoms, art. 8(1), *opened for signature* Nov. 4, 1950, 213 U.N.T.S. 221 (entered into force Sept. 3, 1953).

[515]*Consideration of Reports Submitted by States Parties Under Article 40 of the Covenant,* Human Rights Committee, 53d sess., U.N. Doc. CCPR/C/79/Add.50 (1995), para. 287 (commenting on the United States' initial report).

[516]*See* "U.S. Reservations, Declarations, and Understandings, International Covenant on Civil and Political Rights," *Congressional Record,* vol. 138, p. S4781-01 (daily edition, April 2, 1992). With regard to implementation, the U.S. Senate noted:

[T]he United States understands that this Covenant shall be implemented by the Federal Government to the extent that it exercises legislative and judicial jurisdiction over the matters covered therein, and otherwise by the state and local governments; to the extent that state and local governments exercise jurisdiction over such matters, the Federal Government shall take measures appropriate to the Federal system to the end that the competent authorities of the state or local governments may take appropriate measures for the fulfillment of the Covenant.

Ibid., para. II(5). The Human Rights Committee has observed that the United States' federal structure, "coupled with the absence of formal mechanisms between the federal and state levels to ensure appropriate implementation of the Covenant rights by legislative or other measures may lead to a somewhat unsatisfactory application of the Covenant throughout the country." *Concluding Observations of the Human Rights Committee: United States of America,* para. 271, Human Rights Committee, 53d sess., U.N. Doc. CCPR/C/79/Add.50; A/50/40 (October 3, 1995).

[517]*See* Human Rights Watch, *Modern Capital of Human Rights? Abuses in the State of Georgia* (New York: Human Rights Watch, 1996), p. 155.

The Rights to Freedom of Association and Peaceful Assembly

International law recognizes the rights of everyone to freedom of association and peaceful assembly with others, subject to the same restrictions that may be placed on the freedom of expression: the state may limit the freedom of association only insofar as necessary for the protection of the rights or reputations of others, national security or public order, or public health or morals.[518] Similarly, the First Amendment protects the "right to associate with others in pursuit of a wide variety of political, social, economic, educational, religious, and cultural ends."[519]

Even without the Equal Access Act, students have a constitutionally protected right to form a gay-straight alliance on the same terms as other student groups. As Reps. Don Bonker and William F. Goodling observed in 1994:

> The rights of the lawful, orderly group to meet are not dependent upon the fact that other students may object to the ideas expressed. All students enjoy free speech constitutional guarantees. It is the school's responsibility to maintain discipline in order that all student groups be afforded an equal opportunity to meet peacefully without harassment. The school must not allow a "hecklers' veto."[520]

Similarly, the right to freedom of association protects lesbian, gay, bisexual, and transgender teachers and administrators who join gay rights groups, attend events such as gay pride rallies, or are open about their relationship with their partners. In the case of *Weaver v. Nebo School District,* for example, the federal district court noted, "To the extent the School District may be punishing Ms. Weaver by not assigning her as a volleyball coach because of her private relationship with another woman, this action is unconstitutional."[521]

The Right to Education

The right to education is recognized in both international and domestic U.S. law. Internationally, the right is set forth in the Universal Declaration of Human Rights, the International Covenant on Economic, Social and Cultural Rights, and the Convention on the Rights of the Child. These instruments place an obligation

---

[518]*See* ICCPR, arts. 22, 21; Convention on the Rights of the Child, art. 15.

[519]*Roberts v. United States Jaycees,* 468 U.S. 609, 622 (1984).

[520]Statements of Reps. Don Bonker and William F. Goodling, in *Congressional Record,* vol. 130 (daily edition, October 11, 1994), pp. 32315-18.

[521]*Weaver v. Nebo School District,* 29 F. Supp. 2d 1279, 1290 n.10 (D. Utah 1998).

on states to endeavor to make public education available and accessible to all youth.

Although the U.S. Constitution does not guarantee the right to education, all U.S. states recognize a fundamental right to primary and secondary education in state constitutions or confer the right by statute.[522] As the U.S. Supreme Court has observed,

> education is perhaps the most important function of state and local governments. Compulsory school attendance laws and the great expeditures for education both demonstrate our recognition of the importance of education to our democratic society. It is required in the performance of our most basic public responsibilities, even service in the armed forces. It is the very foundation of good citizenship. Today it is a principal instrument in awakening a child to cultural values, in preparing him for later professional training, and in helping him to adjust formally to his environment . . . .[523]

Under article 26 of the ICCPR, the United States is obligated to respect the entitlement of every person "without any discrimination to the equal protection of the law." Consistent with this nondiscrimination provision, when a state provides education for its children, it may not arbitrarily deny an education to particular groups of children. The state may make distinctions among groups of individuals only to the extent that those distinctions are based on reasonable and objective criteria. In particular, the state may not make distinctions among people on the basis of a quality, such as sexual orientation, that is inherent to individuality and humanity and a deeply rooted element of one's sense of self.[524]

---

[522]The U.S. Supreme Court has rejected the contention that education is a fundamental right guaranteed by the U.S. Constitution: "Education, of course, is not among the rights afforded explicit protection under our Federal Constitution. Nor do we find any basis for saying it is implicitly so protected." *San Antonio Independent School District v. Rodriguez,* 411 U.S. 1 (1973). For a review of the right to education in state constitutions and statutes, see generally Molly McUsic, "The Use of Education Clauses in School Finance Reform Litigation," *Harvard Journal on Legislation,* vol. 28 (1991).

[523]*Brown v. Board of Education,* 347 U.S. 483, 493 (1954). The U.S. Supreme Court has also observed that education "provides the basic tools by which individuals might lead economically productive lives" and "has a fundamental role in maintaining the fabric of our society." *Plyler v. Doe,* 457 U.S. 202, 221-22 (1982).

[524]*See* "Right to Nondiscrimination and Equal Protection of the Laws" section, above.

Further, in providing education, the state is obligated to promote respect for human rights. The preamble to the Universal Declaration of Human Rights declares that "every individual and every organ of society, keeping this Declaration constantly in mind, shall strive by teaching and education to promote respect for" human rights. The Universal Declaration goes on to provide that "education shall be directed to the full development of the human personality and to the strengthening of respect for human rights and fundamental freedoms." Similarly, the Convention on the Rights of the Child provides that the purposes of education include "the development of respect for human rights and fundamental freedoms" and "the preparation of the child for responsible life in a free society, in the spirit of understanding, peace, tolerance, equality of sexes, and friendship among all peoples . . . ."[525]

Protection of Gender Identity in International and U.S. Law

In the course of our research, Human Rights Watch interviewed students who reported suffering harassment or violence, not because of their actual or perceived sexual orientation, but because of their gender identity, expression, or appearance. Young men talked of being perceived as "effeminate," "passive," or "unathletic." Young women reported being called "too aggressive," "butch," "having an attitude," or "a troublemaker." Some of these students identify as gay, lesbian or bisexual and they perceive that their sexual orientation—though not explicitly cited—triggered these attacks. Some of the students we interviewed identify as heterosexual but simply fail to conform to gender-based stereotypes and are coping with harassment and violence for failing to conform to rigid rules dictating how young women and young men "should" act, speak, walk, dress, compete, and look. Still others are questioning their gender identity and may, as adults, identify as transgender.[526]

---

[525]Convention on the Rights of the Child, art. 29(1)(b), (d). The Declaration on the Rights of the Child also provides that the child "shall be given an education which will promote his general culture, and enable him, on a basis of equal opportunity, to develop his abilities, his individual judgment, and his sense of moral and social responsibility, and to become a useful member of society." Declaration on the Rights of the Child, Principle 7, G.A. Res. 1386, U.N. GAOR, 14th sess., Supp. No. 16, p. 19, U.N. Doc. A/4354 (1959).

[526]*Transgender* is an umbrella term that encompasses a continuum from men and women who simply failed to conform to society's rules dictating how men and women should look to people who identify as transsexuals, that is, people who undergo medical treatment, including sex reassignment surgery, in order to change their bodies to conform with their gender identities. *Transsexualism* is recognized by the medical establishment when men or women report a persistent identification that does not conform with their

Gender identity refers to whether a person's innate or perceived sense of self conforms with one's biological sex. *Gender expression* refers to one's active, outward portrayal of one's gender identity, while one's *gender appearance* is how others perceive one's gender.[527] Rigid stereotyping of roles for girls and boys (and men and women) can lead to significant abuse of people who fail to conform to these stereotypes. The rigidity of stereotyped roles for both men and women and their contribution to gender-based discrimination was recognized in the Convention on the Elimination of All Forms of Discrimination against Women, which requires states to:

> take all appropriate measures: (a) To modify the social and cultural patterns of conduct of men and women, with a view to achieving the elimination of prejudices and customary and all other practices which are based on the idea of the inferiority or the superiority of either of the sexes or on stereotyped roles for men and women.[528]

The Committee on the Elimination of Discrimination against Women recognizes the pervasiveness of such stereotyping.[529] Elaborating on the

---

biological sex. Under existing medical protocols, such a diagnosis is made only after a person reaches twenty-one years old.

[527]There is a growing debate regarding the medical establishment's treatment of infants who are born intersex, with ambiguous indicators of their biological sex. However, for the purposes of this report, we have confined ourselves to a discussion of issues related to sexual orientation and gender identity. For more information on intersexuality, see the webpage of the Intersex Society of North America, www.insa.org/ (accessed on March 28, 2001).

[528]Convention on the Elimination of All Forms of Discrimination against Women, art. 5(a), *adopted* December 18, 1979, 1249 U.N.T.S. 13 (entered into force September 3, 1981). The United States has signed but failed to ratify the Convention on the Elimination of All Forms of Discrimination against Women. Nonetheless, as a signatory to the treaty, the United States should respect its object and purpose, especially because it is an elaboration of the prohibition against discrimination on the basis of sex enshrined in the ICCPR, a treaty which the United States has ratified.

[529]*General Recommendation No. 3, Education and Public Information Campaigns,* Committee on the Elimination of Discrimination against Women, 6th sess., U.N. Doc. CEDAW/C/1987/L.1/Add (1987). The general recommendation calls for education and public information programs in light of the fact that every country report has reflected a failure to address article 5. The committee observed that "the reports . . . present features in varying degrees showing the existence of stereotyped conceptions of women . . . that perpetuate discrimination based on sex and hinder the implementation of article 5 of the Convention."

importance of rejecting stereotyped roles for men and women and its contributing role in gender-based violence, it has observed:

> Traditional attitudes by which women are regarded as subordinate to men or as having stereotyped roles perpetuate widespread practices involving violence or coercion, such as family violence and abuse, forced marriages, dowry deaths, acid attacks and female circumcision. Such prejudices and practices may justify gender-based violence as a form of protection or control of women. The effect of such violence on the physical and mental integrity of women is to deprive them of equal enjoyment, exercise and knowledge of human rights and fundamental freedoms.[530]

Although the committee focused on violence against women, the phrase "gender-based violence" includes violence against both men and women so long as the violence is motivated by gender. Thus, men as well as women may be targeted for violence because they fail to conform to stereotypes based on gender or because they claim a gender identity which fails to conform with societal expectations.

The committee noted that "gender-based violence, which impairs or nullifies the enjoyment by women of human rights and fundamental freedoms under general international law or under human rights conventions, is discrimination within the meaning of article 1 of the Convention."[531] The committee expressly recognized violations of the right to life, the right not to be subject to torture or cruel, inhuman or degrading treatment or punishment, the right to equal protection according to humanitarian norms in times of conflict, the right to liberty and security of person, the right to equal protection under the law, the right to equality in the family, the right to the highest attainable standard of physical and mental health, and the right to just and favorable conditions of work.[532]

The committee also reiterated that the convention applies to violence perpetrated by public authorities and requires states to act with due diligence to prevent or at least provide redress for acts of violence by "any person, organization or enterprise."[533]

---

[530]*General Recommendation No. 19, Violence Against Women*, para. 11, Committee on the Elimination of Discrimination against Women, 11th sess., U.N. Doc. CEDAW/C/1992/L.1/Add.15 (1992).

[531]Ibid.

[532]Ibid.

[533]Ibid.

The recognition that gender-based discrimination and persecution is a violation of human rights is also found in the policy of the United Nations High Commission for Refugees that encourages states:

> to adopt the interpretation that women asylum seekers who face harsh or inhuman treatment due to their having transgressed the social mores of the society in which they live may be considered a "particular social group" within the meaning of Article 1 A (2) of the 1951 United Nations Refugee Convention.[534]

Similarly, the European Parliament adopted a resolution in 1984 recognizing that women who "transgress social mores" are a social group for the purposes of the Convention Relating to Refugees.[535]

The growing jurisprudence recognizing gender-based persecution triggered by women failing to conform to societal expectations and the committee's analysis of gender-based violence, provide the basis under international law for protecting both men and women from discrimination and persecution based on their gender identity or expression. Harassment and violence against students who fail to conform to society's preconceptions of how young men and women should act is a violation of not only the rights enumerated by the committee, but also the right to education and the right to freedom of expression.

U.S. courts have also had to grapple with the question of how discrimination or harassment based on actual or perceived gender identity may violate federal prohibitions against sex discrimination. Title VII of the Civil Rights Act of 1964 prohibits employment discrimination based on race, color, religion, sex, and national origin.[536] The jurisprudence surrounding Title VII provides the most extensive exploration of the parameters of sex discrimination in U.S. law. The federal Equal Employment Opportunity Commission promulgated regulations for the enforcement of the law which include the following definition:

> Unwelcome sexual advances, requests for sexual favors, and other verbal or physical conduct of a sexual nature constitute sexual

---

[534]*Executive Committee Conclusion No. 39 (XXXVI), Refugee Women and International Protection,* para. k, U.N. High Commissioner for Refugees (1985).

[535]European Parliament, Resolution on the Application of the Geneva Convention relating to the Status of Refugees, 1984 O.J. (C 127) 137.

[536]Civil Rights Act of 1964, Pub. L. 88-352, Title VII, 78 Stat. 253 (codified as amended at 42 U.S.C. §§ 2000e to 2000e-17 (2001)).

harassment when ... or (3) such conduct has the purpose or effect of unreasonably interfering with an individual's work performance or creating an intimidating, hostile, or offensive work environment.[537]

The lead case in the area of how discrimination based on gender identity may rise to the level of sex discrimination under Title VII is *Price Waterhouse v. Hopkins.*[538] In the *Price Waterhouse* case, the employee, Ann Hopkins, was denied partnership despite a stellar employment record with the firm. When the firm failed to reconsider her for partnership the following year, Hopkins filed a claim for sex discrimination. The defendant argued that she was denied partnership based on a negative assessment of her "interpersonal skills."[539] In deciding this case, the Supreme Court recognized that the legislative history was bizarre, as "sex" as a grounds on which to forbid employment discrimination was added by opponents of the bill with the intent of defeating the legislation.[540] The Court then found that gender stereotyping established the link to the plaintiff's sex that is required under Title VII. Specifically, the Court noted a partner's advice to the plaintiff that she "[w]alk more femininely, talk more femininely, dress more femininely, wear make-up, have her hair styled, and wear jewelry."[541] The Court went on to state:

> It takes no special training to discern sex stereotyping in a description of an aggressive female employee as requiring "a course in charm school." Nor ... does it require expertise in psychology to know that, if an employee's flawed "interpersonal skills" can be corrected by a

---

[537]29 C.F.R. § 1604.11(a) (1996).

[538]490 U.S. 228 (1989). The Civil Rights Act of 1991, enacted "to respond to recent decisions of the Supreme Court by expanding the scope of relevant civil rights statutes in order to provide adequate protection to victims of discrimination," has superceded other aspects of the Court's analysis in *Price Waterhouse. See* Pub. L. No. 102-166, §§ 3(4) (codified at 42 U.S.C. § 1981 note) and 107 (codified at 42 U.S.C. §§ 2000e-2, 2000e-5(g)), 105 Stat. 1071, 1071, 1075-76; *Landgraf v. USI Film Products,* 511 U.S. 244, 251 (1994).

[539]*See Price Waterhouse,* 490 U.S. at 234.

[540]Opponents of the Civil Rights Act of 1964 added the provision prohibiting employment discrimination based on sex to the bill because they were convinced that a sufficient number of lawmakers would balk at guaranteeing equality between men and women and withdraw their support for the measure. *See* ibid., p. 244 n.9 (citing Charles and Barbara Whalen, *The Longest Debate: A Legislative History of the 1964 Civil Rights Act* (Cabin John, Maryland: Seven Locks Press, 1985), pp. 115-17).

[541]Ibid., p. 235.

soft-hued suit or a new shade of lipstick, perhaps it is the employee's
sex and not her interpersonal skills that has drawn the criticism.[542]

The connection between sex or gender stereotyping and sex discrimination
was explored more exhaustively by a federal appeals court in *Doe v. City of
Belleville, Illinois.*[543] In *Doe,* one of the plaintiffs was a teenage heterosexual male
who wore an earring in one ear. He was called "fag" and "queer" and asked if he
was a "girl or a guy"; he was threatened with anal rape; and he had his testicles
grabbed by a heterosexual male co-worker. The court answered the question of
whether a heterosexual male can sexually harass another heterosexual male in the
affirmative, consistent with the Supreme Court's decision in *Oncale.* The court
noted that one of the plaintiffs "was apparently singled out for . . . abuse because
the way in which he projected the sexual aspect of his personality (and by that we
mean his gender) did not conform to his coworkers' view of appropriate masculine
behavior."[544] The court quoted the Supreme Court's observation in *Price
Waterhouse* that:

> We are beyond the day when an employer could evaluate employees by
> assuming or insisting that they matched the stereotype associated with
> their group, for "'in forbidding employers to discriminate against
> individuals because of their sex, Congress intended to strike at the entire
> spectrum of disparate treatment of men and women resulting from sex
> stereotypes.'"[545]

The court also emphasized that when the content of the harassment is explicitly
sexual—as in *Doe,* where the harassers grabbed the plaintiff's testicles, threatened
to rape him, and debated whether he would scream when raped—the plaintiff meets
his burden of proving that he suffers harassment because of his sex. The court's

---

[542]Ibid., p. 256.

[543]119 F.3d 563 (7th Cir. 1997). This decision was subsequently vacated by the
Supreme Court and remanded to the U.S. Court of Appeals for the Seventh Circuit for
further consideration in light of *Oncale v. Sundowner Offshore Services,* 479 U.S. 806
(1998), which held that same-sex sexual harassment is covered by Title VII of the Civil
Rights Act of 1964. The *Doe* case was apparently resolved without a published decision.

[544]*Doe,* 119 F.3d at 580.

[545]*Price Waterhouse,* 490 U.S. at 251 (quoting *Los Angeles Dept. of Water and Power
v. Manhart,* 435 U.S. 702, 707 n.13 (1978) (quoting *Sprogis v. United Air Lines, Inc.,* 444
F.2d 1194, 1198 (7th Cir. 1971))), *quoted in Doe,* 119 F.3d at 581.

holding is consistent with prior decisions in which "it is generally taken as a given that when a female employee is harassed in explicitly sexual ways by a male worker or workers, she has been discriminated against 'because of' her sex."[546] Rejecting the view that same-sex sexual harassment must be based on the harasser's attraction to the victim, another federal court observed in 1996:

> Title VII does not require that sexual harassment be motivated by attraction, only that it be because of sex; indeed harassment, like other forms of victimization, is often motivated by issues of power and control on the part of the harasser, issues not related to sexual preference.[547]

But in the absence of explicit protection from discrimination based on sexual orientation and gender identity, some courts have required a higher burden from lesbian, gay, bisexual, and transgender individuals who are subjected to same-sex harassment. Most recently, a federal court of appeals held in March 2001 that a gay employee who had endured "a panoply of markedly crude, demeaning, and sexually oriented activities" did not demonstrate discrimination based on his gender because he could not show that his harassers were motivated by sexual desire or by "'general hostility to the presence of [men] in the workplace.'"[548] Dissenting from the panel's decision in the case, one judge noted:

> If his attackers were women or if they were gay men—or if Rene were a lesbian attacked by straight men—there is no question that plaintiff's openly gay status would not be a complete defense to his Title VII claim. That Rene's attackers were ostensibly heterosexual men is no basis for a different outcome—the attack was homosexual in nature, and his case involves allegations of sexual abuse that female employees did not have to endure.[549]

In a positive development, the U.S. Department of Justice announced, following the *Oncale* decision, that it would use existing federal civil rights laws

---

[546]*Doe,* 119 F.3d at 574.

[547]*Tanner v. Prima Donna Resorts, Inc.,* 919 F. Supp. 351, 355 (D. Nev. 1996), *quoted in Doe,* 119 F.3d at 588.

[548]*Rene v. MGM Grand Hotel, Inc.,* 243 F.3d 1206 (9th Cir. 2001) (quoting *Oncale,* 523 U.S. at 80).

[549]Ibid. (D.W. Nelson, J., dissenting).

to take legal action against businesses and state and local governments that engage in employment discrimination against transgender persons, based on employer's "expectations of what a male employee should act like, or how he should hold himself out."[550]

Title IX of the Education Amendments of 1972 prohibits sex discrimination in federally funded educational programs.[551] In reviewing claims under Title IX, federal courts have consistently drawn on Title VII jurisprudence to help understand the parameters of sex discrimination. Having found that sex discrimination encompasses discrimination based on violating stereotypes of how men and women are expected to look, dress, talk, walk, and be, it is probable that courts would find sexual harassment or discrimination in similar cases with students.

This conclusion is supported by the guidelines issued by the Office for Civil Rights of the U.S. Department of Education, which echo the analysis of *Doe v. City of Belleville*:

> [I]f harassment is based on conduct of a sexual nature, it may be sexual harassment prohibited by Title IX even if the harasser and the harassed are the same sex or the victim of the harassment is gay or lesbian. If, for example, harassing conduct of a sexual nature is directed at gay or lesbian students, it may create a sexually hostile environment and may constitute a violation of Title IX in the same way that it may for a heterosexual student.[552]

---

[550]"Policy Targets Bias" *Washington Blade*, November 20, 1998.

[551]*See* Education Amendments of 1972, Pub. L. No. 92-318, Title IX, 86 Stat. 374 (codified as amended at 20 U.S.C. § 1681(a) (2000)).

[552]U.S. Department of Education, Office for Civil Rights, "Sexual Harassment Guidance: Harassment of Students by School Employees, Other Students, or Third Parties," *Federal Register*, vol. 62 (March 13, 1997), p. 12039.

XII. CONCLUSION

This is a report about the abject failure of the United States government to protect lesbian, gay, bisexual, and transgender youth who attend public schools from harassment and violence. Government at the local, state, and federal levels has refused to dismantle the laws and policies and to eliminate the practices that effectively discriminate against these youth. The entrenched societal prejudice against lesbian, gay, bisexual, and transgender youth is based on rigidly enforced rules dictating how girls and boys should look, walk, talk, dress, act, think, and feel. The social regime in most schools is unforgiving: Youth who break these rules will be punished. Their peers enforce the rules through harassment, ostracism, and violence. School officials condone this cruel dynamic through inaction or in some cases because they, too, judge gay, lesbian, bisexual, and transgender youth to be undeserving of respect.

Discrimination based on sexual orientation also reinforces the discrimination based on gender that many girls face in schools and places lesbians in a particularly vulnerable position. The discriminatory view that boys are inherently superior to girls pervades many schools, sending boys a message that they should assert their masculinity and prove their heterosexuality by being abusive and disrespectful to girls as well as to gay students. Unfortunately, sexism also thrives in gay communities. Young lesbians not only face harassment and abuse from their heterosexual peers but may also face discrimination from their gay male peers. While gay boys receive some positive messages because they are boys, young lesbians receive the message that they are unworthy both because of their gender and because of their sexual orientation. Thus it is not surprising that youth service providers were concerned that lesbians were less likely to do well in school once they were identified by their peers. Transgender students are the most vulnerable beause they receive both intensely negative messages and almost no peer support or understanding.

The impact of this harassment and discrimination is devastating. In a study conducted in an Iowa school, gay students reported hearing on average antigay epithets every seven minutes. What makes the harassment even more devastating for the students is that the adults and the institutions charged with protecting and educating students turn their backs on them. In many cases, adults who do intervene fear they will themselves become the targets of harassment and will lose their jobs.

Left unchecked, peer harassment escalates into violence. Lesbian, gay, bisexual, and transgender students describe their daily experiences as living in survival mode. Not surprisingly, they lose their focus, their grades drop, some drop out, and a few commit suicide.

There is no possible justification for why school officials turn their backs on these students. The foundational principle of human rights is that all people are born free and equal in dignity and rights. But the more than two million school age youth in the United States who are different from the majority of their peers soon learn that the principle of equality does not apply to them. They are rejected by school officials who either agree with the socially sanctioned prejudice against lesbian, gay, bisexual, and transgender individuals in the United States or cave into pressure from those who actively promote discriminatory practices.

The role of government in defending and promoting the human rights of its citizens is to challenge ingrained prejudice, dismantle legal and de facto discrimination, and ensure that all are treated with dignity and respect. Federal, state, and local governments have failed to fulfill this role.

Despite this failing, the youth we interviewed challenge the climate of prejudice, discrimination, and fear that surrounds them each day in their schools. They demand that school officials protect lesbian, gay, bisexual, and transgender youth from harassment and violence from peers and teachers. It is a demand which must be met.

And it must be met not just for lesbian, gay, bisexual, and transgender youth, but for all youth. The government at all levels, especially school administrators, teachers, and counselors, as well as parents and youth service providers must understand that failing to protect gay youth ultimately harms all youth.

When adults fail to model and teach respect for all youth, and indeed for all human beings, they send a message that it is acceptable to demean, attack, and discriminate against others because they are or are perceived to be different. It is a message that can only hurt its recipients. Part of being a teenager is building one's identity. By tolerating discrimination, harassment, and violence—whether based on gender, gender identity, sexual orientation, race, ethnicity, immigration status, or disability—society imbues this process of learning about one's self with negative judgments. The youth who harass others not only are learning behavior that is ultimately harmful to themselves but are acting out their awareness of society's failure to respect the equality and dignity of all human beings.

In this report, Human Rights Watch calls on state authorities to end legal and de facto discrimination based on sexual orientation and gender identity, to compel school officials to protect all students from harassment and violence, to create models for intervention to stop harassment and its devastating impact on students, and to monitor school systems throughout the country to ensure compliance with

the principle of nondiscrimination. Furthermore, Human Rights Watch calls for
teaching respect for all students and ensuring that teachers and other school
officials have the skills to communicate that no form of identity-based harassment
or discrimination is acceptable.

DECIPHERING LEGAL CITATIONS

International Documents

The first citation to an international treaty in this report gives the full name of the document; the date on which it was opened for signature, approved, or adopted; the abbreviation for the official compilation, or reporter series, in which it is published, usually the *United Nations Treaty Series* (U.N.T.S.), preceded by the volume number and followed by the page number on which the treaty begins; and the date on which the agreement entered into force. If the treaty has not been published in a bound reporter series, the citation gives the U.N. or other organizational document number. For example, the first reference to the ICCPR reads: International Covenant on Civil and Political Rights (ICCPR), *opened for signature* December 19, 1966, 999 U.N.T.S. 85 (entered into force March 23, 1976).

Decisions of the International Court of Justice are published in *Report of Judgements, Advisory Opinions and Orders of the International Court of Justice* (I.C.J.). The decisions of the Inter-American Court of Human Rights appear in *Inter-American Court of Human Rights, Series A: Judgments and Opinions* and *Series C: Decisions and Judgments* (Inter-Am. Ct. H.R.); those of the Inter-American Commission on Human Rights are found in the *Annual Report of the Inter-American Commission on Human Rights* (Inter-Am. C.H.R.). Decisions of the European Court of Human Rights appear in *European Court of Human Rights* (Eur. Ct. H.R.) or in the *Yearbook of the European Convention on Human Rights* (Y.B. Eur. Conv. on H.R.); and the decisions of the European Commission of Human Rights are published in *Collections of Decisions of the European Commission of Human Rights* (Eur. Comm'n H.R. Dec. and Rep.) or in *European Human Rights Reports* (Eur. H.R. Rep.).

Cases decided by the International Court of Justice and other international tribunals are identified by the case name, usually the names of the parties; the volume and abbreviated name of the source in which the case is published; the page on which the case begins; and the date of decision, if it is not given in the case name or volume number:

>   *Advisory Opinion on Namibia,* 1971 I.C.J. 16, 47.
> *The Handyside Case,* 24 Eur. Ct. H.R. (ser. A) (1971).

As in the citation to the Namibia advisory opinion, the initial page number may be followed by another page number or numbers giving the exact location of the material cited.

177

Citations to documents issued by the Human Rights Committee, the Committee on the Rights of the Child, and other U.N. bodies give the document name; the treaty body, committee, or agency that issued the document; the session number (occasionally indicating the session part or meeting number); page number; U.N. document number; and year:

> *Views of the Human Rights Committee under article 5, paragraph 4, of the Optional Protocol to the International Covenant on Civil and Political Rights concerning Communication No. 488/1992: Australia,* Human Rights Committee, 50th sess., U.N. Doc. CCPR/C/50/D/ 488/1992, para. 8.7 (April 4, 1994).

> *Concluding Observations of the Committee on the Rights of the Child: Japan,* Committee on the Rights of the Child, 18th sess., U.N. Doc. CRC/C/15/Add.90 (1998).

> *General Recommendation No. 19, Violence against Women,* Committee on the Elimination of Discrimination against Women, 11th sess., U.N. Doc. CEDAW/C/1992/L.1/Add.15 (1992).

U.S. Documents

U.S. federal laws are published after their enactment in *United States Statutes at Large* (Stat.) and are subsequently compiled in the *United States Code* (U.S.C.). Administrative regulations, executive orders, and presidential proclamations are published in the *Federal Register* (Fed. Reg.) and then compiled in the *Code of Federal Regulations* (C.F.R.).

Each U.S. state publishes its laws in its own official statutory compilation. Most states have a single statutory code that is divided into chapters, sections, or titles—the Official Code of Georgia Annotated (Ga. Code Ann.), Kansas Statutes Annotated (Kan. Stat. Ann.), and the General Laws of the Commonwealth of Massachusetts (Mass. Gen. L.), for example. California, New York, and Texas codify their laws by subject, such as the California Education Code (Cal. Educ. Code), the New York Civil Rights Law (N.Y. Civ. Rts. Law), or the Texas Labor Code (Tex. Lab. Code Ann.). For a comprehensive list of state law sources, see *Columbia Law Review* editors et al., compilers, *The Bluebook: A Uniform System of Citation,* 15th ed. (Cambridge, Massachusetts: Harvard Law Review Association, 1991), pp. 165-218.

U.S. federal court cases are identified by case name, the volume and page of the source in which it is published, the court that issued the decision, and the decision date. Decisions of the U.S. Supreme Court are published in the *United States Reporter* (U.S.). Cases decided by the U.S. courts of appeals are found in the first, second, and third series of the *Federal Reporter* (F., F.2d, and F.3d), and the decisions of U.S. district courts are published in the first and second series of the *Federal Supplement* (F. Supp. and F. Supp. 2d). For example, the U.S. Supreme Court's 1954 decision in *Brown v. Board of Education,* found in volume 347 of the *United States Reports* at page 483, is cited as *Brown v. Board of Education,* 347 U.S. 483 (1954). The citation *Nabozny v. Podlesny,* 92 F.3d 446, 458-59 (7th Cir. 1996), refers to the decision of the U.S. Court of Appeals for the Seventh Circuit in *Nabozny v. Podlesny,* found in volume 92 of the *Federal Reporter, Third Series,* beginning on page 446, with the specific material cited located at pages 458 and 459.

State court cases are published in six regional reporters: *Atlantic Reporter* (A., A.2d), *North Eastern Reporter* (N.E., N.E. 2d), *North Western Reporter* (N.W., N.W. 2d), *Pacific Reporter* (P., P.2d), *South Eastern Reporter* (S.E., S.E. 2d), *South Western Reporter* (S.W., S.W. 2d), *Southern Reporter* (So., So. 2d). Citations to state court cases published in these reporters indicate the state and court that issued the decision. For instance, the decision that invalidated Georgia's sodomy statute, *Powell v. State,* 510 S.E.2d 18, 26 (Ga. 1998), was issued by the Supreme Court of Georgia. In Tennessee, the state court of appeals reached a similar decision in *Campbell v. Sundquist,* 926 S.W.2d 250 (Tenn. Ct. App. 1996).

APPENDIX A
Excerpts from the International Covenant on Civil and Political Rights

Preamble

The States Parties to the present Covenant,

Considering that, in accordance with the principles proclaimed in the Charter of the United Nations, recognition of the inherent dignity and of the equal and inalienable rights of all members of the human family is the foundation of freedom, justice and peace in the world,

Recognizing that these rights derive from the inherent dignity of the human person,

Recognizing that, in accordance with the Universal Declaration of Human Rights, the ideal of free human beings enjoying civil and political freedom and freedom from fear and want can only be achieved if conditions are created whereby everyone may enjoy his civil and political rights, as well as his economic, social and cultural rights,

Considering the obligation of States under the Charter of the United Nations to promote universal respect for, and observance of, human rights and freedoms,

Realizing that the individual, having duties to other individuals and to the community to which he belongs, is under a responsibility to strive for the promotion and observance of the rights recognized in the present Covenant,

Agree upon the following articles:

Article 2

1. Each State Party to the present Covenant undertakes to respect and to ensure to all individuals within its territory and subject to its jurisdiction the rights recognized in the present Covenant, without distinction of any kind, such as race, color, sex, language, religion, political or other opinion, national or social origin, property, birth or other status.

2. Where not already provided for by existing legislative or other measures, each State Party to the present Covenant undertakes to take the necessary steps, in accordance with its constitutional processes and with the provisions of the present Covenant, to adopt such legislative or other measures as may be necessary to give effect to the rights recognized in the present Covenant.

3. Each State Party to the present Covenant undertakes:

(a) To ensure that any person whose rights or freedoms as herein recognized are violated shall have an effective remedy, notwithstanding that the violation has been committed by persons acting in an official capacity;

(b) To ensure that any person claiming such a remedy shall have

180

his right thereto determined by competent judicial, administrative or legislative authorities, or by any other competent authority provided for by the legal system of the State, and to develop the possibilities of judicial remedy;

(c) To ensure that the competent authorities shall enforce such remedies when granted.

Article 3

The States Parties to the present Covenant undertake to ensure the equal right of men and women to the enjoyment of all civil and political rights set forth in the present Covenant.

Article 4

1 . In time of public emergency which threatens the life of the nation and the existence of which is officially proclaimed, the States Parties to the present Covenant may take measures derogating from their obligations under the present Covenant to the extent strictly required by the exigencies of the situation, provided that such measures are not inconsistent with their other obligations under international law and do not involve discrimination solely on the ground of race, color, sex, language, religion or social origin.

2. No derogation from articles 6, 7, 8 (paragraphs 1 and 2), 11, 15, 16 and 18 may be made under this provision.

3. Any State Party to the present Covenant availing itself of the right of derogation shall immediately inform the other States Parties to the present Covenant, through the intermediary of the Secretary-General of the United Nations, of the provisions from which it has derogated and of the reasons by which it was actuated. A further communication shall be made, through the same intermediary, on the date on which it terminates such derogation.

Article 5

1. Nothing in the present Covenant may be interpreted as implying for any State, group or person any right to engage in any activity or perform any act aimed at the destruction of any of the rights and freedoms recognized herein or at their limitation to a greater extent than is provided for in the present Covenant.

2. There shall be no restriction upon or derogation from any of the fundamental human rights recognized or existing in any State Party to the present Covenant pursuant to law, conventions, regulations or custom on the pretext that the present Covenant does not recognize such rights or that it recognizes them to a lesser extent.

Article 6

1. States Parties recognize that every child has the inherent right to life.

2. States Parties shall ensure to the maximum extent possible the survival and development of the child.

Article 7

No one shall be subjected to torture or to cruel, inhuman or degrading treatment or punishment. In particular, no one shall be subjected without his free consent to medical or scientific experimentation.

Article 18

1. Everyone shall have the right to freedom of thought, conscience and religion. This right shall include freedom to have or to adopt a religion or belief of his choice, and freedom, either individually or in community with others and in public or private, to manifest his religion or belief in worship, observance, practice and teaching.

2. No one shall be subject to coercion which would impair his freedom to have or to adopt a religion or belief of his choice.

3. Freedom to manifest one's religion or beliefs may be subject only to such limitations as are prescribed by law and are necessary to protect public safety, order, health, or morals or the fundamental rights and freedoms of others.

4. The States Parties to the present Covenant undertake to have respect for the liberty of parents and, when applicable, legal guardians to ensure the religious and moral education of their children in conformity with their own convictions.

Article 19

1. Everyone shall have the right to hold opinions without interference.

2. Everyone shall have the right to freedom of expression; this right shall include freedom to seek, receive and impart information and ideas of all kinds, regardless of frontiers, either orally, in writing or in print, in the form of art, or through any other media of his choice.

3. The exercise of the rights provided for in paragraph 2 of this article carries with it special duties and responsibilities. It may therefore be subject to certain restrictions, but these shall only be such as are provided by law and are necessary:

(a) For respect of the rights or reputations of others;

(b) For the protection of national security or of public order (ordre public), or of public health or morals.

Article 20

1. Any propaganda for war shall be prohibited by law.

2. Any advocacy of national, racial or religious hatred that constitutes incitement to discrimination, hostility or violence shall be prohibited by law.

Article 21

The right of peaceful assembly shall be recognized. No restrictions may be placed on the exercise of this right other than those imposed in conformity with the law and which are necessary in a democratic society in the interests of national security or public safety, public order (ordre public), the protection of public health or morals or the protection of the rights and freedoms of others.

Article 22

1. Everyone shall have the right to freedom of association with others, including the right to form and join trade unions for the protection of his interests.

2. No restrictions may be placed on the exercise of this right other than those which are prescribed by law and which are necessary in a democratic society in the interests of national security or public safety, public order (ordre public), the protection of public health or morals or the protection of the rights and freedoms of others. This article shall not prevent the imposition of lawful restrictions on members of the armed forces and of the police in their exercise of this right.

3. Nothing in this article shall authorize States Parties to the International Labor Organization Convention of 1948 concerning Freedom of Association and Protection of the Right to Organize to take legislative measures which would prejudice, or to apply the law in such a manner as to prejudice, the guarantees provided for in that Convention.

Article 23

1. The family is the natural and fundamental group unit of society and is entitled to protection by society and the State.

2. The right of men and women of marriageable age to marry and to found a family shall be recognized.

3. No marriage shall be entered into without the free and full consent of the intending spouses.

4. States Parties to the present Covenant shall take appropriate steps to ensure equality of rights and responsibilities of spouses as to marriage, during marriage and at its dissolution. In the case of dissolution, provision shall be made for the necessary protection of any children.

Article 24

1. Every child shall have, without any discrimination as to race, color, sex, language, religion, national or social origin, property or birth, the right to such measures of protection as are required by his status as a minor, on the part of his family, society and the State.

2. Every child shall be registered immediately after birth and shall have a name.

3. Every child has the right to acquire a nationality.

Article 26

All persons are equal before the law and are entitled without any discrimination to the equal protection of the law. In this respect, the law shall prohibit any discrimination and guarantee to all persons equal and effective protection against discrimination on any ground such as race, color, sex, language, religion, political or other opinion, national or social origin, property, birth or other status.

APPENDIX B
Excerpts from the International Covenant on Economic, Social and Cultural Rights

Preamble

The States Parties to the present Covenant,

Considering that, in accordance with the principles proclaimed in the Charter of the United Nations, recognition of the inherent dignity and of the equal and inalienable rights of all members of the human family is the foundation of freedom, justice and peace in the world,

Recognizing that these rights derive from the inherent dignity of the human person,

Recognizing that, in accordance with the Universal Declaration of Human Rights, the ideal of free human beings enjoying freedom from fear and want can only be achieved if conditions are created whereby everyone may enjoy his economic, social and cultural rights, as well as his civil and political rights,

Considering the obligation of States under the Charter of the United Nations to promote universal respect for, and observance of, human rights and freedoms,

Realizing that the individual, having duties to other individuals and to the community to which he belongs, is under a responsibility to strive for the promotion and observance of the rights recognized in the present Covenant,

Agree upon the following articles:

Article 3

The States Parties to the present Covenant undertake to ensure the equal right of men and women to the enjoyment of all economic, social and cultural rights set forth in the present Covenant.

Article 13

1. The States Parties to the present Convenant recognize the right of everyone to education. They agree that education shall be directed to the full development of the human personality and the sense of its dignity, and shall strengthen the respect for human rights and fundamental freedoms. They further agree that education shall enable all people to participate effectively in a free society, promote understanding, tolerance and friendship among all dantional and all racial, ethnic or religious groups, and further the activities of the United Nations for the maintenance of peace.

2. The States parties to the present Convenant recognize that, with a view to achieving the full realization of this right: . . . . b. Secondary education in its different forms . . . shall be made generally available and accessible to all . . . .

APPENDIX C
Excerpts from the Convention on the Rights of the Child

Preamble

The States Parties to the present Convention,

Considering that, in accordance with the principles proclaimed in the Charter of the United Nations, recognition of the inherent dignity and of the equal and inalienable rights of all members of the human family is the foundation of freedom, justice and peace in the world,

Bearing in mind that the peoples of the United Nations have, in the Charter, reaffirmed their faith in fundamental human rights and in the dignity and worth of the human person, and have determined to promote social progress and better standards of life in larger freedom,

Recognizing that the United Nations has, in the Universal Declaration of Human Rights and in the International Covenants on Human Rights, proclaimed and agreed that everyone is entitled to all the rights and freedoms set forth therein, without distinction of any kind, such as race, colour, sex, language, religion, political or other opinion, national or social origin, property, birth or other status,

Recalling that, in the Universal Declaration of Human Rights, the United Nations has proclaimed that childhood is entitled to special care and assistance,

Convinced that the family, as the fundamental group of society and the natural environment for the growth and well-being of all its members and particularly children, should be afforded the necessary protection and assistance so that it can fully assume its responsibilities within the community,

Recognizing that the child, for the full and harmonious development of his or her personality, should grow up in a family environment, in an atmosphere of happiness, love and understanding,

Considering that the child should be fully prepared to live an individual life in society, and brought up in the spirit of the ideals proclaimed in the Charter of the United Nations, and in particular in the spirit of peace, dignity, tolerance, freedom, equality and solidarity,

Bearing in mind that the need to extend particular care to the child has been stated in the Geneva Declaration of the Rights of the Child of 1924 and in the Declaration of the Rights of the Child adopted by the General Assembly on 20 November 1959 and recognized in the Universal Declaration of Human Rights, in the International Covenant on Civil and Political Rights (in particular in articles 23 and 24), in the International Covenant on Economic, Social and Cultural Rights (in particular in article 10) and in the statutes and relevant instruments of specialized agencies and international organizations concerned with the welfare of children, '

Bearing in mind that, as indicated in the Declaration of the Rights of the Child, "the child, by reason of his physical and mental immaturity, needs special safeguards and care, including appropriate legal protection, before as well as after birth",

Recalling the provisions of the Declaration on Social and Legal Principles relating to the Protection and Welfare of Children, with Special Reference to Foster Placement and Adoption Nationally and Internationally; the United Nations Standard Minimum Rules for the Administration of Juvenile Justice (The Beijing Rules) ; and the Declaration on the Protection of Women and Children in Emergency and Armed Conflict,

Recognizing that, in all countries in the world, there are children living in exceptionally difficult conditions, and that such children need special consideration,

Taking due account of the importance of the traditions and cultural values of each people for the protection and harmonious development of the child,

Recognizing the importance of international co-operation for improving the living conditions of children in every country, in particular in the developing countries,

Have agreed as follows:

Article 1

For the purposes of the present Convention, a child means every human being below the age of eighteen years unless under the law applicable to the child, majority is attained earlier.

Article 2

1. States Parties shall respect and ensure the rights set forth in the present Convention to each child within their jurisdiction without discrimination of any kind, irrespective of the child's or his or her parent's or legal guardian's race, colour, sex, language, religion, political or other opinion, national, ethnic or social origin, property, disability, birth or other status.

2. States Parties shall take all appropriate measures to ensure that the child is protected against all forms of discrimination or punishment on the basis of the status, activities, expressed opinions, or beliefs of the child's parents, legal guardians, or family members.

Article 3

1. In all actions concerning children, whether undertaken by public or private social welfare institutions, courts of law, administrative authorities or legislative bodies, the best interests of the child shall be a primary consideration.

2. States Parties undertake to ensure the child such protection and care as is necessary for his or her well-being, taking into account the rights and duties of his or her parents, legal guardians, or other individuals legally responsible for him or her, and, to this end, shall take all appropriate legislative and administrative measures.

3. States Parties shall ensure that the institutions, services and facilities responsible for the care or protection of children shall conform with the standards established by competent authorities, particularly in the areas of safety, health, in the number and suitability of their staff, as well as competent supervision.

Article 4

States Parties shall undertake all appropriate legislative, administrative, and other measures for the implementation of the rights recognized in the present Convention. With regard to economic, social and cultural rights, States Parties shall undertake such measures to the maximum extent of their available resources and, where needed, within the framework of international co-operation.

Article 5

States Parties shall respect the responsibilities, rights and duties of parents or, where applicable, the members of the extended family or community as provided for by local custom, legal guardians or other persons legally responsible for the child, to provide, in a manner consistent with the evolving capacities of the child, appropriate direction and guidance in the exercise by the child of the rights recognized in the present Convention.

Article 6

1. States Parties recognize that every child has an inherent right to life.

2. States Parties shall ensure to the maximum extent possible the survival and development of the child.

Article 12

1. States Parties shall assure to the child who is capable of forming his or her own views the right to express those views freely in all matters affecting the child, the views of the child being given due weight in accordance with the age and maturity of the child.

2. For this purpose, the child shall in particular be provided the opportunity to be heard in any judicial and administrative proceedings affecting the child, either directly, or through a representative or an appropriate body, in a manner consistent with the procedural rules of national law.

Article 13

1. The child shall have the right to freedom of expression; this right shall include freedom to seek, receive and impart information and ideas of all kinds, regardless of frontiers, either orally, in writing or in print, in the form of art, or through any other media of the child's choice.

2. The exercise of this right may be subject to certain restrictions, but these shall only be such as are provided by law and are necessary:

(a) For respect of the rights or reputations of others; or

(b) For the protection of national security or of public order (ordre public), or of public health or morals.

Article 14

1. States Parties shall respect the right of the child to freedom of thought, conscience and religion.

2. States Parties shall respect the rights and duties of the parents and, when applicable, legal guardians, to provide direction to the child in the exercise of his or her right in a manner consistent with the evolving capacities of the child.

3. Freedom to manifest one's religion or beliefs may be subject only to such limitations as are prescribed by law and are necessary to protect public safety, order, health or morals, or the fundamental rights and freedoms of others.

Article 15

1. States Parties recognize the rights of the child to freedom of association and to freedom of peaceful assembly.

2. No restrictions may be placed on the exercise of these rights other than those imposed in conformity with the law and which are necessary in a democratic society in the interests of national security or public safety, public order (ordre public), the protection of public health or morals or the protection of the rights and freedoms of others.

Article 16

1. No child shall be subjected to arbitrary or unlawful interference with his or her privacy, family, home or correspondence, nor to unlawful attacks on his or her honour and reputation.

2. The child has the right to the protection of the law against such interference or attacks.

Article 17

States Parties recognize the important function performed by the mass media and shall ensure that the child has access to information and material from a diversity of national and international sources, especially those aimed at the promotion of his or her social, spiritual and moral well-being and physical and mental health. To this end, States Parties shall:

(a) Encourage the mass media to disseminate information and material of social and cultural benefit to the child and in accordance with the spirit of article 29;

(b) Encourage international co-operation in the production, exchange and dissemination of such information and material from a diversity of cultural, national and international sources;

(c) Encourage the production and dissemination of children's books;

(d) Encourage the mass media to have particular regard to the linguistic needs of the child who belongs to a minority group or who is indigenous;

(e) Encourage the development of appropriate guidelines for the protection of the child from information and material injurious to his or her well-being, bearing in mind the provisions of articles 13 and 18.

Article 18

1. States Parties shall use their best efforts to ensure recognition of the principle that both parents have common responsibilities for the upbringing and development of the child. Parents or, as the case may be, legal guardians, have the primary responsibility for the upbringing and development of the child. The best interests of the child will be their basic concern.

2. For the purpose of guaranteeing and promoting the rights set forth in the present Convention, States Parties shall render appropriate assistance to parents and legal guardians in the performance of their child-rearing responsibilities and shall ensure the development of institutions, facilities and services for the care of children.

3. States Parties shall take all appropriate measures to ensure that children of working parents have the right to benefit from child-care services and facilities for which they are eligible.

Article 19

1. States Parties shall take all appropriate legislative, administrative, social and educational measures to protect the child from all forms of physical or mental violence, injury or abuse, neglect or negligent treatment, maltreatment or exploitation, including sexual abuse, while in the

care of parent(s), legal guardian(s) or any other person who has the care of the child.

2. Such protective measures should, as appropriate, include effective procedures for the establishment of social programmes to provide necessary support for the child and for those who have the care of the child, as well as for other forms of prevention and for identification, reporting, referral, investigation, treatment and follow-up of instances of child maltreatment described heretofore, and, as appropriate, for judicial involvement.

Article 24

1. States Parties recognize the right of the child to the enjoyment of the highest attainable standard of health and to facilities for the treatment of illness and rehabilitation of health. States Parties shall strive to ensure that no child is deprived of his or her right of access to such health care services.

2. States Parties shall pursue full implementation of this right and, in particular, shall take appropriate measures:

(a) To diminish infant and child mortality;

(b) To ensure the provision of necessary medical assistance and health care to all children with

emphasis on the development of primary health care;

(c) To combat disease and malnutrition, including within the framework of primary health care, through, inter alia, the application of readily available technology and through the provision of adequate nutritious foods and clean drinking-water, taking into consideration the dangers and risks of environmental pollution;

(d) To ensure appropriate pre-natal and post-natal health care for mothers;

(e) To ensure that all segments of society, in particular parents and children, are informed, have access to education and are supported in the use of basic knowledge of child health and nutrition, the advantages of breastfeeding, hygiene and environmental sanitation and the prevention of accidents;

(f) To develop preventive health care, guidance for parents and family planning education and services.

3. States Parties shall take all effective and appropriate measures with a view to abolishing traditional practices prejudicial to the health of children.

4. States Parties undertake to promote and encourage international co-operation with a view to achieving progressively the full realization of the right recognized in the present article. In this regard,

particular account shall be taken of the needs of developing countries.

Article 28

1. States Parties recognize the right of the child to education, and with a view to achieving this right progressively and on the basis of equal opportunity, they shall, in particular:

(a) Make primary education compulsory and available free to all;

(b) Encourage the development of different forms of secondary education, including general and vocational education, make them available and accessible to every child, and take appropriate measures such as the introduction of free education and offering financial assistance in case of need;

(c) Make higher education accessible to all on the basis of capacity by every appropriate means;

(d) Make educational and vocational information and guidance available and accessible to all children;

(e) Take measures to encourage regular attendance at schools and the reduction of drop-out rates.

2. States Parties shall take all appropriate measures to ensure that school discipline is administered in a manner consistent with the child's human dignity and in conformity with the present Convention.

3. States Parties shall promote and encourage international cooperation in matters relating to education, in particular with a view to contributing to the elimination of ignorance and illiteracy throughout the world and facilitating access to scientific and technical knowledge and modern teaching methods. In this regard, particular account shall be taken of the needs of developing countries.

Article 29

1. States Parties agree that the education of the child shall be directed to:

(a) The development of the child's personality, talents and mental and physical abilities to their fullest potential;

(b) The development of respect for human rights and fundamental freedoms, and for the principles enshrined in the Charter of the United Nations;

(c) The development of respect for the child's parents, his or her own cultural identity, language and values, for the national values of the country in which the child is living, the country from which he or she may originate, and for civilizations different from his or her own;

(d) The preparation of the child for responsible life in a free society, in the spirit of understanding, peace, tolerance, equality of sexes, and friendship among all peoples, ethnic, national and religious groups and persons of indigenous origin;

(e) The development of respect for the natural environment.

2. No part of the present article or article 28 shall be construed so as to interfere with the liberty of individuals and bodies to establish and direct educational institutions, subject always to the observance of the principle set forth in paragraph 1 of the present article and to the requirements that the education given in such institutions shall conform to such minimum standards as may be laid down by the State.

Article 37

States Parties shall ensure that:

a. No child shall be subjected to torture or other cruel, inhuman or degrading treatment of punishment.

APPENDIX D
Excerpts from the Convention on the Elimination of All Forms of Discrimination against Women

The States Parties to the present Convention,

Noting that the Charter of the United Nations reaffirms faith in fundamental human rights, in the dignity and worth of the human person and in the equal rights of men and women,

Noting that the Universal Declaration of Human Rights affirms the principle of the inadmissibility of discrimination and proclaims that all human beings are born free and equal in dignity and rights and that everyone is entitled to all the rights and freedoms set forth therein, without distinction of any kind, including distinction based on sex,

Noting that the States Parties to the International Covenants on Human Rights have the obligation to ensure the equal rights of men and women to enjoy all economic, social, cultural, civil and political rights,

Considering the international conventions concluded under the auspices of the United Nations and the specialized agencies promoting equality of rights of men and women,

Noting also the resolutions, declarations and recommendations adopted by the United Nations and the specialized agencies promoting equality of rights of men and women,

Concerned, however, that despite these various instruments extensive discrimination against women continues to exist,

Recalling that discrimination against women violates the principles of equality of rights and respect for human dignity, is an obstacle to the participation of women, on equal terms with men, in the political, social, economic and cultural life of their countries, hampers the growth of the prosperity of society and the family and makes more difficult the full development of the potentialities of women in the service of their countries and of humanity,

Concerned that in situations of poverty women have the least access to food, health, education, training and opportunities for employment and other needs,

Convinced that the establishment of the new international economic order based on equity and justice will contribute significantly towards the promotion of equality between men and women,

Emphasizing that the eradication of apartheid, all forms of racism, racial discrimination, colonialism, neo-colonialism, aggression, foreign occupation and domination and interference in the internal affairs of States is essential to the full enjoyment of the rights of men and women,

Affirming that the strengthening of international peace and security, the relaxation of international tension, mutual co-operation among all States irrespective of their social and economic systems, general and complete disarmament, in particular nuclear disarmament under strict and effective international control, the affirmation of the principles of justice, equality and mutual benefit in relations among countries and the realization of the right of peoples under alien and colonial domination and foreign occupation to self-determination and independence, as well as respect for national sovereignty and territorial integrity, will promote social progress and development and as a consequence will contribute to the attainment of full equality between men and women,

Convinced that the full and complete development of a country, the welfare of the world and the cause of peace require the maximum participation of women on equal terms with men in all fields,

Bearing in mind the great contribution of women to the welfare of the family and to the development of society, so far not fully recognized, the social significance of maternity and the role of both parents in the family and in the upbringing of children, and aware that the role of women in procreation should not be a basis for discrimination but that the upbringing of children requires a sharing of responsibility between men and women and society as a whole,

Aware that a change in the traditional role of men as well as the role of women in society and in the family is needed to achieve full equality between men and women,

Determined to implement the principles set forth in the Declaration on the Elimination of Discrimination against Women and, for that purpose, to adopt the measures required for the elimination of such discrimination in all its forms and manifestations,

Have agreed on the following:

Article 1

For the purposes of the present Convention, the term "discrimination against women" shall mean any distinction, exclusion or restriction made on the basis of sex which has the effect or purpose of impairing or nullifying the recognition, enjoyment or exercise by women, irrespective of their marital status, on a basis of equality of men and women, of human rights and fundamental freedoms in the political, economic, social, cultural, civil or any other field.

Article 2

States Parties condemn discrimination against women in all its forms, agree to pursue by all appropriate means and without delay a policy of eliminating discrimination against women and, to this end, undertake:

(a) To embody the principle of the equality of men and women in their national constitutions or other appropriate legislation if not yet incorporated therein and to ensure, through law and other appropriate means, the practical realization of this principle;

(b) To adopt appropriate legislative and other measures, including sanctions where appropriate, prohibiting all discrimination against women;

(c) To establish legal protection of the rights of women on an equal basis with men and to ensure through competent national tribunals and other public institutions the effective protection of women against any act of discrimination;

(d) To refrain from engaging in any act or practice of discrimination against women and to ensure that public authorities and institutions shall act in conformity with this obligation;

(e) To take all appropriate measures to eliminate discrimination against women by any person, organization or enterprise;

(f) To take all appropriate measures, including legislation, to modify or abolish existing laws, regulations, customs and practices which constitute discrimination against women;

(g) To repeal all national penal provisions which constitute discrimination against women.

Article 4

1. Adoption by States Parties of temporary special measures aimed at accelerating de facto equality between men and women shall not be considered discrimination as defined in the present Convention, but shall in no way entail as a consequence the maintenance of unequal or separate standards; these measures shall be discontinued when the objectives of equality of opportunity and treatment have been achieved.

2. Adoption by States Parties of special measures, including those measures contained in the present Convention, aimed at protecting maternity shall not be considered discriminatory.

Article 5

States Parties shall take all appropriate measures:

(a) To modify the social and cultural patterns of conduct of men and women, with a view to achieving the elimination of prejudices and customary and all other practices which are based on the idea of the inferiority or the superiority of either of the sexes or on stereotyped roles for men and women;

(b) To ensure that family education includes a proper understanding of maternity as a social function and the recognition of the common responsibility of men and women in the upbringing and development of their children, it being understood that the interest of the children is the primordial consideration in all cases.

Article 10

States Parties shall take all appropriate measures to eliminate discrimination against women in order to ensure to them equal rights with men in the field of education and in particular to ensure, on a basis of equality of men and women:

(a) The same conditions for career and vocational guidance, for access to studies and for the achievement of diplomas in educational establishments of all categories in rural as well as in urban areas; this equality shall be ensured in pre-school, general, technical, professional and higher technical education, as well as in all types of vocational training;

(b) Access to the same curricula, the same examinations, teaching staff with qualifications of the same standard and school premises and equipment of the same quality;

(c) The elimination of any stereotyped concept of the roles of men and women at all levels and in all forms of education by encouraging coeducation and other types of education which will help to achieve this aim and, in particular, by the revision of textbooks and school programmes and the adaptation of teaching methods;

(d) The same opportunities to benefit from scholarships and other study grants;

(e) The same opportunities for access to programmes of continuing education, including adult and functional literacy programmes, particularly those aimed at reducing, at the earliest possible time, any gap in education existing between men and women;

(f) The reduction of female student drop-out rates and the organization of programmes for girls and women who have left school prematurely;

(g) The same Opportunities to participate actively in sports and physical education;

(h) Access to specific educational information to help to ensure the health and well-being of families, including information and advice on family planning.

Article 11

1. States Parties shall take all appropriate measures to eliminate discrimination against women in the field of employment in order to ensure, on a basis of equality of men and women, the same rights, in particular:

(a) The right to work as an inalienable right of all human beings;

(b) The right to the same employment opportunities, including the application of the same criteria for selection in matters of employment;

(c) The right to free choice of profession and employment, the right to promotion, job security and all benefits and conditions of service and the right to receive vocational training and retraining, including apprenticeships, advanced vocational training and recurrent training;

(d) The right to equal remuneration, including benefits, and to equal treatment in respect of work of equal value, as well as equality of treatment in the evaluation of the quality of work;

(e) The right to social security, particularly in cases of retirement, unemployment, sickness, invalidity and old age and other incapacity to work, as well as the right to paid leave;

(f) The right to protection of health and to safety in working conditions, including the safeguarding of the function of reproduction.

2. In order to prevent discrimination against women on the grounds of marriage or maternity and to ensure their effective right to work, States Parties shall take appropriate measures:

(a) To prohibit, subject to the imposition of sanctions, dismissal on the grounds of pregnancy or of maternity leave and discrimination in dismissals on the basis of marital status;

(b) To introduce maternity leave with pay or with comparable social benefits without loss of former employment, seniority or social allowances;

(c) To encourage the provision of the necessary supporting social services to enable parents to combine family obligations with work responsibilities and participation in public life, in particular through promoting the establishment and development of a network of child-care facilities;

(d) To provide special protection to women during pregnancy in types of work proved to be harmful to them.

3. Protective legislation relating to matters covered in this article shall be reviewed periodically in the light of scientific and technological knowledge and shall be revised, repealed or extended as necessary.

Article 14

1. States Parties shall take into account the particular problems faced by rural women and the significant roles which rural women play in the economic survival of their families, including their work in the non-monetized sectors of the economy, and shall take all appropriate measures to ensure the application of the provisions of the present Convention to women in rural areas.

2. States Parties shall take all appropriate measures to eliminate discrimination against women in rural areas in order to ensure, on a basis of equality of men and women, that they participate in and benefit from rural development and, in particular, shall ensure to such women the right:

(a) To participate in the elaboration and implementation of development planning at all levels;

(b) To have access to adequate health care facilities, including information, counseling and services in family planning;

(c) To benefit directly from social security programmes;

(d) To obtain all types of training and education, formal and non-formal, including that relating to functional literacy, as well as, inter alia, the benefit of all community and extension services, in order to increase their technical proficiency;

(e) To organize self-help groups and co-operatives in order to obtain equal access to economic opportunities through employment or self employment;

(f) To participate in all community activities;

(g) To have access to agricultural credit and loans, marketing facilities, appropriate technology and equal treatment in land and agrarian reform as well as in land resettlement schemes;

(h) To enjoy adequate living conditions, particularly in relation to housing, sanitation, electricity and water supply, transport and communications.

Article 15

1. States Parties shall accord to women equality with men before the law.

2. States Parties shall accord to women, in civil matters, a legal capacity identical to that of men and the same opportunities to exercise that capacity. In particular, they shall give women equal rights to conclude contracts and to administer property and shall treat them equally in all stages of procedure in courts and tribunals.

3. States Parties agree that all contracts and all other private instruments of any kind with a legal effect which is directed at restricting the legal capacity of women shall be deemed null and void. . . .

APPENDIX E
Selected State Statutes

California
Freedom from Violence (California Civil Code, section 51.7)

(a) All persons within the jurisdiction of this state have the right to be free from any violence, or intimidation by threat of violence, committed against their persons or property because of their race, color, religion, ancestry, national origin, political affiliation, sex, sexual orientation, age, disability, or position in a labor dispute, or because another person perceives them to have one or more of those characteristics. The identification in this subdivision of particular bases of discrimination is illustrative rather than restrictive.

This section does not apply to statements concerning positions in a labor dispute which are made during otherwise lawful labor picketing.

(b) As used in this section, "sexual orientation" means heterosexuality, homosexuality, or bisexuality.

Nondiscrimination in Education (California Education Code, section 220)

No person shall be subjected to discrimination on the basis of sex, ethnic group identification, race, national origin, religion, color, mental or physical disability, or any basis that is contained in the prohibition of hate crimes set forth in subdivision (a) of Section 422.6 of the Penal Code in any program or activity conducted by an educational institution that receives, or benefits from, state financial assistance or enrolls pupils who receive state student financial aid.

Nondiscrimination in Employment and Housing (California Goverment Code, sections 12920-21)
§ 12920. Public policy

It is hereby declared as the public policy of this state that it is necessary to protect and safeguard the right and opportunity of all persons to seek, obtain, and hold employment without discrimination or abridgment on account of race, religious creed, color, national origin, ancestry, physical disability, mental disability, medical condition, marital status, sex, age, or sexual orientation.

It is recognized that the practice of denying employment opportunity and discriminating in the terms of employment for these reasons foments domestic strife and unrest, deprives the state of the fullest utilization of its capacities for development and advancement, and substantially and adversely affects the interest of employees, employers, and the public in general.

Further, the practice of discrimination because of race, color, religion, sex, marital status, national origin, ancestry, familial status, disability, or sexual orientation in housing accomodations is declared to be against public policy.

It is the purpose of this part to provide effective remedies that will eliminate these discriminatory practices.

This part shall be deemed an exercise of the police power of the state for the protection of the welfare, health, and peace of the people of this state.

§ 12921. Employment and housing without discrimination as a civil right

(a) The opportunity to seek, obtain and hold employment without discrimination because of race, religious creed, color, national origin, ancestry, physical disability, mental disability, medical condition, marital status, sex, age, or sexual orientation is hereby recognized as and declared to be a civil right.

(b) The opportunity to seek, obtain, and hold housing without discrimination because of race, color, religion, sex, sexual orientation, marital status, national origin, ancestry, familial status,

disability, or any other basis prohibited by section 51 of the Civil Code is hereby recognized as and declared to be a civil right.

Prohibition of Hate Crimes (California Penal Code, section 422.6)

(a) No person, whether or not acting under color of law, shall by force or threat of force, willfully injure, intimidate, interfere with, oppress, or threaten any other person in the free exercise or enjoyment of any right or privilege secured to him or her by the Constitution or laws of this state or by the Constitution or laws of the United States because of the other person's race, color, religion, ancestry, national origin, disability, gender, or sexual orientation, or because he or she perceives that the other person has one or more of these characteristics.

(b) No person, whether or not acting under color of law, shall knowingly deface, damage, or destroy the real or personal property of any other person for the purpose of intimidating or interfering with the free exercise or enjoyment of any right or privilege secured to the other person by the Constitution or laws of this state or by the Constitution or laws of the United States, because of the other person's race, color, religion, ancestry, national origin, disability, gender, or sexual orientation, or because he or she perceives that the other person has one or more of these characteristics.

(c) Any person convicted of violating subdivision (a) or (b) shall be punished by imprisonment in a county jail not to exceed one year, or by a fine not to exceed five thousand dollars ($5,000), or by both that imprisonment and fine, and the court shall order the defendant to perform a minimum of community service, not to exceed 400 hours, to be performed over a period not to exceed 350 days, during a time other than his or her hours of employment or school attendance. However, no person shall be convicted of violating subsection (a) based upon speech alone, except upon a showing that the speech itself threatened violence against a specific person or group of persons and that the defendant had the apparent ability to carry out the threat.

Massachusetts

Right of Students to Freedom of Expression (Annotated Laws of Massachusetts, chapter 71, section 82)

The right of students to freedom of expression in the public schools of the commonwealth shall not be abridged, provided that such right shall not cause any disruption or disorder within the school. Freedom of expression shall include without limitation, the rights and

responsibilities of students, collectively and individually, (a) to express their views through speech and symbols, (b) to write, publish and disseminate their views, (c) to assemble peaceably on school property for the purpose of expressing their opinions. Any assembly planned by students during regularly scheduled school hours shall be held only at a time and place approved in advance by the school principal or his designee.

No expression made by students in theexercise of such rights shall be deemed to be an expression of school policy and no school officials shall be held responsible in any civil or criminal action for any expression made or published by the students.

For the purposes of this section and sections eighty-three to eighty-five, inclusive, the word *student* shall mean any person attending a public secondary school in the commonwealth. The word *school official* shall mean any member or employee of the local school community.

Discrimination in Education Prohibited (Annotated Laws of Massachusetts, chapter 76, section 5)

No person shall be excluded from or discriminated against in admission to a public school of any town, or in obtaining the advantages, privileges and courses of study of such public school on account of race, color, sex, religion, national origin or sexual orientation.

Vermont

Antiharassment (Vermont Statutes Annotated, title 16) § 565. Harassment Policy

(a) Each school board shall develop, adopt and make available in the manner described under subdivision 563(1) of this title a harassment policy which includes:

(1) A statement prohibiting unlawful harassment of a student.

(2) The definition of harassment pursuant to subdivision 11(a)(26) of this title.

(3) Consequences and appropriate remedial action for staff or students who commit harassment.

§ 11. Classifications and definitions

(a) For the purposes of this title, unless the context otherwise clearly requires:

. . . . .

(26) "Harassment" means unlawful harassment which constitutes a form of discrimination. It means verbal or physical conduct based on a student's race, creed, color, national origin, marital status, sex, sexual orientation or disability and which has the purpose or effect of substantially interfering with a student's educational performance or creating an intimidating, hostile or offensive environment. Sexual harassment is also a form of unlawful harassment and means unwelcome sexual advances, requests for sexual favors and other verbal or physical contact of a sexual nature when:

(A) Submission to that conduct is made either explicitly or implicitly a term or condition of a student's education.

(B) Submission to or rejection of such conduct by a student is used as a component of the basis for decisions affecting that student.

(C) The conduct has the purpose or effect of substantially interfering with a student's educational performance or creating an intimidating, hostile or offensive educational environment.